John Dewey and
Our Educational Prospect

John Dewey and Our Educational Prospect

A Critical Engagement with Dewey's *Democracy and Education*

Edited by

David T. Hansen

STATE UNIVERSITY OF NEW YORK PRESS

Published by
State University of New York Press, Albany

For information, address State University of New York Press,
194 Washington Avenue, Suite 305, Albany, NY 12210-2384

Production by Kelli Williams
Marketing by Anne M. Valentine

Library of Congress Cataloging-in-Publication Data

John Dewey and our educational prospect : a critical engagement with Dewey's
    Democracy and education / edited by David T. Hansen.
        p. cm.
    Includes bibliographical references and index.
    ISBN-13: 978-0-7914-6921-7 (hardcover : alk. paper)
    ISBN-10: 0-7914-6921-2 (hardcover : alk. paper)
    ISBN-13: 978-0-7914-6922-4 (pbk. : alk. paper)
    ISBN-10: 0-7914-6922-0 (alk. paper)
    1. Dewey, John, 1859–1952. 2. Dewey, John, 1859–1952. Democracy and
education. 3. Education—Philosophy. 4. Education—Aims and objectives.
I. Hansen, David T., 1952–   .

LB875.D5J627   2007
370.1—dc22   2006003064

10 9 8 7 6 5 4 3 2 1

Contents

Preface

This book features a set of critical responses to John Dewey's greatest educational work, *Democracy and Education*. The contributors address Dewey's claim that education is not a preparation for life, but constitutes a fundamental aspect of the very experience of living. Dewey criticizes the cultural bias of his time, still widespread today, that presumes that what takes place in schools, colleges, and universities is separate or removed from what unfolds elsewhere in life. For Dewey, places set aside for formal teaching do differ from the playground, the home, the workplace, and so forth, but only in the sense that they provide a more systematic, reflective opportunity to learn how to learn. One distinctive way in which they accomplish this purpose is by engaging students with humanity's achievements and shortcomings as embodied in a dynamic curriculum. Whether the subject is mathematics, poetry, science, dance, or woodworking, students can acquire more than information and skills, important as they are. They can also develop the disposition and the ability to think, to inquire, to judge, to question, and to communicate, human qualities that give rise in the first place to the things that people study and value.

Dewey argues in the pages of *Democracy and Education* that those who understand how to learn and who are by habit open to new learning are on the way to becoming democratic citizens. For Dewey, democracy constitutes something richer and more generative than its electoral process and system of political structures, as valuable as they are. Rather, "democratic life" constitutes another name for a life of inquiring, communicating, and learning. In Dewey's outlook, democracy necessitates learning about many things: other peoples' view and hopes, how to resolve problems as they surface, how to anticipate and plan for possibilities, how to remain modest in one's claims to truth, how to think about what is good for individuals, communities, and society itself, and more. In reciprocal fashion, democracy as a mode of associated living makes possible this very process of interactive learning and understanding.

Education is not a preparation for such a life; education constitutes such a life. According to Dewey, education, democratic life, and human flourishing are all one.

Published in 1916, *Democracy and Education* has gone through countless printings and continues to be widely cited in both research and many fields of educational practice. The book has been drawn upon so often over the years that it comes as a surprise to learn that no book-length study has been published that centers directly on the text. The present volume seeks to rectify that omission and to be of service to several audiences of readers. Students in colleges of education and elsewhere will find the chapters collected here to be useful and provocative company as they come to grips with Dewey's still timely educational vision. The same holds for educational researchers in diverse fields who have drawn upon Dewey in the past, but seek a richer horizon of understanding to help guide their scholarship. We also hope to serve scholars of Dewey interested in an intensive focus on particular themes in *Democracy and Education*. In a broad sense, this volume is for any person interested in the relation between education and democracy.

The book derives, in part, from presentations at the John Dewey Society Annual Symposium, which takes place at the yearly meetings of the American Educational Research Association. As president of the John Dewey Society from 2003 to 2005, I asked four of the book's eventual contributors to present their responses to *Democracy and Education* at the annual meeting held in San Diego in 2004. I asked a second group of contributors to do the same at the annual meeting held in Montreal in 2005. The society's annual lecturer for 2005, Herbert M. Kliebard, also agreed to contribute a chapter, and in addition to preparing an introduction to the book I have added a chapter of my own. I thank the contributors both for their presentations at the society meetings and for their chapters. Readers will note that several contributors take pains to emphasize that they are not Dewey scholars. However, I invited them to participate because they are scholars and teachers whose influence has been extensive in their respective fields, which include curriculum studies, philosophy of education, policy studies, and teacher education. They have drawn on Dewey's conception of education at important junctures of their careers. Their willingness to be part of this book attests not only to the continued power in Dewey's work, but to the diverse audience of educators to whom he sought to appeal in *Democracy and Education*.

All references to Dewey's work in the volume are from the critical (print) edition, *The Collected Works of John Dewey, 1882–1953*, edited by Jo Ann Boydston and published by Southern Illinois University Press, Carbondale (1969–1991). The works have appeared in three series, *The*

Early Works (hereafter EW), *The Middle Works* (MW), and *The Later Works* (LW). In the following chapters, a reference to LW.5.270, for example, will mean *The Later Works*, Volume 5, page 270. [The pagination of the print edition has been preserved in *The Collected Works of John Dewey 1882–1953: The Electronic Edition*, edited by Larry A. Hickman and published by InteLex Corporation, Charlottesville, Virginia (1996).]

I am grateful to Jeff Frank, doctoral student in the Program in Philosophy and Education at Teachers College, Columbia University, for his editorial and scholarly assistance on this project.

All royalties earned by this volume will be contributed to the John Dewey Society.

DAVID T. HANSEN
New York City
March 2006

1

Introduction

Reading *Democracy and Education*

DAVID T. HANSEN

What is John Dewey's *Democracy and Education?* In a literal sense, it is a study of education and its relation to the individual and society. Moreover, Dewey tells us, it is a philosophical rather than historical, sociological, or political inquiry. His original title for the work was *An Introduction to the Philosophy of Education.* That was the heading he had in view when he signed a contract to undertake the project on July 21, 1911, with the Macmillan Company of New York (MW.9.377). However, his publishers convinced him to change the title in light of pressing political issues triggered by the cataclysm of World War I. Dewey completed the text in August 1915, and it came out the following year with his original title converted into a subtitle. The book constitutes Dewey's philosophical response to the rapid social, economic, political, cultural, and technological change he was witness to over the course of his long life. Born in 1859, when the United States was largely an agrarian society, by the time Dewey pens his educational treatise the country had become an industrial, urban world undergoing endless and often jarring transformations, a process that continues unabated through the present. Dewey sought to articulate and justify the education he believed people needed to comprehend and shape creatively and humanely these unstoppable changes.

At the same time, Dewey endeavored in the book to respond to what many critics regard as the two most influential educational works ever written prior to the twentieth century: Plato's *Republic* (fourth century B.C.E.) and Jean-Jacques Rousseau's *Emile* (published in 1762). Those two works are monumental, comprehensive treatments of the meaning and purposes of education. They are variously powerful, beautiful, edifying, controversial, off-putting, and unforgettable for anyone who comes to grips with their originality and sheer breadth of concern. In *Democracy and Education*, Dewey makes plain his intellectual debt to Plato and Rousseau, even as he underscores his differences with them. The book becomes an occasion for him to enact Aristotle's dictum that, when it comes to inquiry, the scholar must love truth more than the ideas held by her or his teachers.

Still another response to the question What is *Democracy and Education?* is that it was Dewey's favorite among his many publications (Ryan, 1995, p. 181). In one of his rare autobiographical writings, Dewey remarked that an interest in education resided at the core of his intellectual development. "This interest fused with and brought together," he wrote, "what might otherwise have been separate interests—that in psychology and that in social institutions and social life" (LW.5.156). He juxtaposed that admission with his amazement at how little attention professional philosophers, as a rule, devoted to educational questions. As an intellectual tribe, they simply do not, according to Dewey, acknowledge "that philosophizing should focus about education as the supreme human interest in which, moreover, other problems, cosmological, moral, logical, come to a head" (LW.5.156). In general, Dewey's fellow philosophers ignored *Democracy and Education* (it bears emphasizing that when he published it he was Professor of Philosophy at Columbia University). "Although [this book] was for many years," Dewey opined, "that in which my philosophy, such as it is, was most fully expounded, I do not know that philosophic critics, as distinct from teachers, have ever had recourse to it" (LW.5.156). But if philosophers, with notable exceptions, have tended to ignore the book, the rest of the world has not. Its worldwide audience over the last ninety years has consisted of students in colleges of education, educational practitioners and researchers, humanities and social science faculty in many disciplines, public intellectuals, and readers of countless other stripes and persuasions. The book has been the most widely translated of all Dewey's works, appearing in a dozen languages (Ryan, 1995, p. 181). Whether the book will continue to be read in the decades ahead remains a separate question that I will address at the close of this introductory chapter.

My purposes here are to provide an overview of Dewey's project and to outline the substance and aims of the chapters that follow. However, neither here nor anywhere else is it possible to answer definitively the question, What is *Democracy and Education?* Dewey sets his tasks and goes about them in his usual thorough, insightful, and determined (if not relentless) manner. But his thought, his writing style, his terms, his tone, his trajectory, outrun him, or outdo him, throughout the text. What Karl Jaspers said of Immanuel Kant can be said of Dewey's book, with some adjustment: "Kant is a nodal point in modern philosophy. His work contains as many possibilities as life itself. Consciously, Kant proceeded with rational precision, yet his work is shot through with thoughts that go beyond the 'system' and that Kant in turn strove to understand as part of his doctrine. It remains a source of boundless inspiration" (1962, p. 153). Dewey writes systematically, but he does not seek a critical system in the sense to which Kant aspired (cf. LW.5.155). Dewey strives for rational precision, but his irrepressible passion regarding the gifts of life constantly erupts through his language (this point could also be said for moments in Kant's writing). Jaspers's words are on the mark regarding how "shot through" *Democracy and Education* is with uncontainable insights and provocations. The latter are not always clear or comprehensible. For example, Dewey's statements about "mind" are often opaque and elliptical. This fact reveals Dewey's own struggle to understand the very ideas that emerged on the typewriter page before him. (Just as Orpheus's lyre grew into his shoulder, one could say Dewey's typewriter grew into his arms, given the man's phenomenal published output, which has been issued in thirty-seven volumes.) Dewey's words sometimes shimmer like reflections from a lake on the hanging leaves overhead. At times, he writes as if he's trying to capture a shimmer, yet finds it flashing out of his grasp.

Moreover, Dewey confessed, "probably there is in the consciously articulated ideas of every thinker an over-weighing of just those things that are contrary to his natural tendencies, an emphasis upon those things that are contrary to his intrinsic bent, and which, therefore, he has to struggle to bring to expression, while the native bent, on the other hand, can take care of itself" (LW.5.150). Throughout *Democracy and Education*, Dewey's "native bent" for formal and schematic philosophical writing jostles with his ethical and emotional awareness of the demands of actual human experience. Sometimes there are sparks when these elements meet, and sometimes a quiet fusion. At moments Dewey coolly works his way through an argument. At others he sounds like a poet or orator moved by a vision of what could be. He reveals his emotional, moral, and intellectual aversion to all forms of thinking that, in his view, console, isolate, or narrow the mind, rather than opening it up for a constructive response to human affairs. His impulses are so strong that he has difficulties, at times, in handling certain concepts and ideas, almost as if they felt uncomfortable to the touch.

Readers of American letters will recognize Dewey's joyful, inspired, and maddening challenge. There are recurrent and sometimes explicit echoes throughout the book of Ralph Waldo Emerson, Henry David Thoreau, Walt Whitman, Abraham Lincoln, Jane Addams, and many others driven to enthusiastic if also frustrated distraction by the promise of what the nation could become. Dewey seeks in his book to engage what Emerson (1983/1844) called "this new yet unapproachable America" (p. 485)—an America no longer moored politically and culturally to Europe, yet with its identity confused, uncertain, and undetermined, as remains the case today. Dewey aims to articulate the educational vision needed to help the nation achieve its highest ideals in practice, while keeping those very ideals under criticism so that they function as sources of hope and imagination rather than closed outlooks. However, just as Plato and Rousseau sought to write beyond their own societies, Dewey has in view not just his own country but any community that aspires to be democratic in conduct rather than merely in name. He writes in the spirit of a cosmopolitan, humane world he envisions coming into being. He does not proffer a crude American exceptionalism, so endlessly damaging near and far, any more than do the other figures previously mentioned, even if like them he cannot (and would not want to) leave behind his local horizons. Dewey's disarmingly titled "Introduction to the Philosophy of Education" is at once a sustained, disciplined philosophical inquiry into education, and an epic, poetic evocation of human possibility.

Dewey's Historical Moment:
A Reading of the Book's Preface

Dewey published *Democracy and Education* in the midst of what would come to be called World War I. The United States was still a neutral state, although inching ever closer to joining the Allied side and, in retrospect, moving further down the road that would lead to its current superpower status. Meantime, the nation had been undergoing an astounding transformation since the bloody Civil War of 1861–1865 had nearly sundered it. Urban and industrial growth, waves of immigration and internal migration, the expansion of education, imperial actions overseas, international commerce, new modes of transportation and communication, scientific and artistic breakthroughs, and much more, generated a more or less permanent state of social possibility and experiment, as well as unsettlement and unpredictability. A keen observer and commentator on these rapid changes, Dewey intended his book to shed light on their fundamental educational and sociopolitical consequences. What do the changes exact of us, Dewey asked, with regards to the philosophy of life and education we articulate, criticize, and seek to realize?

Dewey signals his purposes in his brief preface to *Democracy and Education*. The preface consists of the following paragraph, and a subsequent one in which he acknowledges his debt to several generations of students as well as to several critics. "The following pages," Dewey writes,

> embody an endeavor to detect and state the ideas implied in a democratic society and to apply these ideas to the problems of the enterprise of education. The discussion includes an indication of the constructive aims and methods of public education as seen from this point of view, and a critical estimate of the theories of knowing and moral development which were formulated in earlier social conditions, but which still operate, in societies nominally democratic, to hamper the adequate realization of the democratic ideal. As will appear from the book itself, the philosophy stated in the book connects the growth of democracy with the development of the experimental method in the sciences, evolutionary ideas in the biological sciences, and the industrial reorganization, and is concerned to point out the changes in subject matter and method of education indicated by these developments. (MW.9.3; unless otherwise indicated, all subsequent references are to this volume)

Written after the completion of the book itself, these prefatory words sound flat-footed and anticlimatic. The passive voice, the mechanical listing of topics, and the matter-of-fact, almost ho-hum tone, do not amount to much of an invitation to read on. Perhaps Dewey was weary after writing the book's twenty-six chapters, which range over almost every conceivable aspect of educational thought and practice. Or perhaps he was bowing to his publishers, who had put forward the idea for *Democracy and Education* by urging Dewey to write a textbook for teachers. Dewey's curt preface certainly sounds textbookish.

However, if we listen, his language expands, beginning in the first of the three sentences that comprise his remarks. The book will "embody an endeavor to detect and state." It will be an inquiry, an endeavor, rather than a demonstration or proof. Dewey will try to "detect" ideas "implied in a democratic society," suggesting the ever-present possibility of failure in that task. He will "endeavor" to state those ideas, to give them form, but once more the emphasis is on effort, on a trial, on an attempt, rather than on a presumption of accomplishment. Moreover, after undertaking this project, he will then "endeavor" to "apply" the ideas to problems in education, suggesting a final time the risk of being unsuccessful. What sounded mechanical at first glance has become, at second hearing, uncertain, unstable, and unsteady. Moreover, the book will "embody" Dewey's inquiry, meaning that from start to finish it *constitutes* an endeavor rather than a polished post-inquiry product. Dewey all but says the project will feature surprises, openings, unanticipated conclusions, and routes identified but not taken. What a strange text-book to offer readers: an ongoing journey rather than a packaged, contained, and prefigured artifact.

Dewey's second sentence, longer than the first but not as long as the third and last, marks out his interest in public education, an institution that had been growing rapidly in its reach in the United States. Armed with "ideas implied in a democratic society," Dewey plans in the book to highlight "constructive" educational aims and methods, those that both mirror and help bring into being a democratic society. Dewey's qualifier anticipates one of the most familiar claims in the book, that education signifies the "reconstruction" of experience "which adds to the meaning of experience, and which increases ability to direct the course of subsequent experience" (p. 82). Constructing, making, bringing into being that which was not there before, *poesis*, as the Ancient Greeks put it: these terms describe the view of education Dewey will try to "state" (i.e., create, make, build) in the pages to come. Dewey's qualifier also provides a strong hint that he will be criticizing what he regards as *un*constructive or positively destructive aims and methods. He further discloses that strategy in the latter portion of the second sentence, when he refers to theories of knowledge and of morality whose consequences, he tells us, are still at work in society to the detriment of its democratic emergence. I write emergence mindful of Dewey's extraordinary claim that his own and other so-called democratic societies are that *in name only*—they are, he says, "nominally" democratic. To employ Emerson's term, they may be "approaching" democracy, but they have not yet moved into that condition. Dewey conceives his book as an instrument to help further and support the approach. In this process, he will not willfully reject previous conceptions of knowledge and morality, any more than he will crudely toss aside previous views of teaching and learning. Instead, he will reconstruct them. He will draw from them what he sees as vital while excising what he believes "hamper[s]" the realization of democracy. We do not know, at this threshold juncture, why Dewey finds so telling a society's moral and epistemological presuppositions. The entire book will generate his response, culminating in his concluding two chapters that explicitly take up the nature and impact of theories of knowledge and morality.

Dewey's final, and cumbersome, sentence remains not only elliptical but enigmatic. Just as he wrote the preface after writing the book, so it seems that readers can only fathom the preface after reading (and rereading) the text. However, Dewey does anticipate his path. He hopes to "state" how his philosophy of education "connects the growth of democracy" with contemporary forces and trends. Dewey will make plain time and again how crucial is the idea of "connection" in his educational and democratic outlook, along with its associated concepts of communication and continuity. The entire philosophy will pivot around the familiar, provocative, still controversial idea of "growth," which Dewey describes not as *having* an end or outcome but as *itself* the finest end or outcome of education (p. 54). He argues that growth is "relative" to nothing save more growth, and concludes that education thus implies no greater end than the capacity for further education. Correspondingly, the "growth of democracy" to which he refers in the preface embodies its own end. That is, a democratic way of life is not a means to some larger end or outcome. It is itself the *realization* of political, social, and educational ends supportive of growth. As he summarizes: "A democracy is more than a form of government; it is primarily a mode of associated living, of conjoint communicated experience" (p. 93).

Dewey will also argue in the book that this democratic "mode of associated living" emerges naturally and organically from forces such as those he names in the preface: the rise of the experimental method in science, the idea of evolution in biology, and what he calls "the industrial reorganization." Any reader familiar with Dewey will recognize that by "experimental method," he denotes nothing more, nor less, than the process he described through his verb choices in the first sentence of the preface: "endeavor," "detect," "state," "apply," and so forth. He will go on to show just how pregnant with meaning and action are these and related verbs associated with inquiry. Moreover, inquiry remains indispensable to democracy, since the latter obliges people to learn constantly from one another, which means learning to study others' ideas, claims, hopes, and practices, as well as their own.

The idea of evolution remains decisive for democracy, according to Dewey, because it reveals that humanity has no preset or predetermined nature. It is true that humanity's horizon of possibility and creativity remains bounded by physical forces, which may themselves be evolving, but its scope is indeterminate. That fact, for Dewey, leads to democracy precisely because it renders suspect any and all claims that it is natural for one group of people to dominate or control another in autocratic fashion. Posed differently, the idea undermines every dogmatic viewpoint, whether religious or secular, about the presumed meaning of being human. At the same time, the idea of evolution suggests humanity has no predetermined, fixed *telos* or end state. Once more, for Dewey, this idea gives rise to democracy because it dissolves claims to know the final destiny of humanity as well as corresponding assertions about what humanity must do to reach that alleged terminus. The wheel turns, and we discern why Dewey suggests that the aim of democracy is democracy itself, just as the aim of growth is further growth.

These points also illuminate, from another angle, why Dewey esteems inquiry. If human beings are not predetermined entities with pre-set destinies, but rather are persons who can influence their very nature through education and social interaction, then it behooves them to learn to question, to criticize, to converse (whether through word or other media), and to be modest and fair-minded in their claims.

Finally, "the industrial reorganization" encompasses all the economic, social, and technological changes touched on previously. The term may also point to the antitrust legislation, the formation of labor unions, and the like that had been taking place in the years before his book appeared. According to Dewey, the conditions for democracy are a natural, organic outgrowth of this "reorganization." As he writes in chapter 7 of his book: "The widening of the area of shared concerns, and the liberation of a greater diversity of personal capacities which characterize a democracy [as a way of life], are not of course the product of deliberation and conscious effort. On the contrary, they were caused by the development of modes of manufacture and commerce, travel, migration, and intercommunication which flowed from the command of science over natural energy" (p. 93). However, Dewey argues that while these circumstances have created conditions for democracy, they cannot in themselves bring it into being. For that task, education is needed: "But after greater individualization on one hand, and a broader community of interest on the other have come into existence, it is a matter of deliberate effort to sustain and extend them" (p. 93). Dewey adds: "Travel, economic and commercial tendencies, have at present gone far to break down external barriers; to bring peoples and classes into closer and more perceptible connection with one another. It remains for the most part to secure the intellectual and emotional significance of this physical annihilation of space" (p. 92). According to Dewey, education constitutes the vehicle for this intellectual and emotional turn in human perception.

What may strike the reader, at first glance, as a rather wooden opening to *Democracy and Education*, becomes on second glance a striking preview of some key themes Dewey will take up in the text. Although highly compressed and elliptical, his preface remains conjoined with the work as a whole, perhaps especially through his emphasis on the existential need for inquiry. That need entails both openness to the world and critical reflection and response. In a democracy, or in what Dewey calls an associated mode of communicative living, inquiry is not the provenance of a select few. It is the privilege and the obligation of everyone. On the one hand, as Dewey clarifies elsewhere, full-time scholars and researchers should make available to the public the results and findings of their work. On the other hand, the task of citizens is to influence policy by judging the outcomes of formal inquiry in light of shared public concerns (LW.2.365). In sum, Dewey does not contend that everyone must become a researcher in a formal sense, in part because there are countless other important social roles and activities in a complex society. He does suggest that a spirit of inquiry characterizes a genuine democracy.

Dewey may also highlight the fact that the book constitutes an inquiry because he is mindful of how challenging readers will find his claims. For example, some may be thrown from the very start by the notion that the United States is a democracy in name rather than in practice. Others readers, as they make their way through the early chapters, may find jarring Dewey's comparisons between so-called savage and civilized groups, until they discern that he is not making empirical claims but rather a theoretical distinction between groups that willingly adapt to change as contrasted with those that do not or will not. Posed differently, he distinguishes groups that seek or accept genuine contact with others from those that reject it out of hand. Given the inexorable changes he witnessed in his lifetime, which he believed would become even more accelerated in the future, Dewey did not believe it possible to achieve complete communal isolation.

However, in perceiving this outlook some readers may be unsettled by Dewey's further suggestion that the United States is not only still on the road to becoming a democracy, rather than having arrived, but is also not yet civilized. It does not yet feature an ethos, in his view, in which groups and communities—especially those with the greatest political and economic resources—deliberately seek out contact with others who differ in outlook and practice, in part so that society can transform itself peacefully rather than violently. Moreover, time and again in the early chapters Dewey emphasizes that technological, scientific, and economic prowess does not in itself constitute civilization. Rather, it is the uses to which this expertise is put that determine the question—in particular, whether these vaunted tools and powers are deployed to enhance and expand the experience of everyone rather than of only a few (see, e.g., pp. 42, 8, 9, 10). In his preface, Dewey implies that readers will need to take on the posture of inquirers themselves if they are to engage these and other arguments. He does not expect agreement as the outcome of the process, but he does hope for the engagement.

The Scope and Structure of *Democracy and Education*

Each of the twenty-six chapters in Dewey's book ends with what he calls a summary. That organizational feature reflects his intent, at his publishers' request, to write a textbook for educators. However, any reader of *Democracy and Education* swiftly discovers that Dewey's so-called summaries are more than that. They do take a look back at the themes and ideas he has put forward. But they also advance his arguments. Many of them contain expressions, formulations, conjectures, and hopes not found in the preceding sections of the respective chapter. If the twenty-six summaries were extracted from the book and bound into a text of their own, they would make for fascinating reading in their own right.

I offer here an interpretive synopsis, but not a summary, of the book so that readers can have it in hand as they work through the chapters that lie ahead. *Democracy and Education* features four primary sections, although they are not identified as such in the preface or table of contents. They form, Dewey says, a logical perspective toward the book's structure. Dewey himself offers a snapshot of the first three parts, in a set of pages that appears to embody the advice of one or more critics of a draft of the work (pp. 331–333). Someone may have said to him that, at this point in the text, readers could use a platform to gather themselves before climbing the final steps to the summit.

In chapters 1–5 of the book, Dewey examines why education is fundamental to the nature and perpetuation of any human community, however humble or vast it may be in size and scope of activity. According to Dewey, education is decisive for *renewal* of human culture and society. The idea of renewal constitutes the very first theme Dewey takes up in the book, as he compares differences between living and inanimate things. That beginning captures one of the primary passions informing the project. *Democracy and Education* constitutes a wake-up call, a sometimes harsh reminder that too much human existence remains, in metaphorical terms, inanimate as contrasted with truly alive. From the start, Dewey criticizes social customs, traditions, and ideals that he believes suppress the flowering of human thought, imagination, creativity, and individuality. In so doing, they suppress the emergence of democracy itself and its organic commitment to the growth of all persons. For Dewey, unexamined customs and traditions, however beloved, can render human life less *animate* than it might otherwise be: less artful, meaningful, joyful, hopeful, and sublime. Dewey never advocates the wholesale repudiation of convention. Far from it: inquiry and communication may affirm long-standing ideals and practices. However, for Dewey such a process implies that the conventional would no longer be merely conventional. It will have been revitalized, or reanimated, precisely by undergoing the democratic crucible of inquiry and criticism.

In the opening chapters, and at several points elsewhere in the book, Dewey pays tribute to precursors such as F. W. A. Froebel and J. F. Herbart for their generative ideas, even as he unsparingly points out limitations he detects in their outlooks. The chapters introduce concepts that Dewey will employ throughout the inquiry, among them communication, environment, direction, control, and growth. He puts them to work immediately in the subsequent part of the book, encompassing chapters 6–14. Chapter 6 (more precisely, its second half) and chapter 7 highlight, respectively, the idea of education as the continuous, expansive reconstruction of human experience, and the idea of democracy as a way of life. Dewey shows how the idea of democracy as "a mode of conjoint, communicated experience" establishes a criterion for the reorganization of contemporary educational practice. Democracy can only exist if practice is reconstructed so that all persons can, in principle, realize their potential as human beings. Conversely, Dewey argues that the very idea of democracy is implied in the core understanding of education as reconstruction, as the continuous growth of all persons. If that process is taking place, democracy itself emerges all the more substantively. Thus, Dewey titles his pivotal chapter 7, "The Democratic Conception *in* Education" (my emphasis). He establishes an ecological, symbiotic relation between democracy and education.

Guided by these ideas, chapters 8–14 constitute an artful, imaginative, and powerful study of factors that reside at the heart of teaching and learning: aims, motivation, interest, self-discipline, social interaction, thinking, method, subject matter, and more. Dewey works tirelessly to establish organic continuity between these terms because he believes they are all, without exception, no more than heuristics for understanding and advancing education. As such, they have immense value. However, the terms do not describe discrete, separate phenomena. They denote aspects or phases of the total experience of teaching and learning.

For example, subject matter literally exists only *in* methods of teaching, learning, inquiring, and communicating, just as those methods only come into being, or exist, *in* subject matter. Divorced from method, subject matter is better characterized as inert stuff, no more animate than stones and steel. Divorced from subject matter, method becomes mythological, a term Dewey employs throughout the book to identify ideas and beliefs that have been reified (or deified) and that, as such, denote absolutely nothing about experience (p. 67). According to Dewey, for instance, there is no such thing as perception without perceiving *something* (p. 70). Certainly, there are particular biological and physical conditions that make sight possible. However, those conditions are not synonymous with perception. They do not cause, for example, one person to perceive sunsets while another person does not. People can single out the concept perception for many valuable heuristic purposes. But they need to be on guard against drawing the conclusion that because they can isolate and discuss the concept, there must be something discrete in the universe called perception apart from percepts.

After presenting the core of his view of genuinely educational practice, Dewey examines in chapters 15–23 a wide array of historical and contemporary assumptions about education and human experience that he argues are hampering what he called in his preface "the adequate realization of the democratic ideal." These chapters read like a philosophical critique of the entire history of Western thought and action. Their reach is as remarkable as Dewey's ability to sustain control over his analysis and not become submerged in either details or too many large ideas at once. He seeks to illuminate both the origins and the deleterious consequences of dualistic thinking that separates mind from body, intellectual from physical work, thought from action, individual from society, social class from social class, humanism from naturalism, and more. He examines the place of specific subjects in education, including geography, history, science, art, and the humanities. He highlights the human values both embodied in and expressed through these subjects. At the same time, he argues for the organic unity of values. He criticizes educational schemes predicated on the assumption that only subjects like literature have aesthetic value, and that only so-called vocational subjects like auto mechanics have practical value. Dewey shows that any well-taught subject yields aesthetic, intellectual, moral, and practical values and meanings. He connects this part of the inquiry to the activities of people after they complete school. He examines connections between play and work, occupations and human growth, labor and leisure, appreciation and production, and more. He continues to root his philosophical criticism in cultural, economic, political, and sociological observations of the current scene. Along the way, he pauses to consider and criticize ideas from Plato, Rousseau, G. W. F. Hegel, Immanuel Kant, and other influential thinkers.

In the fourth and final part of the book, encompassing chapters 24–26, Dewey takes up philosophy, knowledge, and morals. In contrast with the often decontextualized, theoretical treatment of these topics in the history of ideas, Dewey remains grounded in his view of the contemporary world. That fact does not imply his discussion lacks complexity or philosophical sophistication. Quite on the contrary. But it may help explain why professional philosophers have tended to ignore the book. In a nutshell, it does not employ their lingo. Instead, Dewey refers to specific societal assumptions, divisions, and aspirations regarding everything from the purposes of schools to what it means to lead a morally worthy life. He criticizes prior and current conceptions of philosophy, knowledge, and morals, and, through the lens of his democratic criterion of growth, offers his own considered interpretation of each.

According to Dewey, philosophy "might almost be described as thinking which has become conscious of itself—which has generalized its place, function, and value in experience" (p. 336). More substantively, Dewey claims, philosophy is another name for "the general theory of education" (p. 338). He recalls the historic fact that European philosophy, in fundamental respects, originated with the response by the Greeks to pressing educational concerns. One of Plato's most influential dialogues, *Meno*, opens with the question, "Can you tell me Socrates—is virtue something that can be taught?" (1961, p. 354). Meno's question not only highlights content, in this case what we would today call moral education, but also spotlights a perplexing problem of pedagogy: is teaching the same thing as telling? For Dewey, philosophy describes the deliberate criticism of ideas, values, methods, and actions with a view toward extracting from them all that might prove generative of growth for individuals and for society alike. He enacts that very conception of philosophy throughout *Democracy and Education*.

Knowledge is another name for conduct carried out with intelligence, foresight, and awareness of the outcomes of preceding conditions and actions. Knowledge does not mean the same thing as a storehouse of information (cf. p. 195). It is not the possession of a spectator removed from all action. It is not a possession, period. For Dewey, knowledge describes an ability to act effectively in the world. Such action may involve working with others, raising a family, cultivating friendships, and building a career. It can involve undertaking a painting, interpreting a poem, driving a car, and preparing a meal. A knowledgeable person, Dewey avers, is a person who knows her or his way about a particular scene of life: the kitchen, the gymnasium, the chemistry laboratory, or the book, the film, the poem. In the broadest sense, a knowledgeable person habitually seeks connections and continuity across the doings of her or his life. Dewey carries this image into the final chapter of his book, on theories of morals.

Morals describe what people variously call obligations to others, duties, justice, virtue, character, and so forth. Dewey catalogues theories of morals that privilege one or another of these terms—and then punctures all the balloons. *None* of the terms, he contends, marks out a separate realm of life to be dubbed "morality." He argues that the terms capture aspects or phases of human experience in which questions of the goodness or rightness of ideas and actions have become prominent. Thus, concepts like justice and virtue are useful for understanding and, thereby, expanding experience, but they confuse and intimidate people if they are divorced from other facets of experience. "All of the separations which we have been criticizing," Dewey declaims, "spring from taking morals too narrowly—giving them, on one side, a sentimental goody-goody turn without reference to effective ability to do what is socially needed, and, on the other side, overemphasizing convention and tradition so as to limit morals to a list of definitely stated acts. As a matter of fact, morals are as broad as acts which concern our relationships with others. And potentially this includes all our acts. . . . For every act, by the principle of habit, modifies disposition—it sets up a certain kind of inclina-- tion and desire" (p. 367).

Dewey dramatizes his view of the unity of experience by referring to "moral knowledge," thereby fusing terms often treated as separate and unrelated in the history of both ideas and human practices. "The knowledge of dynamite of a safecracker may be identical in verbal form with that of a chemist," Dewey writes; "in fact, it is different, for it is knit into connection with different aims and habits, and thus has a different import" (p. 365). Knowledge does not exist in a vacuum apart from values and commitments. All knowledge, according to Dewey (keeping in mind that it is not synonymous with information), "connects" with people's aims, habits, aspirations, and more. All of the latter, implicitly, harbor moral meaning because they all presume 'this is better than that' or 'this is good and that is bad' or 'it is right to value or do this rather than that.' Summarizing his book-length outlook on education, and echoing yet again the democratic criterion he has articulated, Dewey writes that "what is learned and employed in an occupation having an aim and involving cooperation with others is moral knowledge, whether consciously so regarded or not. For it builds up a social interest and confers the intelligence needed to make that interest effective in practice" (p. 366). For Dewey, an "occupation" describes any sustained undertaking inside or outside school, from interpreting a story to building a dam, that draws out intelligent action in communicative association with others. The moral aspect stands out when this analysis weds with his previous argument (p. 43) that building dams, operating transportation systems, and engaging in all the other productive doings of a would-be civilized society should draw not on technical mastery alone but on communicated values regarding how to enhance the lives of all. Moral knowledge fuses technical know-how with social consciousness.

Dewey's concluding studies of philosophy, knowledge, and the moral, which I have only touched on in this all-too-brief synopsis, constitute a fitting bookend with his preface and his initial reflections on the idea of renewal in chapter 1. In his preface he had anticipated undertaking "a critical estimate" of historic and still influential theories of knowledge and morality. As we have seen, for Dewey questions about knowledge and the moral ultimately derive from, and ultimately must feed back into, educational problems and needs. This perspective sheds light on why he had selected as the title for his book, "An Introduction to the Philosophy of Education." Dewey's entire book embodies the meaning he ascribes to philosophy, beginning with his verbs "endeavor," "detect," "state," and the like, and concluding with his still timely criticism of the meaning of moral education. For Dewey, no education can be moral unless it cultivates the capacity to criticize intelligently. Effective, humane methods of inquiry and communication are so vital in his outlook that it may not be accidental that his analysis of method, in chapter 13, resides literally in the center of the book. It is no coincidence that his discussion of philosophy, knowledge, and the moral come after the bulk of the project has been completed, for his sense of them springs from the experience of inquiry rather than predetermining its trajectory and outcome.

In between his preface and conclusion, in his role as a philosopher Dewey criticizes numerous past and contemporary ideas and practices. They all stand or fall depending on whether they serve the essential, one might say universe-all need of renewal. As Dewey argues, the very meaning of renewal deepens in both complexity and urgency the more a society aspires toward democratic growth. In making this case, Dewey does not shy away from calling into question ideals and customs his contemporaries revere. But he never questions the fundamental need for reverence. Dewey's sense of reverence for human possibility and his achievement in expressing it in *Democracy and Education* remain unsurpassed in the history of writing on education.

Organization of this Book

I have sketched in rapid strokes possible answers to the question What is *Democracy and Education*? Among other things, the book is a philosophical inquiry, a vision of education, a critique of Dewey's contemporary society, and a judgment on the significance of the history of ideas in and for human life. In the chapters ahead, the contributors to this volume provide substantive, panoramic, and provocative perspectives of their own. They do not always see eye to eye with one another, nor will readers accept all of their claims. However, the diversity of themes they take up from Dewey's book, their interpretive standpoints, and their styles and modes of writing, reveal how comprehensive and unfathomable Dewey's educational reach is. The contributors attest to the truth in Jaspers' terms, applied to *Democracy and Education*, that it is "shot through" with generative ideas, insights, and questions.

The sequence of chapters parallels, in a rough fashion, the sequence of topics Dewey takes up in *Democracy and Education*. The contributors have been asked to stay close to Dewey's text, even while touching on other writings by Dewey as well as secondary sources to make their arguments. They have also been encouraged to link their analyses of Dewey's claims with contemporary educational concerns and problems. The latter encompass what the curriculum for children and youth should be, how to organize and implement formal teacher education, what modes of pedagogy are most sensible given societal if not global trends, and how to think about the purposes of school. These issues constitute our educational prospect today.

In chapter 2, Gert Biesta focuses on what he regards as the centrality of communication in Dewey's philosophy of education. Biesta traces the intellectual origins of Dewey's ideas on communication, and argues that they make their first pivotal appearance in the pages of *Democracy and Education*. Biesta describes Dewey's emphasis on communication, rather than on learning, as a "revolutionary" conception of education. Dewey looks beyond discrete theories of learning and instruction to a larger tableau, wherein human beings express and cultivate their humanity through a wide tapestry of communicative modes. Biesta provides a response to a long-standing question about the book, especially among teachers, as to why Dewey makes so little *direct* mention of teachers and teaching. Rather than centering education around the teacher, or around the student for that matter, Dewey places communication at the core, or so Biesta contends. Especially in working with children and youth, it is through the medium of the educational environments teachers set up that they exert their strongest influence. Rather than flowing directly from teacher to student, pedagogical influence flows into environments that fuel communication, consistently and persistently, such that students experience situations that challenge them to learn rather than merely go through the motions or mimic the teacher.

In chapter 3, Reba N. Page takes up Dewey's conception of curriculum in order to examine how he treats the relation between formal and informal education—a major theme in the early chapters of *Democracy and Education*. Like Dewey, Page does not underplay how tenuous the relation often turns out to be. It is not simply a matter of fine-tuning pedagogical methods or curricular content. The distinction between the formal and the informal points to fundamental aspects of human experience, of how unpredictable, disjointed, surprising, and confounding it can turn out to be. The distinction underscores why education and schooling are not synonyms, and why school is a place where informal education occurs as surely as does formal tuition. In developing her argument, Page draws on an array of examples, from her young daughter's reaction to first noticing the moon to Eleanor Duckworth's widely cited approaches to teaching science, in which she also draws upon the moon as an object of interest. Page shines a light on why Dewey regarded curriculum planning as difficult, challenging, and utterly indispensable, even as he appreciated how the best laid plans can both go awry and yield unanticipated benefits.

Larry A. Hickman, in chapter 4, elucidates the distinctive meaning Dewey attaches to three closely related, core terms in *Democracy and Education*: socialization, social efficiency, and social control. Hickman takes up each concept in turn, showing how it adds to Dewey's overall picture of educational and democratic life. Each term captures an element in why both education and democracy are interactive and interpersonal processes. They are not means to some distant ends. For example, social control does not imply a top-down, authoritarian structure. Rather, for Dewey, control emerges through communication, interaction, and conjoint attempts to resolve problems and create structures of meaning and satisfaction. Genuine social control resides *in* these processes, such that people learn to adapt to change, as well as instigate it, in ways that do not lead to violence or chaotic disorder. Dewey makes a similarly creative move with concepts of socialization and social efficiency, whose meanings also derive from the democratic criterion he articulates in the book. Hickman contrasts these views with contemporary conceptions of efficiency and control that he regards as narrow and constraining on our educational prospects.

In chapter 5, Naoko Saito reconstructs Dewey's widely admired and widely criticized concept of growth. Saito shows how the concept brings to a head, in a culminating, consummatory manner, many educators' deep intuitions regarding the distinctiveness and humanity of each student. In addition, Dewey's way of characterizing the idea of growth makes not just ample but essential room in teaching and learning for the imaginative, the creative, and the constructive, rather than solely for rote learning. However, Saito also makes plain how widely criticized Dewey's concept has been because of its alleged emptiness. When Dewey claims that the purpose of growth is further growth, some critics reply that the claim begs the fundamental question, Growth toward what or for what? Saito draws on Ralph Waldo Emerson's notion of perfectionism, as well as Stanley Cavell's trenchant remarks on that notion, to reconceive how we might regard the idea of growth. She argues that Emerson's thought helps retain the nonfoundational character of growth that was important to Dewey, since he viewed preordained outcomes of education as problematic. He insisted that part of the educational process is learning to criticize education itself. At the same time, Saito presents a case for why an Emersonian take on growth can also rescue the idea from the charge of being an empty concept.

Gary D. Fenstermacher argues, in chapter 6, that *Democracy and Education* constitutes a powerful reminder about the centrality of the student in education. Even though the book does not always explicitly place the student in the forefront, Fenstermacher shows how Dewey highlights the student's agency and the need for educators to respect that agency. Dewey regards students as purposive beings who merit substantive autonomy in fashioning their educational experience. Students are capable of enhancing their own being through exercising their agency, intentionality, reasoning, and more, in the work of education. Fenstermacher contrasts this focus on Dewey's part with contemporary educational policy and research, which in his view remains virtually silent about the student-as-agent, or student-as-full-human-being. Instead, much of today's policy and research pivots around things that should be done *to* students. *Democracy and Education* illuminates the vibrant agency of students, and, for Fenstermacher, reading the book provides a penetrating view on how educators can restore a focus on the student in the discourses of policy and research.

Herbert M. Kliebard begins chapter 7 by reminding us that no school has ever existed without having something to teach. He points out that Dewey, in founding and directing the famed Laboratory School in Chicago in the 1890s, turned to his contemporaries for answers to the primordial question, What should we teach? He was satisfied with none of the theories he came upon. Through analysis and criticism of those extant positions, he began to forge his own. Kliebard concentrates on chapters 13–15 in *Democracy and Education* to elucidate how Dewey develops his distinctive outlook. He traces the movement of Dewey's thought through those chapters, which focus, respectively, on method, subject matter, and the relation between play and work. Kliebard concludes that while Dewey's educational philosophy embodies both deep integrity and persuasive power, it failed to influence in any fundamental or enduring way American schooling. The system has proven to be intractable, Kliebard contends, and has relegated to its margins and interstices Deweyan approaches to curriculum and pedagogy. Nonetheless, he implies that a permanent value in studying *Democracy and Education* is that it challenges conventional assumptions and practices, serving in a metaphorical sense as a textual, Socratic gadfly stinging the body politic into awareness.

In chapter 8, Sharon Feiman-Nemser examines *Democracy and Education* through the eyes of a teacher educator. She elucidates Dewey's concept of education as "the reconstruction of experience" and considers what that concept implies for the education of teachers. She also contrasts this take on teacher education with what the latter would look like if approached through two classic theories of learning that Dewey criticizes, namely, education as preparation and as unfolding from within. In the second part of her chapter, Feiman-Nemser considers two proposals for the reform of teacher education, written one hundred years apart, which she presents as different embodiments of Dewey's core ideas. The first, written by Dewey himself, takes theory as its starting point. The second, written by Deborah Ball and David Cohen, situates professional education "in" practice. Both proposals share a commitment to fostering an investigative stance toward teaching and both embrace the reconstruction rather than the reproduction of experience in learning to teach.

Elizabeth Minnich, in chapter 9, sketches a portrait of Dewey's philosophy of life that she finds expressed throughout the pages of *Democracy and Education*. Minnich examines primordial notions of reproduction and renewal, the latter a term Dewey himself takes up. These two notions differ from replication; both reproduction and renewal point to transformation within continuity. Minnich suggests that the terms illuminate why we might conceive life as, in her words, adaptive, cocreative, and communicatively reproductive. In this process, relation is central—relation between persons and world, and between persons and other people. Relation makes possible individuation, just as dependence makes possible independence. Dewey emphasizes that societal presuppositions about the supposed weakness implied by the idea of dependence can lead to confusion about the educational process. For Dewey, dependence signals the very possibility of relation with others and the world, and thus the emergence of genuine individuality and the best meanings embedded in the treasured term independence. Minnich infuses her argument with several examples from her teaching, in order to interpret why the idea of experience figures so prominently in Dewey's philosophy of life.

In the final chapter, I take up the question why Dewey closes his book by bequeathing readers an image of the moral self. I suggest that the image has its origins in Emerson's idea of "reception," which resides at the core of the latter's vision of what it means to become a human being. With this background in place, I examine how and why Dewey fuses the concepts of self and "interest." That fusion mirrors his book-length criticism of theories, and the social practices he associates with them, that separate mind from body, individual from society, and school from life. Dewey argues that self and interest are two names for the same fact, namely, that the self literally becomes a self only through engagement in the world. In the final chapter of *Democracy and Education*, Dewey employs these ideas as well as others he has articulated to criticize moral theories and schemes of moral education predicated upon them. As an outcome of his critique, the fusion of self and interest metamorphoses into an image of the moral self. The concept of the moral—the very last concept Dewey examines in his epic inquiry—becomes crucial in elucidating the kind of education, and the kind of person, Dewey imagines grows from and makes possible a democratic life.

Conclusion: Dewey and the Teacher's Legacy

In a recent essay on what it means to be a teacher, George Steiner writes that "there have been, there are, great American teachers: Ralph Waldo Emerson, first and foremost, Oliver Wendell Holmes Jr., Charles Eliot Norton, John Dewey, Martha Graham" (2003, p. 124). Steiner means that these figures not only were personal influences on many others, but that their work—as expressed, for example, in their writing—was educative, edifying, and pedagogical in structure and overtone. That description fits *Democracy and Education*. Dewey's publishers had asked for a textbook for teachers, but he gave them much more. He produced a book that teaches, even as it articulates from Dewey's point of view the elements of an education in and for a democratic society. Readers may not accept his lessons, and they may disagree with his methods. However, they can only reach those judgments by entering the inquiry with him. In so doing, they put themselves in a position to learn—to grow. They may even learn lessons about how to grow in ways that deepen the impulse to inquire and to learn. Dewey would contend that that process also holds the promise of their developing their democratic dispositions. Democracy implies interaction, not agreement. According to Dewey, it implies like-mindedness, which he characterizes as a willingness and an ability to communicate, but it does not imply identical-mindedness.

As the previous section forecasts, the chapters ahead address many features of Dewey's argument and vision in *Democracy and Education*. The authors make plain the continued power and pertinence of the book, even while raising many questions about it. In rereading the text as part of their preparation to write their chapters, the authors also make clear what they have learned this time around. Their example attests to the living quality of the book. Every return to it can generate new layers of meaning about life and education, new layers of questioning regarding one's contemporary times, new ways of arguing with Dewey, and more.

That outcome triggers the question, What future is there for *Democracy and Education*? Will people who care about education continue to turn to it? The contributors to this volume attest to how original and majestic the book remains and to how helpful it is in criticizing the current educational scene. However, it is not clear that the field of education will continue to engage its traditions, of which Dewey is a part, in a serious, thoughtful way. The explosion of information in the world today, the rapidity of interaction via contemporary modes of communication, the continued blurring of the lines between providing education and offering marketable degrees and diplomas: these and other forces conspire to push educators into a mode of incessant busyness, with increasingly scarce time for the solitude and the conversation so indispensable for thoughtful study and reflection. Such accelerated circumstances generate professional amnesia and, as a consequence, uninformed and unrooted attachment to passing educational theories and programs. The fact that genuine education continues to take place, at all levels of the system, attests to the underlying quest for meaning and purpose that animates many teachers and students. That quest must compete today with an intense array of pressures that militate against its realization.

Educators need not read their traditions eulogistically, as if turning to Dewey is like sitting in on the weekly sermon, or standing to honor the flag during the seventh inning stretch. On the contrary, to read tradition critically is to reanimate, revitalize, and redirect it (Hansen, 2001, pp. 114–156). It is to gain precious distance both from the impulse toward traditionalism—the uncritical embrace of the past—and from the demands of the pressing present. The aim is not to escape or withdraw from the latter but to hold it up against a broader backdrop than it is itself capable of providing. Only the engagement with tradition can make possible this critical distance; there is no other way. The attempt to reject tradition and start over from scratch is merely a guaranteed method of hardening present assumptions about what is good, proper, appropriate, needed, and so forth. The critical engagement with tradition, of which this entire volume is an enactment, puts the spotlight on what is at stake in considerations about the purposes of education.

Dewey once wrote, in words that ended up on his headstone where he is buried in Vermont, "The things in civilization we most prize are not of ourselves. They exist by grace of the doings and sufferings of the continuous human community in which we are a link. Ours is the responsibility of conserving, transmitting, rectifying and expanding the heritage of values we have received that those who come after us may receive it more solid and secure, more widely accessible and more generously shared than we have received it" (LW.9.57–58). What does Dewey mean by the remarkable fusion of terms such as conserving, transmitting, rectifying, and expanding? How can a process of conserving simultaneously be one of expanding? How can transmitting cohere with rectifying? What does Dewey intend by linking terms such as "prizing," "grace," "heritage," and "values"? One approach to answering these questions is to read or re-read *Democracy and Education*. Any person who takes up that task positions him- or herself to better understand the indispensability of tradition for any meaningful educational scheme. Without traditions of thought and practice, people would be tongue-tied and unable to withstand the latest craze that clamors for attention. Part of engaging tradition is reading it sympathetically, mindful of Dewey's reminder of what all people owe to their precursors. The other part of the process is reading it critically, and here the challenge, the joy, the frustration, and the accomplishment derive from confronting what it means to "rectify" that which has harmed humanity and to "expand" that which has enhanced its prospect. If the present volume contributes to the reconstruction of educational tradition, in the form of continued critical attention to *Democracy and Education*, it will have fulfilled its purpose.

References

Dewey, John. (1985). Democracy and education. In J. A. Boydston (Ed.), *John Dewey, the middle works 1899–1924: Vol. 9. Democracy and education 1916* (pp. 3–370). Carbondale: Southern Illinois University Press.

Dewey, John. (1988). From absolutism to experimentalism. In J. A. Boydston (Ed.), *John Dewey, the later works 1925–1953: Vol. 5. Essays* (pp. 147–160). Carbondale: Southern Illinois University Press.

Dewey, John. (1989). A common faith. In J. A. Boydston (Ed.), *John Dewey, the later works 1925–1953: Vol. 9. Essays* (pp. 1–58). Carbondale: Southern Illinois University Press.

Emerson, Ralph Waldo. (1983/1844). "Experience." In *Ralph Waldo Emerson. Essays & lectures* (pp. 471–492) New York: The Library of America.

Hansen, David T. (2001). *Exploring the moral heart of teaching: Toward a teacher's creed*. New York: Teachers College Press.

Jaspers, Karl. (1962). *Kant*. New York: Harcourt Brace.

Plato. (1961). *Meno*. In E. Hamilton & H. Cairns (Eds.), *The collected dialogues of Plato* (pp. 353–384). Princeton: Princeton University Press.

Ryan, Alan. (1995). *John Dewey and the high tide of American liberalism*. New York: W. W. Norton.

Steiner, George. (2003). *Lessons of the masters*. Cambridge: Harvard University Press.

2

"Of all affairs, communication is the most wonderful"

The Communicative Turn in Dewey's *Democracy and Education*

GERT BIESTA

The Communicative Turn in Dewey's Philosophy

Democracy and Education is not a book that gives itself easily to its readers. I have to confess that when I first read the book as an undergraduate, I found it quite boring. In its attempt to cover almost everything there was to say about education past and present, the book didn't stand out—or at least not to me and not at the time—as making a particular point in the educational discussion or taking a particular position in the educational field. I had to make quite a detour to arrive at a point at which I began to see that in between the chapters and passages that have remained challenging up to the present day, Dewey was actually doing something that was quite unique if not revolutionary, both from an educational and a philosophical point of view. The detour I took first led me to Dewey's writings on knowledge, such as *Studies in Logical Theory* (1903), *Essays in Experimental Logic* (1916), *The Quest for Certainty* (1929), *Logic: The Theory of Inquiry* (1938), and *Knowing and the Known* (1949, with Arthur F. Bentley); then to his work on social psychology, most notably *Human Nature and Conduct* (1922); and from

23

there to what I still consider to be Dewey's most fascinating and most important book: *Experience and Nature* (1925). It was through my reading and rereading of the latter book that I slowly began to see what Dewey was actually trying to do. In *Experience and Nature* I found a Dewey who was trying to move modern philosophy away from its Cartesian preoccupation with mind and consciousness and who was instead putting *communication* at the very center of his thinking.

When Dewey opened "Nature, Communication and Meaning," chapter 5 of *Experience and Nature,* by stating that "(o)f all affairs, communication is the most wonderful" (Dewey, 1958[1929], p. 166), it was not because he had found a new topic to philosophize about. It was because he had come to the conclusion that mind, consciousness, thinking, subjectivity, meaning, intelligence, language, rationality, logic, inference, and truth—all those things that philosophers over the centuries have considered to be part of the natural makeup of human beings—only come into existence through and as a result of communication. "When communication occurs," Dewey wrote, "all natural events are subject to reconsideration and revision; they are re-adapted to meet the requirements of conversation, whether it be public discourse or that preliminary discourse termed thinking" (ibid.). And, in a slightly more daring passage: "That things should be able to pass from the plane of external pushing and pulling to that of revealing themselves to man, and thereby to themselves; and that the fruit of communication should be participation, sharing, is a wonder by the side of which transubstantiation pales" (ibid.).

Chapter 5 of *Experience and Nature* contains many passages that exemplify the 'communicative turn' in Dewey's philosophy. He introduced his views by noting that "(s)ocial interaction and institutions have been treated as the products of a ready-made *specific* physical or mental endowment of a self-sufficient individual" (ibid., p. 169; emphasis in original). But this is not how Dewey saw it. He argued instead that "the world of inner experience is dependent upon an extension of language which is a social product and operation" (ibid., p. 173), which means that "psychic events . . . have language for one of their conditions" (ibid., p. 169). In Dewey's view, language is itself "a natural function of human association" and its consequences "react upon other events, physical and human, giving them meaning or significance" (ibid., p. 173). Failure to see this, so Dewey argued, led to the "subjectivistic, solipsistic and egotistic strain in modern thought" (ibid., p. 173). Yet for Dewey "soliloquy is the product and reflex of converse with others; social communication not an effect of soliloquy" (ibid., p. 170). This ultimately means that "communication is a condition of consciousness" (ibid., p. 187). As Dewey explained: "If we had not talked with others and they with us, we should never talk to and with ourselves" (ibid.). Along similar lines, Dewey argued that "the import of logical and rational essences is the consequence of social interactions" (ibid., p. 171), just as intelligence and meaning should be seen as "natural consequences of the peculiar form which interaction sometimes assumes in the case of human beings" (ibid., p. 180).

Dewey was well aware that putting communication at the very center and the very beginning of his philosophy meant that he had to think differently about the process of communication itself as well. He could no longer rely on the idea—still so common in our days (see, e.g., Biesta, 2004a; Mcquail & Windahl, 1989)—that communication "acts as a mechanical go-between to convey observations and ideas that have prior and independent existence" (ibid., p. 169). In chapter 5 of *Experience and Nature* he therefore unfolded an understanding of communication in thoroughly *practical* terms (see Biesta, 1994; 1995). He presented communication "as the establishment of cooperation in an activity in which there are partners, and in which the activity of each is modified and regulated by partnership" (Dewey, 1958[1929], p. 179). Against this background, he defined communication as a process in which "(s)omething is literally made in common in at least two different centres of behavior" (ibid., p. 178). He explained communication as a process in which person A and person B coordinate their actions around a thing in such a way that "B's understanding of A's movement and sounds is that he responds to the thing from the standpoint of A," that is, perceiving the thing "as it may function in A's experience, instead of just egocentrically" (ibid., p. 178). In this situation B responds to the *meaning* of A's movement and sounds, rather than to the movement and sounds itself. Similarly, "A . . . conceives the thing not only in its direct relationship to himself, but as a thing capable of being grasped and handled by B. He sees the thing as it may function in B's experience" (ibid.). This view of communication as a meaningful or, better, a *meaning-guided* process led Dewey to the conclusion that meaning itself "is primarily a property of behavior," but the behavior of which it is a "quality is a distinctive behavior; cooperative, in that response to another's act involves contemporaneous response to a thing as entering into the other's behavior, and this upon both sides" (ibid., p. 179). It is this process, so Dewey argued, that effects "the transformation of organic gestures and cries into . . . things with significance" (ibid., p. 176) or, as he put it elsewhere, into events with meaning.

What does all this have to do with *Democracy and Education*? For me personally it was only when I had to come to appreciate the pivotal role of communication in Dewey's philosophy, and to understand the particularities of his specific view of communication, that I was able to see that this whole theory of communication was actually already there in the first three chapters of *Democracy and Education*, a book published nine years before *Experience and Nature*, and probably written and conceived well before that date. As a matter of fact, the contract for *Democracy and Education* was signed on July 21, 1911 and in the summer before the book finally appeared Dewey wrote that he had been "working away fragmentarily at a philosophy of education for four or five years" (LW.9.377). But what is important here is not so much my personal odyssey—although it may well be that I am not the only one who initially overlooked the significance of the first three chapters of *Democracy and Education*. There are two other aspects of *Democracy and Education*, however, that are of a much wider significance. The first is the fact that Dewey seemed to have presented his philosophy of communication for the first time in the context of a discussion about education; the second is that he developed his theory of education as a theory of communication. I want to argue that this double relationship between education and communication not only gives *Democracy and Education* a special place in Dewey's writing career in that it is the book in which the 'communicative turn' in his work actually occurs; it also makes the book stand out as a rather unique contribution to the theory and philosophy of education. Let's look at these two points in more detail.

The Communicative Turn in *Democracy and Education*

As far as I have been able to investigate, *Democracy and Education* is the first publication in which Dewey presents his account of communication as a process of social cooperation and coordination in full detail. The index to Dewey's collected works shows that communication was discussed in two earlier publications, one probably dating from 1895 (*Plan of Organization of the University Primary School*; 1895, EW.5.224–243) and one from 1899 (*The School and Society*; 1899, MW.1.1–109). In both cases, however, the discussion bears little or no resemblance to the ideas that Dewey was going to unfold in *Democracy and Education*. In the *Plan of Organization of the University Primary School* the word "communication" is mentioned on page 231, but only in a very general way. A slightly more precise comment is made on page 226 when Dewey writes that language "is not primarily expression of *thought*, but rather social *communication*" (1895, EW.5.226). This, however, is not followed up with any detailed discussion about the *process* of social communication. In *The School and Society* "communication" is mentioned on page 29 as one of the manifestations of the child's social instinct, but again without any further discussion of the communicative process. It seems safe to conclude, therefore, that the theory of communication did not yet exist at the time of these publications.

This does raise questions about the development of Dewey's thinking up to the publication of *Democracy and Education*. My investigations suggest that *Democracy and Education* is *not* the culmination of a line of thought that was already worked out in earlier publications. The treatment of communication in *Democracy and Education* is distinctively new and different from what Dewey had written before, which suggests that the book marks a decisive step in the development of Dewey's thought. In earlier publications there is a general awareness of the social nature of the individual and the social function of language (see, e.g., 1895, EW.5.226). And in *My Pedagogic Creed* (1897, EW.5.84–95) Dewey is aware of the importance of participation in the educational process ("I believe that all education proceeds by the participation of the individual in the social consciousness of the race"; 1897, EW.5.84). But not even in articles with such titles as "The Bearings of Pragmatism upon Education" (1909, MW.4.178–191), and "Education from a Social Perspective" (1913, MW.7.113–127), nor in relevant sections of the first edition of *How We Think* (e.g., the section Language and the Training of Thought; 1909, MW.6.314–327) is there any explicit discussion of the idea that communication is a process of social coordination and cooperation or that this process not only effectuates common understanding and a common, shared world, but that it is also the origin of reflection and reflective consciousness. The only exception I have been able to find is in a series of lectures on the psychology of social behavior that was given in 1914 and of which a summary was published in the same year (for the summary, see Dewey, 1914, MW.7.390–408; the text of the lectures was never published). In these lectures, Dewey is much more explicit about the communicative conditions under which language, meaning, and reflection originate and seems to have presented a view that is close to what was going to appear two years later in *Democracy and Education* (see particularly MW.7.395–397), yet, given the date of these lectures, it is reasonable to assume that Dewey had by then already written a substantial part of *Democracy and Education*, particularly the chapters on communication.

Any further explanation for the emergence of the communicative turn in *Democracy and Education* will have to remain more speculative. One factor that may have contributed to the development of Dewey's ideas about communication is the influence of colleagues at Columbia University where Dewey moved after leaving the University of Chicago in 1904. Dewey's biographer George Dykhuizen particularly mentions the influence of Franz Boas, "whose reputation in anthropology rivaled that of Dewey in philosophy" (Dykhuizen, 1973, p. 123). Boas, according to Dykhuizen, helped Dewey see "that a sound philosophy of experience could not restrict itself within the confines set by biology and psychology but had to include also institutional and cultural factors, which play a role as decisive in determining what experience is and will be" (ibid.). "Hegel had earlier introduced Dewey to very similar notions; now Boas and other anthropologists, including Ruth Benedict at Columbia, helped guide Dewey's thinking further toward the cultural anthropology that was to be such an important feature of his later philosophy" (ibid.).

A second influence that may have shaped Dewey's thinking on communication can be found in the collaboration with Dewey's former colleague at the Universities of Michigan and Chicago, James Hayden Tufts. Their book *Ethics*, published in 1908 (see MW.5), contains an extensive discussion of group life and the "rationalizing and socializing agencies in early society" (see MW.5.41–53). Here we can find some of the ideas that were to become central in Dewey's understanding of communication, most notably the claim that "cooperation implies a common end" and that in cooperation "each is interested in the success of all," which makes the common end to be "a controlling rule of action" (ibid., p. 46). The irony is that the discussion about group life and socialization primarily occurs in part I of the book which, as the authors make clear, was written by Tufts (see MW.5.6). While the collaboration on *Ethics* did expose Dewey to questions about cooperation and coordination of action and the importance of this for the emergence of group mores and customs, it was not Dewey himself who put pen to paper in writing about these particular topics.

The third influence on Dewey's ideas about communication has to be the interaction with George Herbert Mead who also was a close colleague both at the University of Michigan and the University of Chicago. As I have discussed in detail elsewhere (see Biesta 1998; 1999a; 2005), Mead had already developed a fairly detailed understanding of communication in terms of coordination of action in the first decade of the twentieth century. Although Mead is not mentioned in *Democracy and Education*, Meadian ideas about the role of gesture in human cooperation and interaction play a central role in Dewey's account of the process of communication, which makes it difficult to believe that Dewey did not have Mead's ideas in mind when he developed his account of communication.

The fact that the communicative turn in Dewey's work came to fruition in a book on education rather than a book on philosophy proper highlights the importance of education for Dewey's intellectual development. The case of *Democracy and Education* suggests that it was only when Dewey had to reflect on the fundamental 'mechanisms' of the educational process, when, in other words, he was trying to formulate an answer to the question of how education is actually *possible*, that he came to develop his theory of communication. Interestingly enough, this is precisely the point Dewey made in 1930 when, in an autobiographical piece called "From Absolutism to Experimentalism" (1930, LW.5.147–160), he wrote that it was his interest in the practice and theory of education that "fused with and brought together what might otherwise have been separate interests—that in psychology and that in social institutions and social life" (ibid., p. 156). It is also the position he put forward in chapter 24 of *Democracy and Education* when he reached the conclusion that philosophy is essentially "*the general theory of education*" (1916, MW.9.338, emphasis in original) since education "offers a vantage ground from which to penetrate to the human, as distinct from the technical, significance of philosophical discussions" (ibid.) so that we can think of education as "the laboratory in which philosophical distinctions become concrete and are tested" (ibid., p. 339) and of philosophy as "the theory of education in its most general phases" (ibid., p. 341). This, then, brings me to the second point: the role of communication in Dewey's understanding of education.

Education as a Practice of Communication

A question one may want to ask is why Dewey came up with a theory of *communication*, and not, for example, a theory of instruction or a theory of learning. Part of the answer can be found in some of Dewey's earliest writings on education, particularly in the way in which he 'framed' the "problem of education" as neither being about individual development nor about adaptation to the existing social order—or, in more disciplinary terms: as neither a psychological nor a sociological problem. In the *Plan of Organization of the University Primary School* Dewey put it as follows: "The ultimate problem of all education is to co-ordinate the psychological and the social factors" (1895, EW.5.224). Some years later, in *My Pedagogic Creed* (1897), he argued along similar lines that "the psychological and social sides [of the educational process] are organically related," so that "education cannot be regarded as a compromise between the two, or a superimposition of one upon the other" (1897, EW.5.85). In a sense we can read Dewey's theory of communication as his answer to a question he asked twenty years earlier, namely, how the interplay between the individual and the social factors, between 'the child' and 'the curriculum' can be brought about.

In the first three chapters of *Democracy and Education*, Dewey focused this discussion on a central educational question, namely, how meaning can be communicated. Although he wrote that "education consists primarily in transmission through communication" (1916, MW.9.12), he hastened to add that this is not a process of "direct contagion" or "literal inculcation" (ibid., p. 14). Communication should rather be understood as "a process of sharing experience till it becomes a common possession" (ibid., p. 12). This means that the central educational 'mechanism' is *participation*, or, to be more precise, "the communication which insures participation in a common understanding" (ibid., p. 7). The latter point is crucial for Dewey. Participation is neither about physical proximity nor the situation in which all work toward a common end (see ibid., pp. 7–8). It is only when all "are *cognizant* of the common end and all [are] interested in it" that there is real participation, and it is only this kind of participation "which modifies the disposition of both parties who undertake it" (ibid., p. 12, emphasis added). This means that education does not simply follow from *being in* a social environment. Education follows from *having* a social environment, and to have a social environment means to be in a situation in which one's activities "are associated with others" (ibid., p. 15). As Dewey explained: "A being connected with other beings cannot perform his own activities without taking the activities of others into account. For they are the indispensable conditions of the realization of his tendencies" (ibid., p. 16).

It is along these lines that Dewey suggested a crucial difference between *education* and *training*. Training is about those situations in which those who learn do not really share in the use to which their actions are put. They are not a *partner* in a shared activity. Education, on the other hand, is about those situations in which one really shares or participates in a common activity, in which one really has an interest in its accomplishment just as others have. In those situations, one's ideas and emotions are changed as a result of the participation. In such situations, "(one) not merely acts in a way agreeing with the actions of others, but, in so acting, the same ideas and emotions are aroused in [oneself] that animate the others" (ibid., p. 17). It is not, therefore, that meaning is transmitted from one person to another. It is because people share in a common activity that their ideas and emotions are transformed as a result of and in function of the activity in which they participate. This is how things are literally made in common. "Understanding one another means that objects, including sounds, have the same value for both with respect to carrying on a common pursuit" (ibid., p. 19).

The crucial point for Dewey is that common understanding is *not* a condition for cooperation. It is not that we first need to come to a common understanding and only then can begin to coordinate our actions. For Dewey it is precisely the other way around: common under-standing is produced by, is the outcome of successful cooperation in action. This is why he wrote that "the bare fact that language consists of sounds which are *mutually intelligible* is enough of itself to show that its meaning depends upon connections with a shared experience" (ibid., p. 19). In this respect there is no difference between the way in which the thing "hat" and the sound "h-a-t" get their meaning. Both get their meaning "by being used in a given way, and they acquire the same meaning with the child which they have with the adult because they are used in a common experience by both" (ibid., p. 19). In sum: "The guarantee for the same manner of use is found in the fact that the thing and the sounds are first employed in a *joint* activity, as a means of setting up an active connection between the child and a grown-up. Similar ideas or meanings spring up because both persons are engaged as partners in an action where what each does depends upon and influences what the other does" (ibid., emphasis in original).

In *Democracy and Education*, the theory of communication not only figures in Dewey's account of how meaning can be communicated, it also provides the framework for a social or communicative *theory of meaning* itself. While participation in a joint activity is central in Dewey's account of communication, he emphasized the importance of the role played by things—both the things around which action is coordinated and the sounds and gestures that are used in the coordination of action. Dewey noted that it is often argued "that a person learns by merely having the qualities of things impressed upon his mind through the gateway of the senses. Having received a store of sensory impressions, associations or some power of mental synthesis is supposed to combine them into ideas—into things with a *meaning*" (ibid., p. 34). But the meaning of stones, oranges, trees, and chairs is not to be found in the things themselves. As a matter of fact, "it is the characteristic *use* to which the thing is put . . . which supplies the meaning with which it is identified" (ibid., p. 34). And to have the same ideas about things that others have is "to attach the same meanings to things and to acts which others attach" (ibid., p. 35)—something that is precisely brought about through communication, through conjoint action.

The educational significance of Dewey's communicative theory of meaning is first and foremost found in a rejection of the idea that the child can simply discover the meaning of the world—and of the things and events in the world—through careful observation from the 'outside.' For Dewey, the meaning of the world is, after all, not located in the things and events themselves, but in the social practices in which things, gestures, sounds, events play a role. We could therefore say that because meaning only exists *in* social practices, it is, in a sense, located *in-between* those who constitute the social practice through their interactions. This is why communication is not about the transportation of information from point A to point B, but all about participation. If it is the case that meaning only exists *in* social practices, then it also follows that meaning can only be (re)presented in and through social practices. For education this implies, among other things, that we should approach questions about the curriculum in terms of the representation of *practices* inside the walls of the school and not in terms of the representation of formal abstractions of these practices. This means, for example, that the teaching of mathematics should be about bringing the practice of mathemat*izing* into the school and allowing for students to take part in this practice, just as, for example, the teaching of history should be about engaging students with the practice of *historizing*.

The educational implications of the participatory theory of communication are not only programmatic. The idea that students learn from the practices in which they take part is also helpful in understanding why the hidden curriculum is so effective—and often far more effective than the official curriculum. The hidden curriculum is, after all, located in the very practices in which children and students take part during their time in school, while the official curriculum is a much more artificial add-on to the real "life in schools." This also explains why one of the things that children and students learn most effectively during their time in schools and other educational institutions is the practice of schooling itself, that is, how to be a 'proper' student and how to 'play the game' of schooling.

Dewey's theory of communication also has implications for how we understand teaching and the impact of the teacher on the student. A crucial implication of the idea of communication as participation is that the effect of the teacher on the student is not direct but only indirect. Teaching is not a kind of input that goes directly into the mind of the student without any noise, disturbance, or transformation. Teaching is about the construction of a social situation and the effects of teaching only result from the ways in which students take part in the social situation. We can take this point further and ask the question: who actually educates? Common sense would dictate that educators educate—and in a certain sense this is, of course, true. But if it is the case that there is no direct relationship between the activities of the educator and the learning of the student, that teaching is not direct input into the minds of the students, then the conclusion has to be that it is the social situation which emerges from the interaction between the teacher and the student that actually educates. Or, as Dewey put it:

"We never educate directly, but indirectly by means of the environment" (ibid., p. 23).

Dewey's ideas about the social origin and 'location' of meaning also imply that reflection itself has a social origin, in that reflection only becomes possible once one is able to make a conscious distinction between things and their possible meanings. "The difference between an adjustment to a physical stimulus and a *mental* act," Dewey wrote, "is that the latter involves a response to a thing in its *meaning*; the former does not." This gives one's behavior "a mental quality" (ibid., p. 34). And it is only when one has an *idea* of a thing that one is able "to respond to the thing in view of its place in an inclusive scheme of action" (ibid., p. 35). It becomes possible "to foresee the drift and possible consequences of the action of the thing upon us and of our action upon it" (ibid.), and this makes the transition from action to intelligent action possible—itself a crucial transition in Dewey's educational thought.

This is, of course, not all there is to say about the theory of education that Dewey developed in the first three chapters of *Democracy and Education*. But it suffices as an indication of the kind of educational theory that Dewey presented in these chapters. What is unique about this theory, and about Dewey's approach to education more generally, is first and foremost the simple fact that Dewey approaches education as a process of communication. Contrary to a long-standing tradition in educational theory and practice, Dewey's theory does not focus on questions about teaching or instruction as such. He does not conceive of education as something that is done to children and students instead of with them. But Dewey also doesn't end up in the other extreme, which would be a theory of learning, that is, a theory that only looks at the activities of 'learners' without recognition of the contributions of others (a popular but problematic move in our days; see Biesta, 2004b). While Dewey does acknowledge the crucial role of the activities of the student in the educational process, the configuration of this process as a process of *communication*—of participation in a conjoint activity—is the central idea of Dewey's educational philosophy. Dewey's philosophy of education is therefore not a child-centred approach but a thoroughly *communication-centered* philosophy. This is what makes him stand out in the canon of progressive education—as he would make very clear in his 1938 *Experience and Education*. I believe that it makes him, and more specifically *Democracy and Education*, also stand out in the history of educational theory and practice more generally. This is not to say that Dewey has remained the only one who made communication the central principle of his educational approach, but he may well have been one of the first to do so.[1] This, then, is the other reason why *Democracy and Education* is such an important book.

Democracy and Education and our Educational Future

Where does all this leave us today? Can *Democracy and Education* still speak to us? Can Dewey's theory of communication still function as a reference point for contemporary educational theory and practice? In conclusion, let me make three observations.

First, as I have argued in this chapter, *Democracy and Education* is an important book in Dewey's oeuvre because it inaugurated the communicative turn in his philosophy. I believe that it is important to remind ourselves that Dewey's philosophy is first and foremost a philosophy of communication—or, as I have argued elsewhere, a philosophy of communicative *action* (see Biesta, 1995). If I were to say what makes Dewey prominent in the canon of Western philosophy, it is not the fact that he is a fallibilist, an antifoundationalist, or a postpositivist but first of all that he is a philosopher of communication. Maybe this is one of the less well understood and appreciated aspects of Dewey's philosophy, in which case *Democracy and Education* can function as an important reminder. There is, however, a proviso in that Dewey's philosophy of communication is a *naturalistic* philosophy of communication, one that understands communication as something emerging from natural processes (see Biesta & Burbules, 2003).

In this respect, Dewey's approach differs from the approach of the other major philosopher of communication, Jürgen Habermas, whose work is guided by a *transcendental* conception of communication. A problem with Habermas's approach is the coercive character of (his understanding of) communicative rationality. Here Dewey's approach to communication is far more open and definitely less coercive and provides an alternative starting point for a philosophy of communication. The main problem with Dewey's naturalistic approach, however, is that it seeks a foundation for communication in (human) nature, in something that itself lies outside the confines of communication. In my own work I am trying to develop a more consistent and in a sense more radical understanding of communication, one that tries to think of communication itself in communicative terms (see Biesta, 1999b; 2004a). This version of pragmatism, which I refer to as deconstructive pragmatism, may lead to an understanding of communication that is neither naturalistic nor transcendental and might help us to develop a pragmatist philosophy of communication that is ready and relevant for the twenty-first century.

Second, I believe that *Democracy and Education* remains important for education precisely because it places communication at the very heart of educational theory and educational practice. One important implication of this approach, as I have shown, involves our understanding of the location of meaning. Dewey convincingly shows that meaning is not to be found in 'the world' itself, but is located in human practices. Schools still tend to focus on the end products of such practices (in the form of knowledge, skills, or values), and tend to represent these end products as discoveries rather than human constructions. In doing so, they continue to create an artificial distance between the learner and the curriculum.

Dewey's communicative approach urges educators to ask how learners can get in touch with human practices rather than with their end products. It urges educators to ask how students can become engaged with the practice of historiz*ing* or mathematiz*ing*, rather than with history or mathematics (see also Biesta, 2005). The idea of such a communicative curriculum also has repercussions for the learner. If learning takes place in and through participation and communication, then the role of the learner changes from being a meaning-taker to being a meaning-maker. If students are really allowed to participate in human practices, if, to put it in Dewey's words, they can engage in education rather than training, then this must imply that education can no longer simply be a reproductive process, but must acknowledge that the learner can be a source of new meanings and new insights as well. In both respects, Dewey's communicative approach as laid out in *Democracy and Education* still stands out as a critical reminder of a different, more humane, and in a sense more realistic approach to education.

Finally, we should not forget that the philosophy of communication spelled out in the first three chapters of *Democracy and Education* also provides the framework for an approach to democracy that is both communicative and educative. For Dewey, democracy *is* participation, and the key question he asks when defining democracy is about the opportunities for communication and participation, thereby making the principle of shared interests the primary test of the worth of any form of human association (see chapter 7 of *Democracy and Education*). Dewey may well have been too optimistic about the extent to which communication and participation, the sharing in a conjoint activity, can bring and keep people together. But it is important not to confuse optimism with naivete. A philosophy of communication can never guarantee social harmony or peaceful coexistence, and it would be naive to expect that it could. But if there is any reason for optimism, it has to come from the belief that at the end of the day communication and interaction are to be preferred over isolation and disengagement. Our vulnerable planet has simply become too small for the latter to be a viable option. In this respect, I do believe that a philosophy of communication like the one presented in *Democracy and Education* can still be a source of inspiration for our educational efforts today.

Note

1. One of the best studies on this topic remains Klaus Schaller's *Pädagogik der Kommunikation* (1987). Although Schaller's theory of education as communication has its roots in Continental philosophy, primarily the work of Heidegger, he does acknowledge the importance of Dewey's work.

References

Biesta, G. J. J. (1994). Education as practical intersubjectivity. Towards a critical-pragmatic understanding of education. *Educational Theory* 44(3), 299–317.

Biesta, G. J. J. (1995). Pragmatism as a pedagogy of communicative action. In J. Garrison (Ed.), *The new scholarship on John Dewey* (pp. 105–122). Dordrecht/Boston/London: Kluwer Academic Publishers.

Biesta, G. J. J. (1998). Mead, intersubjectivity, and education: The early writings. *Studies in Philosophy and Education 17*, 73–99.

Biesta, G. J. J. (1999a). Redefining the subject, redefining the social, reconsidering education: George Herbert Mead's course on Philosophy of Education at the University of Chicago. *Educational Theory* 49(4), 475–492.

Biesta, G. J. J. (1999b). Radical intersubjectivity. Reflections on the "different" foundation of education. *Studies in Philosohpy and Education 18*(4), 203–220.

Biesta, G. J. J. (2004a). "Mind the gap!" Communication and the educational relation. In Charles Bingham & Alexander M. Sidorkin (Eds.), *No education without relation* (pp. 11–22). New York: Peter Lang.

Biesta, G. J. J. (2004b). Against learning. Reclaiming a language for education in an age of learning. *Nordisk Pedagogik 23*, 70–82.

Biesta, G. J. J. (2005). George Herbert Mead und die Theorie der schulischen Bildung. In D. Troehler & J. Oelkers (Eds.), *Pädagogik und Pragmatismus. Gesellschaftstheorie und die Entwicklung der Pädagogik* (pp. 131–150). Zürich: Verlag Pestalozzianum.

Biesta, G. J. J., & Burbules, N. (2003). *Pragmatism and educational research*. Lanham, MD: Rowman and Littlefield.

Dewey, J. (1895). *Plan of organization of the university primary school*. In J. A. Boydston (Ed.), *John Dewey, the early works, 1882–1898: Vol. 5* (pp. 224–243). Carbondale: Southern Illinois University Press.

Dewey, J. (1897). *My pedagogic creed*. In J. A. Boydston (Ed.), *John Dewey, the early works, 1882–1898: Vol. 5* (pp. 84–95). Carbondale: Southern Illinois University Press.

Dewey, J. (1899). The school and society. In J. A. Boydston (Ed.), *John Dewey, the middle works, 1899–1924: Vol. 1* (pp. 1–109). Carbondale: Southern Illinois University Press.

Dewey, J. (1909). The bearings of pragmatism upon education. In J. A. Boydston (Ed.), *John Dewey, the middle works, 1899–1924: Vol. 4* (pp. 178–191). Carbondale: Southern Illinois University Press.

Dewey, J. (1909). How we think. In J. A. Boydston (Ed.), *John Dewey, the middle works, 1899–1924: Vol. 6.* Carbondale: Southern Illinois University Press.

Dewey, J. (1913). Education from a social perspective. In J. A. Boydston (Ed.), *John Dewey, the middle works, 1899–1924: Vol. 7* (pp. 113–127). Carbondale: Southern Illinois University Press.

Dewey, J. (1914). The psychology of social behavior. In J. A. Boydston (Ed.), *John Dewey, the middle works, 1899–1924: Vol. 7* (pp. 390–408). Carbondale: Southern Illinois University Press.

Dewey, J. (1916). Democracy and education. In J. A. Boydston (Ed.), *John Dewey, the middle works, 1899–1924: Vol. 9.* Carbondale: Southern Illinois University Press.

Dewey, J. (1930). From absolutism to experimentalism. In J. A. Boydston (Ed.), *John Dewey, the later works, 1925–1953: Vol. 5* (pp. 147–160). Carbondale: Southern Illinois University Press.

Dewey, J. (1958[1929]). *Experience and nature* (2nd ed.). New York: Dover.

Dewey, J., & Tufts, J. H. (1908). Ethics. In J. A. Boydston (Ed.), *John Dewey, the middle works, 1899–1924: Vol. 5* (pp. 3–540). Carbondale: Southern Illinois University Press.

Dykhuizen, G. (1973). *The life and mind of John Dewey.* Carbondale: Southern Illinois University Press.

Mcquail, D., & Windahl, S. (1989). Models of communication. In E. Barnouw, G. Gerbner, W. Schramm, T. L. Worth, & L. Gross (Eds.), *International encyclopedia of communication* (pp. 36–44). New York/Oxford: Oxford University Press.

Schaller, K. (1987). *Pädagogik der Kommunikation.* Sankt Augustin: Richarz.

3

Curriculum Matters

REBA N. PAGE

Suppose you are interested, as I am, in the curriculum in U.S. schools today—would there be any value in your consulting John Dewey's *Democracy and Education*? After all, the title does not mention curriculum, and the book was published almost eighty years ago, at a quite different point in American and world history.

My own recent experience in rereading Dewey's classic leads me to a positive answer. This may not be particularly surprising because many students of education know that curriculum is one of the central topics in *Democracy and Education*, notwithstanding the word's absence from the book's title and all the chapter titles save one. Dewey puts subject matter at the heart of education, and curriculum at the heart of schooling, along with teaching and administration. As he makes clear, one cannot teach or learn without teaching or learning *something*. That "something" is subject matter, and the subject matter of the school is the curriculum.

As Dewey also makes clear, curriculum is an important means by which societies define and maintain themselves. A democratic society, he adds, is particularly dependent on a "humanized curriculum" in which knowledge is meaningful to youth because it "connects with the common interests of men as men" (MW.9.200).

But we have problems with humanized curriculum. For example, yesterday's *Albuquerque Journal* headlined, "School's at Home for More U.S. Kids," and reported that somewhere between 1.2 and 2 million youth are now homeschooled. Although this number represents only

39

about 2.2% of the school-age population, it has increased 29% since 1999. The article reports that parents say they turned to homeschooling, when they could afford to, because they are worried about safety in schools, want the flexibility to teach religious and moral lessons, and/or are dissatisfied with academic instruction. Although news articles are necessarily inconclusive, I see the parents' responses mirroring the problem with curriculum that Dewey reiterates throughout *Democracy and Education*—the knowledge taught in schools is remote from and dead to concerns of life that are crucial to our humanity. When single-minded— "abstract and bookish, to use the ordinary words of depreciation" (MW.9.11)—school curriculum ignores our longing for connection between knowledge and action, self and other, and mind and heart.

My positive answer regarding the continuing value of *Democracy and Education*, however predictable it may seem, only emerged after I encountered several surprises while revisiting Dewey's book. For one thing, I was overwhelmed this time around by the sheer abundance of ideas the book contains, the comprehensive if largely implicit model of curriculum those ideas constitute, and the fresh and intriguing possibilities the ideas seem to offer for thinking about, and rethinking, our present school curriculum.

For another, I was startled by how emotionally engaged I was by *Democracy and Education*. One always expects an intellectual challenge from a Dewey text, but this experience was also deeply moving. Differently than in earlier readings, the book evoked a stream of personal and professional memories—even some Emily Dickinson-like reveries. I realize Dewey would not have been surprised because he saw personal interest and the emotions as just as fundamental in inquiry as "pure intellect" (MW.9.345). But I was surprised.

I believe my response to Dewey's book testifies to its *careful intelligence*. Thoughtfulness saturates its language for curriculum, as does profound concern for students and teachers, and for all knowledge and all humanity. The book's mindfulness stands in stark contrast to our current, coercive discourse in the United States about uniform standards, "high-stakes" accountability measures, and centralized control. If nothing else, the contrast gives us purchase on exactly where we are located today.

For example, for me *Democracy and Education* provoked two questions: (1) *Is* America a democracy or, better perhaps, do we still aspire to democracy—or is America now a plutocracy, governed by the rich, for the rich, as more than 40% of the country's astronomical wealth is owned by a mere 1% of the population (Phillips, 2002), and (2) *Is* present schooling educative—or is it strictly legalistic, as we now find ourselves reduced to requiring, by law, that youth *will* learn and schools *must* teach? On both counts, our present course would seem to be "high-stakes" not only for students and schools, but "high-stakes" for a democratic society.

In commenting on the value in rereading *Democracy and Education* for understanding and acting on curriculum today, I draw principally from chapter 14, "The Nature of Subject Matter." There Dewey treats subject matter theoretically, particularly its intellectual aspects (a short section is devoted to social aspects). But I also refer occasionally to other portions of *Democracy and Education* because Dewey's discussion of curriculum is threaded throughout the book, most notably perhaps in the nine chapters following chapter 14, in which he works out the practical implications of his theoretical discussion in relation to the subjects schools typically teach. Along with analysis, my commentary also includes some of the personal memories that arose as I reread *Democracy and Education* this time around. They helped me ground various of Dewey's propositions about subject matter and curriculum, and I hope they may provide readers some ballast, too.

I center my discussion on a single pair of ideas from the vast store in *Democracy and Education*: informal and formal education. I choose this pair because Dewey emphasizes it, in an odd remark that "a proper balance" between the "incidental" education that occurs in our everyday associations with others and the "intentional" education that occurs mostly in schools is "one the weightiest problems with which the philosophy of education has to cope" (MW.9.12). I was struck by this emphatic claim—and baffled by what Dewey meant by it. I cannot recall much attention to formal and informal education or the issue of their balance in current educational research and policy.[1] The article in the Albuquerque paper assumes a division between homeschooling and schools, not a connection. Therefore, in tackling Dewey's curious assertion, I imagined that it might throw a fresh light on our present ideas and practices in education and, particularly, curriculum, which we have trouble seeing because they are so familiar we take them as obvious or commonsensical. After a century of building a mass, public, K–12 system, we readily take for granted that all education is formal and therefore synonymous with schooling, and that the more access to schooling for all youth the better. However, reading *Democracy and Education*, we may begin to see a different question: *What* are all youth gaining access to?[2]

As Dewey indicates in chapter 14, this is a question about the subject matter of the school—the curriculum, and the school studies that make up its content. Specifically, it is a question about how it is possible that the knowledge taught in schools, in contrast to subject matter in informal education, so often proves to be of uncertain, if not downright negligible, value, and how such a state of affairs is of consequence for both individuals and American society.[3]

Informal Education: A Family Road Trip

Let me begin with one of the personal memories that recurred throughout my reading of *Democracy and Education*, one that persisted even when I tried to ignore it because it seemed, erroneously as it turned out, a diversion from Dewey's ideas rather than a move into them. It is a memory of a family road trip. I retell it, thinking it exemplifies some of Dewey's thinking about informal education.

In August 1969, my husband and I, along with our eighteen-month-old daughter, Katie, as well as my two teen-aged sisters and our large dog, Ruggs, were piled into an unair-conditioned station wagon, heading from the deep humidity of the corn fields of northwestern Illinois to the even thicker swamp of Baltimore, where my husband was going to begin a doctoral program in English literature. It was late in the day on the second day of our trip and we were all a little the worse for wear—windblown yet unable to close the windows, stuck to the car upholstery as we were stuck in the car. We were riding together/alone, silent, hoping the dog wouldn't breathe on us, intent only on arrival and deliverance.

And then, just as we made our way over a pass in the Appalachians, a small voice from the backseat announced excitedly, "Munn"! The one-and-a-half-year-old, perched in one of those old, unsafe, car seats we used back then—the kind with metal arms that hooked over the back of the seat of the car—repeated and pointed, a little demandingly: "Munn! Munn"! And so we parents roused ourselves and nodded, "Yes," we echoed "The moon," and even the teenagers joined in in their slightly supercilious way, "Yes, there's that ol' summertime moon." And, with Katie pointing, yes, there *was* the moon—full, creamy-white, floating up out of the brooding purple of the coastal plain to the east.

But, then, as Katie turned to the teenage aunties sitting beside her, she caught sight of the sky to the west, out the back window of the station wagon and, with equal excitement, she announced "Sun! Sun"! And, sure enough, as we all turned to look back, there was the orange fireball that had dogged us through a long summer day, descending in all its glory into the western horizon. Less lethargic now, we acknowledged the child again, and again, we repeated her talk, the way adults often do with young children. "Yes," we said, "There's the sun going down."

And then Katie expanded the play, reaching out her hand and pointing us to the east, with "Munn! Munn!" and then, swiveling around and throwing back her head with, "Sun! Sun!" And as she continued pointing and chortling and looking to us to see that we were noticing, too, we reassured her that we were, and we laughed, and we chanted with her—"Munn! Munn! Sun! Sun!"

I tell this story—and perhaps I recalled it when reading *Democracy and Education*—because it seems to capture something of Dewey's notion of the children we adults must care to educate. Not empty or passive children, even when very young, but active children engaged intelligently with the things and people of their worlds, children who, as Dewey puts it, are quite capable of self-direction in the proper situation, meaning an educative situation.

I tell the story, too, because it captures some facets of Dewey's view of the nature and value of subject matter and knowledge. Our young daughter had a subject she was studying as she pursued her interests, such as getting others in the car to join her in making sense of the evening sky. She used words, along with her eyes and arms, to reach bodily toward qualities and relationships in the things and people in the world around her, naming them and handling them and thereby connecting with them. She wasn't merely responding to physical stimuli that impressed themselves on her retinas—she was engrossed in the spectacular beauty of an evening sky, and wanted to communicate about it and thereby share it with the family around her. It's even distantly possible, although I think this is the mother–teacher speaking now about some older Katie, that our daughter's excitement reflected some vague sense on her part that there was something a little odd about those two otherwise familiar objects, because how could both the sun and the moon be visible in the sky at the same time?

Of course, Katie had no knowledge of what Dewey describes as the formal, abstract, logically organized subject matter of the academic disciplines, such as astronomy. And, equally, none of us in the car responded to her interests by offering a lecture on the laws governing the movement of celestial phenomena. However unconsciously, we knew that such abstractions would "no more represent the living world of [Katie's] experience than the astronomer's knowledge of Mars represents a baby's acquaintance with the room in which he stays" (MW.9.190).

Instead, what is today called a "teachable moment," along with its materials, were incidental and informal, not intentionally selected or planned as formal education is, whether in schools or other settings such as a homeschool. We adults knew the child and we responded to her and the subjects that mattered to her, not to some generalized timetable of child development or standardized knowledge from a text-and-test. Put simply, we did what adults do when they teach in what Dewey terms informal education. We laughed and shared our daughter's infectious joy in the evening, and we concurred that, yes, what she had noticed was indeed marvelous and that she was marvelous, too, in the noticing, and that, yes, we were all happy to be there with her and with each other on our long trip to Baltimore. The subject matter we shared in that stifling automobile was part of a family curriculum—a curriculum so "familiar" (MW.9.193) that we relied on it without recognizing that we were. It was engaging, sociable, vital—in a word, meaningful.

In subsequent days, we adults continued enlarging and giving direction to Katie's particular interest in the sun and munn, although not with a deliberate outcome or scope and sequence of materials in mind. I tried to dredge up knowledge I had once learned in school about how, exactly, it *is* possible for both the sun and the moon to be visible simultaneously in the sky. Once settled in Baltimore, Katie's father and I resumed reading her the best-ever bedtime story, *Good Night, Moon*, which is where Katie probably learned the word. We also retold the story of the road trip, so often that it is now a part of our family history. My husband and I even happened across some of Piaget's descriptions of his children's explanations for the sun and moon and, following his lead, talked to our daughter about her "theories" while sitting out on the balcony of our row house, as bricks on all sides exuded the heat of the day into the heat of the night.

In all these informal ways, we parents confirmed the value of our daughter, her interests, and her engagement with the world, by offering loving attention, along with facts and ideas from other sources we knew about to which she might connect her own observations and thoughts. Although necessarily limited, this early "curriculum" provided a base for Katie's subsequent education, as she moved out into the more diverse experiences and knowledge furnished in the formal curriculum in public schools. Just as Dewey suggests, her experience, like that of each of us, was amplified and made meaningful in communication with others and the world.

I also tell this personal story about informal education because it may represent the kind of engaging lessons we schoolteachers hope for every time we enter a classroom to engage deliberate, formal education.

Subject Matter in Informal and Formal Education

But what happens in those classrooms, as opposed to family station wagons, that makes school knowledge so often less than vital, sociable, and meaningful, despite our high hopes and deep longing?

Dewey offers an explanation in chapter 14 by comparing subject matter in informal and formal education. As he puts it, "one of the weightiest problems with which the philosophy of education has to cope is the method of keeping a proper balance between intentional [formal] and incidental [informal] education" (MW.9.12). His is a markedly different formulation of the issue of curriculum quality than we typically use today that may help us re/cognize our present course.

The way Dewey goes about explicating the "weighty" problem is different, too. He constructs an elaborate web of ideas about subject matter in informal and formal education, beginning simply enough with a logical definition, but then going on to use other tools, such as literary analysis of the phrase, empirical categorizations of subject matter, and a cultural history of formal schooling. I describe Dewey's method at some length because it itself is the message, showing us what subject matter is, including the school's subject matter. More complex and evolved than the list of seemingly tried and true school subjects we usually take it to be, school curriculum exemplifies the social as well as intellectual precepts and practices that govern how we would live together and, as such, it warrants more care and thought than we who say we aspire to a democratic society ordinarily give it.

A Logical Definition

Dewey begins with a consideration of what all subject matter has in common, whether in informal or formal education. He offers a "definition in principle" (MW.9.188), theorizing that subject matter "consists in the facts observed, recalled, read and talked about, and the ideas suggested, in course of a development of a situation having a purpose" (MW.9.188). Subject matter is "the stuff" (MW.9.162), or the "data" (MW.9.197), that humans both think about and think with.

Seen theoretically, subject matter does not refer narrowly to the school studies, however readily we today make that assumption. Indeed, as Dewey's definition suggests, no topic or object is automatically or inherently subject matter because materials *become* subject matter. In the course of everyday living, people are continuously engaged in noticing and assembling particular "facts" and developing "ideas" because they seem of use in addressing some problem or perplexity persons are interested in. This means that anything—any topic or object—can become subject matter, when it is picked up and "reckoned with in the process of a person carrying forward an active line of interest" (MW.9.141). This expansive conception of subject matter, far greater than there is time to teach or learn it all, might prompt us to take a closer look at the studies schools teach, and to pose the central question of curriculum: What knowledge *should* our schools teach, and why?[4]

Connotations of Subject Matter

Dewey then elaborates the general definition of subject matter by spinning out some of the specific connotations of the quaint, almost lumpish, two-word phrase. For example, the phrase directs us to consider the *materiality* of "facts" and "ideas," rather than regarding them as ethereal or disembodied phenomena located in a mind or set apart from the practical concerns of the world in an "ivory tower." The phrase also connotes that which *matters*—and it matters to an identifiable *subject* or person; it is personally interesting and of consequence in someone's specific inquiry. As well, subject matter is *subjected* matter (MW.9.172), because people work on facts and ideas, including those of others as well as their own. They apprehend and grasp them, integrate them with other ideas they already have, bend them to particular purposes and uses and, in these various ways, make the facts and ideas into knowledge of their own.

By closely analyzing *subject matter,* Dewey calls our attention to the importance of meanings carried in the unexceptional phrase that we may not be aware of but which, once noticed, signal connections that are telling for a more fruitful understanding of the wide reach of subject matter and curriculum. For example, Dewey links the connotations of the phrase to some of the qualities of informal education, such as that going on in our family station wagon—knowing involves the intellect and also the body; knowledge is a crucial resource for dealing with real-world problems, not just valuable for its own sake, schooling, or credentials; and teaching and learning in everyday life are active, constructive processes rather than a mechanical transfer of one person's ideas to another person.

Although these qualities could also apply in formal education, more often they do not, and, as Dewey notes, instead of balance or "continuity" (MW.9.343) between the two kinds of education, there is a "split" (MW.9.12).[5] Thus, subject matter in formal education is usually regarded as the province of mind, reason, theory, headedness, and so forth, while action, the emotions, the practical, and handedness find their place in informal education. The contemporary "split" mirrors long-standing "dualisms, or antitheses" (MW.9.343), which we inherit from past eras when social conditions were more sharply stratified and formal education was reserved for an elite. But because we are unaware of traces of the dualisms that recur in our present educational theories and practices—as Dewey shows us, playing with the phrase, *subject matter*—we continue to construct a segregated rather than open society, with schooling that "creates only 'sharps' in learning—egoistic specialists" (MW.9.12) pursuing "academics," rather than youth who are response-able to others and the world and, therefore, responsible "for the consequences of their actions, including thought" (MW.9.187).[6]

Categories of Subject Matter

In addition to a logical definition of subject matter and an elaboration of some of its connotations, Dewey also undertakes a direct comparison of subject matter in informal and in formal education, principally by naming and juxtaposing various categories or types of subject matter.

For example, Dewey distinguishes *subject matter in informal education* (MW.9.188), *subject matter of the student* (MW.9.189), and *subject matter of life-experience* (MW.9.11). Subject matter in informal education, he says, is "incidental and unplanned" (MW.9.12). It is the "education one gets from living with others" (MW.9.12), rather than by direct tutelage—education in which both knowledge and intellectual and social dispositions are formed unconsciously, by "the surrounding atmosphere and spirit" (MW.9.21). Subject matter in informal education is whatever people notice as they pursue particular interests in everyday interactions, and knowledge is therefore seamlessly and immediately pertinent. No one has to make sure the subject matter is "relevant" in informal education.

Furthermore, subject matter in informal education is "carried directly in the matrix of social intercourse. It is what the persons with whom an individual associates do and say" (MW.9.188). Thus, our daughter Katie was learning to "walk the walk and talk the talk"[7] that prevailed in our family, and there was no division on that moonstruck evening between knowledge about the sun and munn and knowledge about self and others.

Dewey suggests an affinity between *subject matter in informal education* and the different category, *subject matter of the student* (MW.9.189). In both, subject matter is local, idiosyncratic, and organized "in connection with direct practical centers of interest" (MW.9.191). For example, the knowledge young students bring to school is referenced to a particular "matrix" of their own activities, their families and friends, and their homes and neighborhoods, just as knowledge in the station wagon was peculiar to my family's circumstances.

In a similar move, Dewey poses the subject matter of informal education and of the student as versions, or instances, of the *subject matter of life-experience* (MW.9.11). All of these subject matters are "knowledge of *how to do*" (MW.9.192). We develop this knowledge unconsciously, seemingly by absorption or saturation and without effort, as we engage in the mundane activities of everyday living—observing, talking, joking, walking and running, ordering others around, and so forth. In such ordinary activities, we become intimately "familiar" with the things and people in our world and how they operate—and, simultaneously, familiar with ourselves as able to affect our world and desirous of affecting it. This informal subject matter, Dewey says, remains our "most deeply-ingrained knowledge" (MW.9.192).

Yet we today don't often think about the young as having to learn how to laugh or tell a joke or observe. Nor do we acknowledge that we adults have to teach youth these seemingly "natural" or "human" activities or how they figure in our particular culture. Especially, we do not recognize the part that "unplanned subject matter" plays in children's development of habits of curiosity, confidence, and responsibility, both in and out of schools.[8] Because we do not typically credit the value of "knowledge of 'how to do,' " we do not expect schools to integrate it in the planned curriculum. *Democracy and Education*, however, highlights the fundamental importance of incidental knowledge for our sense of self, our relations with others, and our very stance in the world. It is the base upon which "the relatively superficial means" (MW.9.7) of intentional schooling is appended.

On the other side, Dewey develops a parallel set of categories of subject matter to point up the different characteristics of formal education, including *subject matter of formal education* (MW.9.189), *subject matter of the school* or the curriculum (MW.9.11), *subject matter of the curriculum* or the school studies (MW.9.188), and *subject matter of the instructor* (MW.9.191). In all of these, and in contrast to informal education, subject matter is "definitely formulated, crystalized, and systematized" (MW.9.190). It is consciously selected, planned, and organized so as to ensure the representation of the most "prized" meanings of a social group, those meanings "identified with their conception of their own collective life" (MW.9.188). Because it may include little directly personal or useful, and hence, obviously relevant knowledge— youth are likely to pick up *that* kind of knowledge in the course of ordinary living—formal subject matter is "consciously impressed upon youth . . . often with intense emotional fervor" (MW.9.189). In contrast to subject matter in informal education, the *subject matter of the school*— the curriculum, and the studies that furnish its content—and the *subject matter of the instructor* are abstract, "standardized"(MW.9.190) in disciplines, and organized logically, according to how various facts and ideas relate to each other rather than to particular circumstances. As Dewey explains, our everyday conception of water is related to its instrumental uses in drinking, washing, swimming, and so forth, whereas the chemist's H_2O connects the nature of water with other knowledge about "the structure of things" (MW.9.198).

A Cultural History of Education

As Dewey distinguishes these several categories of subject matter, associating some with informal education and others with formal education, he adds yet another layer to his analysis of subject matter by outlining a cultural history that spells out the origins and functions of formal education, including both its promises and perils. His unusual move to a cultural history provides a "long view" of curriculum and schooling, one that points us toward issues we may easily overlook, such as the possibility of a society in which schools do not exist, the possibility of abandoning public schools,[9] or the possibility of fundamentally "reorganizing" (MW.9.257) our present schools so that the "interests of life and the studies which enforce them enrich the common experience of men instead of dividing men from one another" (MW.9.257).

The promise of subject matter in formal education. Education originates, as Dewey explains, because a social group can only maintain its "form of life" (MW.9.189) if it passes on knowledge about it to the young. Groups do this educating informally until certain social conditions develop: the group grows complex and the young are unable to share in adult activities; it accumulates an "immense bulk of communicated subject matter" (MW.9.194) that is far too large for any human to master; it sees present competencies depending on "standard ideas" (MW.9.189) developed by past generations; and some of the accumulated information is so specialized that youth will not be able to pick it up simply by participating in the ordinary pursuits of everyday life. Under these conditions, the group turns to formal education and deliberately selected and organized subject matter.

The promise of subject matter in formal education is that, in contrast to subject matter in informal education, it can open a group's young to experiences, including collective humanity's, that are more diverse and enriching than those a single family or neighborhood can offer. These experiences are embodied in the knowledge produced by past generations in response to practical problems in living and are saved for future use in what are today called bodies of knowledge, including the academic disciplines. Differently from informal education, schools translate this cross-generational knowledge into a consciously designed course of study that can connect youth, with their idiosyncratic and contemporary interests, to the expansive resources of humankind.

More specifically, schools elaborate and extend children's "primary or initial subject matter"(MW.9.192)—the "knowledge of *how to do*" (MW.9.192), which is usually *not* the result of deliberate or planned study—by introducing two additional "stages in the growth of subject matter" (MW.9.192) in human history. The first addition is "communicated subject matter, or information" (MW.9.194), which is knowledge amassed by others with more experience and stored in the "rows and rows" (MW.9.194) of texts housed in such repositories as libraries or the Web. Informational knowledge "has the office of an intellectual middleman. It condenses and records in available form the net results of the prior experiences of mankind, as an agency for enhancing the meaning of new experiences"—that is, our contemporary experiences (MW.9.196). The third stage of subject matter is the "specialized" (MW.9.198) knowledge called science or rationalized knowledge (MW.9.196). It is "ascertained knowledge" because the results of inquiry are themselves subjected to systematic and self-conscious tests so as to verify their warrant and, thus, to distinguish them from the "opinion, guesswork, speculation, and mere tradition" (MW.9.196) humans are prone to rely on.[10]

Dewey's key point is that *subject matter in education* (MW.9.200) consists in all three of these forms, or stages, of knowledge, not in any one of them.[11] Without deep "familiarity" with things in the world, youth will have difficulty understanding the significance of information and science, just as, without information and science, they will be limited by their local circumstances in what they can do and know. Therefore, the school's curriculum should be "reconstructed" (MW.9.325) so that youth learn how they and all humans, across time, are connected in knowledge:

> Organized subject matter [the bodies of knowledge humans have created, and the school studies derived from them] represents the ripe fruitage of experiences like theirs [students'], experiences involving the same world, and powers and needs similar to theirs. It does not represent perfection or infallible wisdom; but it is the best at command to further new experiences which may, in some respects at least, surpass the achievements embodied in existing knowledge and works of art. (MW.9.190)[12]

The kind of amplification and integration of present and past experience that formal education promises reflects Dewey's democratic ideal and, in addition, is a crucial means for realizing and maintaining a "democratic mode of associated living" (MW.9.93). In contrast to other social arrangements, a "democratically constituted society" (MW.9.93) signifies, first, that members have "more numerous and more varied points of shared common interest" and that, consequently, there is "greater reliance upon the recognition of mutual interests [rather than on external authority] as a factor in social control" (MW.9.92). In other words, in responding to others, a person is acting responsibly, considering the effects of her actions on others and, because she is related to those others, the effects on herself. Second, a democratic society engages in "full and free" (MW.9.88) interactions with other social groups. As a result, it changes its "social habit" so that it "flexibly adjusts and evolves" (MW.9.105) as it encounters "the new situations produced by varied intercourse" (MW.9.92). Rather than circling the wagons and holding fast to the world that is, citizens in a democracy expect life to consist in changes that they can shape to enrich that which is. On both counts, education for democracy provides for intellectual and social dispositions such as having one's own interests and ideas and pursuing them with integrity, being continuously open to and curious about others' ideas and the world, and having respect and, therefore, responsibility for oneself and for diverse others (MW.9.187).

The perils of subject matter in formal education. However, Dewey also sees just as clearly the perils of subject matter in formal education, and his insights are a key source of leverage in regard to our own educational and societal conditions. According to Dewey, the chief hazard in school lessons is that "the bonds which connect the subject matter of school study with the habits and ideals of the social group are disguised and covered up" (MW.9.189).

When this disconnection between school knowledge and society occurs, two deleterious consequences follow. First, and most important, the manifest curriculum in school becomes a *hiding curriculum.* The school hides the value of knowledge from youth when it presents *school* science or *school* literature—knowledge that, divorced from human purposes, is "merely academic" (MW.9.12), seems to exist only for its own sake (MW.9.141) or for more schooling, is "compartmentalized" (MW.9.255) in separate subjects, and requires only "mental" operations and "pure intelligence" (MW.9.345) that proceed without the distractions of the world's practical constraints. In short, presented a hiding curriculum, students learn, *in school,* to see knowledge as merely the school's gambit, not as a resource that they and all people depend on in better making their way in a precarious world.

It is worth pointing out that Dewey is not talking here about the "hidden curriculum" that has occupied so much scholarly attention in recent decades—the knowledge schools convey tacitly and in tandem with formal subject matter, such as the largely unspoken institutional rules for how, not just what, "good" students will speak in classrooms (Jackson, 1968) or the differentiating structures in schools, such as tracking, that subtly elevate one group's manners and knowledge to a position of greater power or status than those of other groups (Apple, 1979).[13] Rather, Dewey is talking here about the *formal, explicit curriculum*—the three Rs, social studies, algebra, what we sometimes call academic content knowledge. And his claim is that *all* students—the advantaged along with the disadvantaged and the high-scoring along with the low-scoring— are turned away from studies if they are merely scholastic, rather than humane, because they will not see knowledge as a tangible, material resource that humans make and use when they wrestle with particular problems in everyday life—even such as understanding the moon and sharing its beauty. Furthermore, a hiding, formal curriculum will only exacerbate the operation and effects of the "hidden curriculum" because, if turned away from school knowledge, students will turn toward their necessarily limited personal, familial, peer, and popular resources. Then the differentiated social resources students bring to school will have even more influence on school success and, because schools are gatekeepers, subsequent life chances.

An example of the hiding curriculum. Consider an illustrative example of schooling that hides knowledge. The customs of the eighteenth century readily seem exotic to us today, even though they arose as people then confronted uncertainties in living and created solutions to manage those uncertainties, just as we do today. Ostensibly, a humane curriculum would connect us with these people who differed from us in the particular uncertainties they encountered and the solutions they devised, but not in their human "powers and needs" (MW.9.189).

Longitude was one of the mysteries people in the eighteenth century faced. Navigation proceeded like a throw of the dice, and being "lost at sea," whether that meant being misplaced, puzzled, or drowned, was an ever-present possibility. So huge were the human and economic costs resulting from the lack of ascertained knowledge about longitude that, in 1714, the king of England offered a prize equivalent to $12,000,000 to the person who could provide a solution. Now, that is "prized" knowledge!

However, so huge were the social as well as conceptual and technical roadblocks that, despite the grand prize, it took several decades for a solution to be generated, and then several more for it to be fully accepted. In other words, longitude was a subject that mattered, both socially and intellectually. It was not circumscribed in the compartment we blandly refer to as "the natural sciences," but traversed political machinations, vanity, hard work, social class conflict, careful design, wrong turns, ingenuity, imagination, personality clashes, and moral struggles (was longitude a function of the "clock of heaven," as astronomers and clerics argued, or of a manmade, mechanical, marine chronometer as a lone clockmaker thought?).[14]

Yet think about how the subject matter, longitude, is usually presented in our schools. Typically, it is a vocabulary word usually confined to lessons in the subject demarcated as geography. Students are required to learn to spell the word, to recite its definition, and, perhaps, to mark designated degrees of longitude on mimeographed maps. Selected students, well-behaved perhaps, or those at wealthier schools, may be allowed to find extra reference materials about longitude in the library or on the Web. But it is unlikely that any students, whether with microcomputers or mimeographs, will learn about longitude as a life-and-death matter in the past, or still today, a "factor upon which the accomplishment of human purposes depend" (MW.9.141).

Dewey offers three explanations for the propensity of school knowledge to be uprooted from its social origins and uses. All three present the "split" as a function of societal conditions and the ideas that grow up in those conditions, not as failings of the schools alone or of particular individuals. First, the continuing explosion of knowledge, along with accelerated means of reproducing and distributing it, dispose schools to skate lightly over as much knowledge as possible or, as we teachers say, to "cover the curriculum." In the process, however, we "swamp" (MW.9.194) students with indiscriminate bits and pieces of information, such as the dictionary definition of longitude. Rather than being integrated with the student's "world of personal acquaintance, [school knowledge] forms another strange world which just overlies [it]" (MW.9.194).

Second, the very processes of formal education—the "special selection, formulation, and organization of subject matter" (MW.9.201)— lead to school knowledge being seen, by educators and the public alike, as a thing of value in itself, to be collected, and not as a resource from the past that people can use in "a developing future" (MW.9.85). In California, for example, the current curriculum framework in language arts and the tests aligned with it stipulate that second-graders, if they are properly knowledgeable, will be able to identify "alliteration" in a selection of poetry. This is ludicrous, and not just because second-graders are highly unlikely to know the word, but because requiring knowledge simply for the school's and the state's testing purposes trivializes the knowers along with knowledge.[15]

The third reason subject matter is readily separated from its social roots is that we are seldom conscious of the ways that ideas and practices from the past shape our present language for curriculum. For instance, when we select and distribute subject matter according to "utilitarian ends narrowly conceived for the masses" and "the traditions of a specialized, cultivated class for the few," the differentiated curriculum based in social class works against our espoused concern about how to live together democratically.

In sum, when formal education disguises and covers up the bonds between the school curriculum and societal ideals and practices, youth are left unmoved by, and even disdainful of, the knowledge humans have accumulated throughout history and which we continue to rely on in order to survive. They learn *in school* that the school's knowledge and the cultural heritage it translates are arcane, useless, and meaningless, and they turn away to more appealing, yet limited, subject matter in informal education, such as that of their peer group, family, or the media.

Dewey's point is not that formal education is superior to or should replace informal education, but that they must be in balance. Otherwise, our so-called knowledge society will be a know-nothing society, as even youth who achieve high grades or test scores will learn "mechanical[ly] and without interest or discipline because the school's subject matter is apparently of little use in accomplishing anything of real value" (MW.9.141). To achieve balance, the school's subject matter—the curriculum—must be "reorganized" (MW.9.256).

Formal Education: Eleanor Duckworth's Moon Project

In thinking about Dewey's discussion of our fond if often unrealized hopes for subject matter in formal education, I found myself musing on a teacher, Eleanor Duckworth, whom I met in Harvard's Graduate School of Education (HGSE) when I was a visitor there for a couple of years and who, by all accounts, seems to have achieved a "reorganized" course of study such as the one Dewey urges.[16] Hers is an accomplishment worth considering, given how infrequently school lessons fulfill their educational and democratic promise.

I learned about Eleanor's introductory graduate course from students I met who were enrolled in it or who had previously completed it.[17] The course usually enrolls about 100 students, most of them graduates of prestigious colleges or universities. They arrive at HGSE well equipped with what is sometimes referred to as "high-status knowledge," which they will presumably be able to cash in for high grades in graduate school and, eventually, high-status jobs and/or high-level salaries.

My informants told me that on the first day of class, Eleanor poses two straightforward, specific questions: Where and when will the moon appear this evening and what will it look like, and where and when will it appear the following evening and how will it look then? Eleanor may point out that her questions are hardly arcane. After all, the moon is a familiar object and readily available for observation, depending, of course, on Boston's cloud cover and smog. What, Eleanor asks students, do they know about this celestial body that has been part of their environment for their entire lives?

Eleanor might also justify her questions with a Deweyan touch by adding that sky-gazing is one of humanity's fundamental preoccupations. People have engaged in it for centuries, including not just the Johnny-come-lately specialists we call scientists, but shepherds, sailors, seers, and today's amateur astronomers. The last includes people like Jay McNeil, whose paying job is satellite dish maintenance but whose passion is the universe. McNeil just recently knocked the socks off the astronomy community by discovering what he called a "funky-looking, tiny, elongated object" that turned out to be the birth of a star 1,500 light years away, now appropriately named the McNeil Nebula (Kudos, 2004). However it is produced, the knowledge derived from sky-gazing influences human lives, by leading to valuable technological advances and sometimes by impeding them, too, as with longitude's long evolution. Equally, knowledge about the heavens reflects and occasionally revolutionizes our social views and practices. Indeed, it has sparked radical changes in who we humans think we are and how we view our place at the center or on the margins of the universe.

Usually, my informants told me, they and the other students in the class are a little unsettled by Eleanor's questions. (Maybe some readers are feeling a bit queasy too, thinking, "Well, do *I* know when and where the moon will rise here, tonight?") It turns out that most of the students in Eleanor's class, despite impeccable scholastic records, have no idea when or where the moon will rise in Boston that evening or the next. Those who do may have heard it on the Weather Channel or they recall information learned in school, but in neither case are students confident in predicting the moon's pattern.

In Deweyan terms, and I think Eleanor might put it this way, too, most of these academically successful students have never *studied* the moon. They may have aced Astronomy 101 at Haverford, but they do not seem to have learned about the night sky in a way that makes them feel more at home in their world.

Having established a context to spark students' interest in the moon—they assumed they knew about it, but it turns out they don't—

Eleanor ends the first class meeting by assigning the moon project. Eleanor asks that every evening throughout the semester, at the same time, say, 8 or 9 P.M., students will stop whatever they are doing and go outside and observe the moon—and this, even though all the students are well past Piaget's concrete operational stage. They are to record the data from their observations and ideas in a journal and, in class, they should be ready to discuss what they have learned about how the moon moves in the sky, as well as any other observations they find interesting. On occasion, they should expect to be assigned moon-related readings, including poetry and stories as well as technical, scientific articles representative of "rationalized knowledge" (MW.9.197). In all, the moon serves as a tangible, readily available object that all the students in Eleanor's course can explore individually, following their own idiosyncratic predilections, and sociably, as experiences are shared in class discussions. The course engages students in all three of the stages of knowledge Dewey describes: knowledge of *how to do*, communicated knowledge, and logically organized knowledge.

In addition to the subject matter of the moon, students in Eleanor's course study the subjects of teaching and learning. Thus, in observing the moon, they concomitantly observe themselves learning about it and teaching about it in conversations with others. Teaching and learning are subjects of perhaps more obvious interest to the students, given that they are enrolled in Harvard's Graduate School of Education, not a program in astronomy. However, teaching and learning are fleeting processes, and they are easily talked about abstractly and judgmentally. The moon serves as a vehicle to ground and generate specific observations and reflections on teaching and learning that can then be compared, including students' own and those of others.[18]

Eleanor's course can be seen as what Dewey calls a "learning environment which is able to stimulate responses and direct the learner's course" (MW.9.188). It is designed in light of Eleanor's own expert knowledge of *her* subject matters (*subject matter of the instructor*), that is, the psychology of teaching and learning and knowledge about the moon. But Eleanor does not teach her subjects directly. As Dewey notes, that would be to fail "to bear in mind the difference in subject matter from the respective standpoints of teacher and student [which] is responsible for most of the mistakes made in the use of texts and other expressions of preexistent knowledge" (MW.9.190). Instead, Eleanor translates her subjects into the *subject matter of instruction* (MW.9.191).

The process of translation entails two considerations, according to Dewey: a teacher must understand her students' particular interests and needs, and she must understand the knowledge she has that best connects with students' interests and can thereby direct and expand them. Thus, the subject matter of instruction is a bridge that can link the particular, practical, locally organized experiences of the students who are observing and discussing the moon, teaching, and learning, on the one hand, with the abstract, standardized, logically organized experiences of the human race that are embodied in particular disciplines, such as psychology, on the other. Moreover, because Eleanor has knowledge of her subject matter "at her fingers' ends" (MW.9.191), she is free to concentrate on the interplay between student responses and subject matter and, thus, can identify opportune junctures for redirecting students to materials that can amplify their present interests.[19] As this may suggest, popular characterizations of Dewey's views on education as solely student- or child-centered are mistaken. They ignore Dewey's equal attention to the cultural heritage and the need to put it in relation to students' present experiences through deliberate curriculum design.

The "learning environment" Eleanor designs is particularly notable for its emphasis on students' "firsthand knowledge" (MW.9.195)—the knowledge that students construct as they pursue "facts" and "ideas" in inquiries they are interested in. I know few teachers who give it such care and respect. Eleanor focuses on the development of firsthand knowledge with her scholastically adept students because she regards it as an essential disposition for teachers, as well as for learning. Teachers need to understand how they themselves learn and use knowledge, if they are to develop ways to teach others how to learn and use knowledge.

Firsthand knowledge, however, is usually the kind of knowledge that teachers, and students, too, pay lip service to and hurry over in order to get to "information," or "secondhand knowledge"(MW.9.195)—the knowledge others have created that we today typically regard as "real" knowledge. But Eleanor is especially careful not to preempt her students by prematurely introducing the general knowledge of "experts"(MW.9.190), including her own. As Dewey might put it, she has not only the knowledge and the arts to take the reorganization of curriculum seriously, but the "courage"—the heart.

Thus, in weekly class meetings, under Eleanor's light-handed but steady guidance, students traverse a wide array of epistemological issues in discussions that are neither haphazard nor lock-step. Beginning discussions may involve their comparing different data sets, different ways of seeing, and conflicting explanations of the moon's movement. Later, students may consider the social as well as intellectual competence entailed in comprehending someone else's experiences or conveying their own, whether in conversation or written texts. They may ask how they integrate another's experiences with their own so that they are not just memorizing "ready-made knowledge" (MW.9.216) produced by others. Other discussions may focus on how one is able to change one's mind, what it takes to be able to say one knows something in contrast to having an opinion about it, what implications one's own learning strategies in regard to the moon or any subject matter may have for how one might teach about the subject in schools, or how one connects personal and school knowledge.

Throughout, the environment in Eleanor's course stimulates and directs students to be self-conscious and systematic in their inquiries and reflections, to appreciate knowing as both a specialized and ordinary process and, in all endeavors, to be responsive and, therefore, responsible, in their actions. This may make Eleanor's course sound like it is all "sweetness and light," but from student reports, it seems to follow what Dewey sets down as the most "severe standard"(MW.9.186) for schooling: to teach students to be clear about "what is involved in really knowing and believing a thing" (MW.9.186). As he notes, this standard cannot be learned through didactic admonition, but only through practice and reflection on practice, such as those offered in the discussions and other activities in Eleanor's class.

Eleanor's thoughtfully designed curriculum avoids the "split" in which the "material of formal instruction [is] merely the subject matter of the schools, isolated from the subject matter of life-experience" (MW.9.11). Students I talked with told me that directly observing and reflecting on the moon, teaching, and learning proved to be an increasingly engrossing experience for them and many of their classmates. They commented that they thought nothing of leaving weekend parties to undertake the moon watch and, in fact, they said that often many of the people at the parties knew about Eleanor's course and joined them in their lunar observations and speculations. A common, lively discourse about the moon, and about learning and teaching about it, developed in Eleanor's classroom and extended beyond it into the haunts of Longfellow Hall and Cambridge.

Furthermore, Eleanor is genuinely interested in the data students gather and is respectful of the conversation and insights each contributes. In her view, as in Dewey's, each individual apprehends the world uniquely, even when she or he is presented "the same" curriculum and "the same" teaching. Because Eleanor respects students' uniqueness, they learn what it means to be respected. Being respected themselves, they develop the disposition to respect others for *their* unique contributions and on *their* terms. This is a radically different orientation from our present coercive efforts to *make* schools teach and kids learn a standardized curriculum, at at least a minimum level of proficiency. Eleanor seems to understand that no one can make another person learn without seriously mis-educative effects. As Dewey puts it, "In last analysis, *all* that the educator can do is modify stimuli so that [the student's] response will as surely as is possible result in the formation of desirable intellectual and emotional dispositions" (MW.9.188).

Using *Democracy and Education* Today

Dewey's comparison of the often lifeless subject matter in formal education and the typically vital subject matter in informal education is particularly provocative for our present situation. With his multilayered method of analyzing subject matter, we gain a variety of contexts, or vantage points, from which to "see" what we are about today and reconsider whether our educational ideas and practices are what we intend. *Does* our curriculum reflect and recreate the democratic "form of life" we say we prize?

Dewey's analysis suggests it does not, as he concludes his comparison with an argument for a thoroughly "reorganized" (MW.9.256) curriculum. First, Dewey indicates that deliberate education can succeed only if we are cognizant of how much we learn unconsciously, how difficult such "habitudes" (MW.9.22) are to change once formed, and the crucial foundation such "deeply-ingrained knowledge" furnishes for intentional education. Second, and equally important, the school's specialized knowledge cannot be neglected because, more than subject matter in informal education, it can expand our connections with diverse others and their knowledge, allow us to reflect on the trustworthiness of our most cherished ideas and practices and possibly change them, and, on both counts, deepen the meaningfulness of our lives.

However, putting the two subject matters in relation is no easy task and, rather than a generative hybrid that has its own integrity (Cohen, 1990; Kliebard, 2004; Page, 1999, 2000), most often, integrated curriculum is simply a "conglomerate" (MW.9.256) in which opposing ideas, set side by side, cancel each other out and, thus, contribute to students' sense that there is little knowledge to learn in school. Curriculum's effective redesign will require steep resources, including money and time, as well as ideas and the courage to embrace progressive change.

We typically think of integrated curriculum in relation to kindergartens and early childhood education and, on this account, Dewey's call for curriculum reorganization may seem dated and of relatively limited import. After all, we can still find at least some youngsters learning "how to do" in interest centers, the arts, and human occupations such as gardening, sky-gazing, and so forth. However, Eleanor's course with doctoral students indicates that moongazing is no idle reverie or just for young children like my daughter Katie. As Dewey himself points out in a footnote (MW.9.191), the three stages of growth in subject matter are "relative, not absolute." Accordingly, even very knowledgeable people, when they begin with a new subject matter, will "learn by doing" (MW.9.192), and that first stage of subject matter will be as necessary and empowering for their studies as for those of very young learners. Furthermore, because we in the United States seem to be intent on extending formal education for all to both preschool and college, it is all the more important that we ask the central curriculum question: *To what will all these very young and older students be getting access?* If it is just another hiding curriculum of memoriter work and mechanical "academics" driven by testing, is anything gained?

Dewey's analysis of subject matter in formal and informal education also illuminates another thorny question about curriculum—should schools distribute different kinds of knowledge to different groups of students, as in tracking, special education, vocational education, and other forms of curriculum differentiation? We see the contemporary answer in mandatory lessons and benchmarks for all, as in No Child Left Behind (NCLB). Dewey's is quite different.

Throughout *Democracy and Education*, Dewey deplores a differentiated curriculum that forecasts narrowly "utilitarian" ends for the children of the laboring classes and therefore provides them only "mechanical essentials," while foreseeing "the traditions of a specialized cultivated class" for advantaged children of the leisure class and providing them only the "liberal arts." Such class-based differentiation "is equivalent to the setting up of different types of life-experience, each with isolated subject matter, aim, and standard of values" (MW.9.343). Thus, Dewey describes the educational and social perils in what we today would call the lower-track curriculum:

> The notion that the "essentials" of elementary education are the three R's mechanically treated . . . unconsciously assumes that [democratic] ideals are unrealizable [and that] in the future, as in the past, getting a livelihood, "making a living," must signify for most men and women doing things which are not significant, freely chosen, and ennobling to those who do them; doing things which serve ends unrecognized by those engaged in them, carried on under the direction of others for the sake of pecuniary reward. (MW.9.200)

Then, Dewey describes the typical regular- or upper-track curriculum but, in contrast to most research and policy today, he is as critical of it as of the lower track:

The education called liberal [is infected] with illiberality. [It is] a somewhat parasitic cultivation bought at the expense of not having the enlightenment and discipline which come from concern with the deepest problems of common humanity (MW.9.200). . . . [It prepares] the few for a knowledge that is an ornament and a cultural embellishment (MW.9.265). . . . Those who are not only much better off in worldly goods, but who are in excessive, if not monopolistic, control of the activities of the many are shut off from equality and generality of social intercourse. They are stimulated to pursuits of indulgence and display, they try to make up for the distance which separates them from others by the impression of force and superior possession and enjoyment which they can make upon others. (MW.9.327)

Dewey concludes succinctly: "Democracy cannot flourish where [assumptions about social class are the] chief influences in selecting subject matter of instruction" (MW.9.200). Therefore, to resolve the disconnections produced in tracking by replacing the lower-track curriculum with "a college-prep curriculum for all," as California's Superintendent of Public Instruction recently pronounced, or with a "high-status" or "curriculum of power" for all, which some scholars have proposed (Angus & Mirel, 2000; Apple, 2001; Ravitch, 2000), is senseless. Such a move would simply keep in motion the "oscillation" in curriculum reform between "fads and frills" on the one hand, and "the good old curriculum" of the three Rs, math, and the classics on the other (MW.9.256), along with accompanying oscillation in societal organization.[20]

Instead, Dewey urges a focus on what is valuable in both "utilitarian" and "cultivated" curricula, and proposes their conscious reorganization. He urges the reconstruction of the long-standing dualisms in curriculum and the social stratification it reflects and recreates in a school curriculum that connects individualism *and* community, practice *and* theory, mind *and* action, and head *and* heart. Inventing practices that honor these connections, whether in schools or other social institutions, has long been America's distinctively ambitious agenda and, as Dewey says, even though "the peculiar problem in present education [is that] the school cannot immediately escape from the ideals set by prior social conditions . . . it should contribute through the type of intellectual and social dispositions which it forms to the improvement of those conditions" (MW.9.144).[21]

A human curriculum built on diversity *and* the common good has rarely held sway in America, but rereading *Democracy and Education* provides stark evidence of just how hell-bent we now are on "mechanical efficiency" alone. We have no time for the "slow" (MW.9.144) work of learning environments that first honor students' individual experiences and then bridge to the social experiences stored in the bodies of knowledge. Indeed, we seem to have lost sight of "slow" education altogether, along with the value of its intimate, delicate touch and its trust in youth and teachers. Who today, for example, would echo Dewey that "in last analysis, *all* that the educator can do is modify stimuli so that response will as surely as is possible result in the formation of desirable intellectual and emotional dispositions" (MW.9.188). Instead, we are intent on directly modifying people. We use the "frontal assault" as we pursue equality and excellence by aligning prescribed content standards for all, one method of teaching for all, and one minimum benchmark for all on high-stakes tests, even though "the frontal assault is as ineffectual in education as in war"(MW.9.176). Furthermore, we take pride in our zero tolerance for flexibility, divergent opinions, or inquiry in regard to the unintended as well as intended results of these measures, even in the face of evidence that would suggest the value of reconsideration: "We plume ourselves upon our firmness in clinging to our conceptions in spite of the way in which they work out" (MW.9.197).

Democracy and Education speaks in a different tenor and from a broader vantage point to let us re/cognize the measures we now prescribe, such as No Child Left Behind, state and federal curriculum standards, and other versions of systemic reform. Serious debate is overdue regarding the federal government's recent reentry into curriculum on a grand scale, along with its simultaneous retreat from traditional interests in religion and civil rights (Kaestle, 2003; Page, 2003). Can a democratic society and educative schools prosper when curriculum is managed by the external authority of the nation-state?

A second and related matter is that we in the university need to re/cognize how we, including Dewey, have never succeeded in making a convincing case for humane curriculum to the public, or to school practitioners, policymakers, or even within the educational research community. A particular issue in this regard entails demonstrating the "reality" of the social and the tacit dimensions of curriculum, in both the hiding curriculum I speak of earlier and in the hidden curriculum described by scholars such as Michael Apple (1979) and Philip Jackson (1968). Another facet of the research agenda should be to develop fuller understanding of practices in ordinary school lessons, with specific attention to how and in what circumstances the loosening of bonds between subject matter in formal education and social ideals occurs, and the academic and social consequences of that loosening for both individuals and school communities. Without such work on our part, curriculum will continue to be treated as a technical matter, similar to making trains run on time.

The most forceful message in *Democracy and Education* may well be Dewey's faith in the very possibility of democracy and education. Herve Varenne (1986) describes Dewey as one of America's prophets, calling us back to our best hopes and ideals. This has certainly been my experience in rereading *Democracy and Education* in these stark times. I find the book powerful because it exemplifies the careful intelligence Dewey proposes as both the means to and the result of a democratic way of life and educative schools. I also find *Democracy and Education* powerful because it calls us to action to realize these ideals and, as I have tried to show, provides us abundant intellectual and emotional resources to do the work. Although written almost eighty years ago, *Democracy and Education* speaks to our times. We might hearken to it.

Notes

1. Contemporary research that does attend to the balance between formal and informal education, albeit not necessarily with reference to Dewey, includes Lave and Wenger, 1991; McLaughlin, Irby, and Langman, 1994; and McNeil, 2000.

2. Kliebard (1992) poses this question in the introduction to his collection of essays.

3. See my (1999) empirical study of the uncertain value of school knowledge.

4. Kliebard (1977) identifies this and three other questions as defining the field of curriculum studies. The other three are: Should schools provide different kinds of knowledge to different groups of students? How should knowledge be taught to effect particular habits of mind? What scope and sequencing of knowledge will support the development of an "educated person"?

5. The "split" we are most concerned with today is "the achievement gap"—the difference in scores on standardized tests received by children from advantaged versus disadvantaged environments. *Democracy and Education* gives little, if any, attention to testing. Furthermore, the manner in which schools today are being urged to close "the achievement gap" risks reproducing the very pedagogical and societal "split" Dewey sees as the root of the negligible engagement with school knowledge of many, if not most, students.

6. Spivak (1993) plays on response-able and responsible. See also Ricoeur (1976). For a curricular application of the play, see Page (1997).

7. As Dewey puts it, conscious teaching of manners and morals will only be effective if instruction "falls in with the general 'walk and conversation' " (MW.9.22) of the child's group.

8. One person who has thought deeply about these matters is Jane Roland Martin (1992, 2002).

9. Illich (1971) argues for deschooling society; Americans are proving willing to abandon public education.

10. Dewey's sanguine view of science is questioned in postmodern, poststructural, and feminist critiques of the Enlightenment and Modernism, and in some empirical research conducted in the social studies of science.

11. Geertz (1983) also offers a three-stage model of the growth of subject matter. Using the metaphor of a metropolis, he likens the primal knowledge of the human species to the old city with its inchoate streets and byways, the modern disciplines to the rationalized grid typical of the suburbs, and, in between the two, the obliquely organized commonsense knowledge. Like Dewey, Geertz sees all three productions as constitutive of our humanity.

12. Kliebard (1977) explains that, for Dewey, the correspondence between student experiences and the experiences of the human race is epistemological, not literal.

13. The hidden curriculum is chiefly the concern of scholars; it does not figure in federal or state curriculum standards, for example.

14. Dava Sobel's *Longitude* is the source for this story.

15. I heard this example from an elementary schoolteacher who is also a doctoral student in education at the University of California, Riverside.

16. I, not Eleanor, am responsible for looking at her course in Deweyan terms.

17. Eleanor comments on the course in her book (1987).

18. Sometimes Eleanor chooses a topic other than the moon. After all, any topic can become subject matter if it must be "reckoned with" (MW.9.141) as one pursues events one is interested in and affected by.

19. Interested students can follow the introductory moon course with an advanced seminar Eleanor teaches that focuses on the "rationalized knowledge" of Piagetian theory.

20. See Page (2000) for a description of the oscillation in "the tracking wars."

21. Dewey notes that schools must combat exploitation of one class by another through modification of curriculum and teaching methods, but also by securing equal school facilities and supplementing family resources so that all children can take advantage of free schooling.

References

Angus, D., & Mirel, J. (2000). *The failed promise of the American high school, 1890–1995*. New York: Teachers College Press.

Apple, M. (1979). *Ideology and curriculum*. Boston: Routledge & Kegan Paul.

Apple, M. (2001). Standards, subject matter, and a romantic past. *Educational Policy, 5*(2), 323–334.

Cohen, D. (1990). A revolution in one classroom: The case of Mrs. Oublier. *Educational Evaluation and Policy Analysis, 12*, 479–502.

Duckworth, E. (1987). *"The having of wonderful ideas" and other essays on teaching and learning*. New York: Teachers College Press.

Geertz, C. (1975/1983). Common sense as a cultural category. In *Local knowledge: Further essays in interpretive anthropology* (pp. 73–93) New York: Basic Books.

Illich, I. (1971). *Deschooling society.* New York: Harper & Row.

Jackson, P. (1968). *Life in classrooms.* New York: Holt, Rinehart.

Kaestle, C. (2003). *Mobilizing school reform from above: Five decades of federal and national strategies.* Distinguished Lecture, American Educational Research Association, Chicago.

Kliebard, H. (1977). Curriculum theory: Give me a "for instance." *Curriculum Inquiry, 6,* 257–276.

Kliebard, H. (1992). *Forging the American curriculum: Essays in curriculum history and theory.* New York: Routledge.

Kliebard, H. (2004). *The struggle for the American curriculum, 1898–1958* (3rd ed.). New York: Routledge.

Kudos for the minor stars. (2004, March 29). *Los Angeles Times,* p. B4.

Lave, J., & Wenger, E. (1991). *Situated learning: Legitimate peripheral participation.* Cambridge: Cambridge University Press.

Martin, J. R. (1992). *The schoolhome.* Cambridge: Harvard University Press.

Martin, J. R. (2002). *Cultural mis-education: In search of a democratic solution.* New York: Teachers College Press.

McLaughlin, M., Irby, M., & Langman, J. (1994). *Urban sanctuaries: Neighborhood organizations in the lives and futures of inner-city youth.* San Francisco: Jossey-Bass.

McNeil, L. (2000). *Contradictions of school reform: The educational costs of standardized testing.* New York: Routledge.

Page, R. (1997). Teaching about validity. *International Journal of Qualitative Studies in Education, 10,* 145–156.

Page, R. (1999). The uncertain value of school knowledge: Biology at Westridge High. *Teachers College Record, 100*(3), 554–601.

Page, R. (2000). The tracking show. In B. Franklin (Ed.), *Curriculum and consequence: Herbert M. Kliebard and the promise of schooling* (pp. 103–127). New York: Teachers College Press.

Page, R. (2003). Invitation to curriculum. Vice-Presidential Address, American Educational Research Association. *Division B Newsletter.* www.aera.net/ Div B.

Phillips, K. (2002). *Wealth and democracy: A political history of the American rich.* New York: Broadway Books.

Ravitch, D. (2000). *Left back: A century of failed school reforms.* New York: Simon & Schuster.

Ricoeur, P. (1976). *Interpretation theory: Discourse and the surplus of meaning.* Fort Worth: Texas Christian University Press.

School's at home for more U.S. kids. (2004, August 4). *Albuquerque Journal,* pp. A1–A2.

Sobel, D. (1995). *Longitude: The true story of a lone genius who solved the greatest scientific problem of his time.* New York: Walker.

Spivak, G. (1993). *Outside/in the teaching machine.* NY: Routledge.

Varenne, H. (Ed.) (1986). *Symbolizing America.* Lincoln: University of Nebraska Press.

4

Socialization, Social Efficiency, and Social Control

Putting Pragmatism to Work

LARRY A. HICKMAN

Given the assaults on public education that are currently being waged by the Bush administration, it is highly appropriate that we should revisit a key text of one of public education's greatest champions: John Dewey's *Democracy and Education*. For the purposes of this chapter I have selected three central terms from that text. They are terms that have been broadly misunderstood. They are the terms of my title: "socialization," "social efficiency," and "social control."

Socialization

In chapter 7 of *Democracy and Education*, Dewey tells us what he means by socialization: "Any education given by a group tends to socialize its members, but the quality and value of the socialization depends upon the habits and aims of the group" (MW.9.88).

Unlike some of the critics of socialization who have linked the term to dark and sinister plots, Dewey here employs the term in a neutral sense. Socialization occurs in a madrassa in Pakistan, a public school in Peoria, a Christian homeschool in Phoenix, a graduate school in Palo

Alto, and countless professional societies as well. His point can be expressed with bumper-sticker precision: "socialization happens."

In this connection, Dewey was highly critical of the claims of social contract theorists such as Hobbes, Locke, and Rousseau. In his view, socialization is not the result of independent, presocial individuals coming together to form a covenant, whether it be among themselves or together in contract with a sovereign. As early as 1888, he was already criticizing what he termed the "aggregation" thesis: "The notion, in short, which lay in the minds of those who proposed [the social contract] theory was that men in their natural state are non-social units, are a mere multitude; and that some artifice must be devised to constitute them into political society. And this artifice they found in a contract which they entered into with one another" (EW.1.231). Further, he suggested, the theory "that men are not isolated non-social atoms, but are men only when in intrinsic relations to men, has wholly superseded the theory of men as an aggregate, as a heap of grains of sand needing some factitious mortar to put them into semblance of order" (EW.1.231).

Murray G. Murphey put this matter about as succinctly as it could be put in his introduction to the critical edition of *Human Nature and Conduct.* "Human beings," he noted, "are social because they must be social or dead; feral fantasies notwithstanding, there are no solitary hunters" (MW.14.10).

Dewey was also critical of the arguments put forward by the advocates of "rugged individualism" as an antidote to socialization. Socialization per se does not carry a germ corruption. Nor is the term synonymous with "collectivism," as some have charged. Dewey reminded us that, like socialization, individualism can take many forms. Historically, the predatory, social Darwinist ideology of America's Gilded Age inspired by Herbert Spencer constitutes one unfortunate example. In our time, Ayn Rand's claim that we become more virtuous as we become more selfish provides another.

Dewey's criticism of classical liberalism included a repudiation of the first of these ideologies directly, explicitly, and at some length. His criticism pertains to the second one by implication. By rejecting the type of individualism urged on us by classical liberalism, however, Dewey was by no means issuing a call for a type of collectivism that would submerge or destroy individuality. On the contrary, he was calling for a newer, reconstructed type of individualism that would marshal the energies of communities in ways that would serve to develop the talents and interests of each member of those communities in an effort to develop potential and encourage growth. He was, in short, calling for community efforts to foster the flowering of individuality—a type of individuality, moreover, that would in turn foster a greater flowering of community life.

The fact is that socialization happens early and it happens often. More generally, it is not the *fact* of socialization that concerns the educator, but its *context*, its *means*, and its *consequences*.

But what, more specifically, does this mean? A gang of thieves is a society. The same is true of a political party and a book club. It is not difficult to find examples of each of these three types of societies. Each socializes its members for better or worse, and, more important, each furnishes the materials by means of which it can be judged as exhibiting desirable or undesirable traits.

At this point it seems appropriate to ask, "What are the desirable traits of social groups that provide the standard by means of which the effects of efforts at socialization can be judged?" Dewey offers two such standards. First, he asks, "How numerous and varied are the interests which are consciously shared?" And second, "How full and free is the interplay with other forms of association?" (MW.9.89).

In other words, Dewey invites us to judge a madrassa, a public school, a Christian homeschool, a graduate school of education, and a professional society in terms of these two criteria: the extent to which they produce a form of socialization that is *reductive*, and the extent to which they produce a form of socialization that is *exclusive*. Restated in terms that are positive, Dewey thought that it is possible to judge the value of a particular case of socialization in terms of whether an individual's intellectual, emotional, and aesthetic horizons enjoy expansion, and whether the individual and the group of which he or she is a member becomes more comprehensive in terms of their connections and interrelations with other socializing forces.

Dewey developed these themes in his book *The Public and Its Problems*, when he characterized publics as both organized around common interests and interacting with other publics in ways that are designed to lead to compromise or even consensus. Applied more specifically to the central themes of *Democracy and Education*, this was Dewey's prescription for educational success: growth occurs when a child is socialized in ways that expand his or her intellectual, emotional, and aesthetic horizons and that develop in the child an awareness of connections and interrelations with other socializing forces.

Once these two criteria have been applied, that is, once a judgment has been made regarding whether or not the manner in which a society socializes its members is not simply desired but desir*able*, then second term of my title, namely "social efficiency" comes into play.[1]

Social Efficiency

In chapter 9 of *Democracy and Education*, Dewey tells us what he means by social efficiency: "In the broadest sense," he writes, "social efficiency is nothing less than that socialization of mind which is actively concerned in making experiences more communicable; in breaking down the barriers of social stratification which make individuals impervious to the interests of others" (MW.9.127).

Seen from one angle, this is just a statement of what occurs when the two criteria of successful socialization just described are satisfied. If "interests which are consciously shared" are numerous and various, and if "interplay with other forms of association" is full and free, then wider avenues of communication will have been created. Superficially, this remark appears to be a truism or, perhaps even worse, a tautology. When given careful appraisal, however, it addresses several complex issues.

First, where there is social efficiency, physical and social objects and events are no longer simply immediately experienced; they are instead experienced as meaningful. As Dewey reminds us in chapter 5 of *Experience and Nature*, such objects and events "acquire representatives, surrogates, signs and implicates" (LW.1.132). Brute and immediate sensations and passions "become capable of survey, contemplation, and ideal or logical elaboration. . . . Learning and teaching come into being, and there is no event which may not yield information" (LW.1.133).

Second, the advance of social efficiency is correlative with the emergence of mind. In a remark that clearly draws on the work of his friend and colleague George Herbert Mead, Dewey writes that "through speech a person dramatically identifies with potential acts and deeds; he plays many roles, not in successive stages of life but in a contemporaneously enacted drama. Thus mind emerges" (LW.1.135).

Mead's work in fact provides further insight into the thinking of his close friend and colleague on these matters. For Mead, communication is essential to the formation of a self. As he reminds us, it is only through communication that a self becomes an other to himself or herself, and this in virtue of the fact that he or she *perceives* himself or herself as communicating (SW.146).[2] Moreover, the formation of such a self, in order to be generous, must take place in a context that is both broad and varied. Here is Mead: "the inner response to our reaction to others is . . . as varied as is our social environment" (SW.146). In addition, if a developing self is to enjoy the benefits of thinking that transcends what is concrete, banal, and ineffectual, it must develop a relation to what Mead calls a generalized other. It is only through conversations with this generalized other that thinking can become abstract, impersonal, and objective.[3]

In short, social efficiency is the result of expanded avenues of communication. Intellectual, emotional, and aesthetic horizons are expanded, and the connections and interrelations of individual and group with other individuals and other groups become more comprehensive. Whenever social efficiency is defined or understood in ways that ignore these considerations, its practice becomes hard and metallic, mechanically utilitarian, or even totalitarian. But when social efficiency is understood in terms of the recrudescence of mind, in terms of enlarged powers of understanding things physical and social in terms of the use to which they are put in shared situations, then mind comes to be understood as the method of social control (cf. MW.9.38).

Social Control

In chapter 3 of *Democracy and Education*, Dewey tells us what he means by social control: "genuine social control," he writes, "means the formation of a certain mental disposition; a way of *understanding* objects, events, and acts which enables one to participate effectively in associated activities" (MW.9.41).

This remark relates the expanded opportunities for communication that are involved in the growth of social efficiency to mental discipline and consciously controlled habit-formation. Socialization occurs, for good or ill. Beyond that, when socialization meets the two criteria that Dewey has suggested, social efficiency emerges and grows, expressing itself as the expansion of mind. And, beyond that, when experimental habit-formation enters the picture, then it may properly be said that there is social control.

The term "control" is, to say the least, currently out of favor. This may be due in part to the many disastrous ends-dominated industrial, commercial, political, and military programs of the twentieth century. Failed attempts at "social engineering," including architectural failures such as the now-demolished Pruitt-Eigo low-cost housing project in Saint Louis and disastrous military failures such as the American ordeal in Southeast Asia during the 1960s and 1970s, have encouraged many contemporary writers—especially those who have been inspired by various forms of "postmodernism" as developed within the French academy—to deprecate the notion of "control" and to place blame for such failures at the door of the technosciences. Literary metaphors have thus taken pride of place and the language of control as management through experimentation has become the object of derision. In such circles, the term "control" has become pejorative.

Viewed in terms of Dewey's version of pragmatism, however, this trend constitutes an overreaction to admitted excesses. His strong commitment to experimentation led him to utilize the term "control" as denoting the intelligent management of circumstances that are not what we wish them to be. The only alternatives to control as intelligent management, he suggested, are tenacity with respect to received views, subservience to external authority, or the application of a priori and therefore untested methods.

In Dewey's lexicon, social control involves a progressive reconstruction of habits, including institutions, through the application of carefully controlled experimental processes. The technosciences may provide successful models of such undertakings, but they by no means establish a hegemony over other areas of inquiry in the process of doing so. Dewey is clear enough about this point in his little book *The Sources of a Science of Education* (LW.5.1–40). The sources of a science of education lie not in the technosciences, and not even in the aims and plans of the educator. They lie instead in the educational process itself—namely, in that interaction between teacher and learner that generates the unanticipated circumstances that, when distilled in the alembic of disciplined experimentation, become capable of promoting growth.

In all this it is as if Dewey were replying in advance to those of his critics who continue to this day to criticize his approach to education as preoccupied with "social engineering." What those critics have missed is the fact that in Dewey's lexicon, social control is neither top-down nor bottom-up. It is neither narrowly authoritarian nor mindlessly populist. It is an activity that enlarges understanding of matters as they are and as they can be, and thereby promotes the growth of individuals and communities. It is a method for the dissemination of power on the basis of the ability to employ it in ways that are broadly beneficial.

I have chosen to emphasize these themes because I believe that American education from kindergarten through postgraduate programs is currently in crisis. Further, I am convinced that the ideas that Dewey presented in *Democracy and Education*—a book that he did not shy from describing as one of his most important efforts—provide tools for dealing with our current difficulties.

Because there is perhaps no American educator who has been more frequently and extensively misread, misunderstood, and even demonized, it is imperative that we be clear about what Dewey actually said. On the fringes of the religious right, for example, one finds Web pages both numerous and copious in which Dewey is featured for all practical purposes as horned and hoofed. Here is one example: "Relativism and positivism are destructive ideologies that sheer (*sic*) men away from the truth a little at a time. These ideas were used by John Dewey and Carl (*sic*) Marx and even Joseph Stalin to lead people astray."[4] Further, "Dewey knew how to change the schools so our customs would not be passed on to our children . . . [which was] all for the intent of cutting off America's children from their inheritance."[5] What was Dewey's purpose in all this? "He believes (*sic*) in the collective society like socialist of (*sic*) Russia and China being more important than any individualism."[6] *The central complaint of this attack from the religious right thus seems to come down to this: Dewey wanted to undermine tradition by promoting relativism and he wanted to use the schools as a platform for social engineering.*

From the other end of the political spectrum, it was not so long ago that Dewey's pragmatism was being assailed by his Marxist–Stalinist critics as the "main-line philosophy of U.S. imperialism" (Wells, p. 131).[7] One critic charged that instead of recognizing that "a well rounded person is first of all a product of what is brought to him from outside himself . . . Dewey's formula would withhold this social heritage. It would do this by making the instincts of the child rather than the humanism of mankind the source of education" (Wells, p. 78).

But wait. There is more. Dewey's view is glossed as follows: "If the schools could only imbue the workers with the idea that their deepest 'instincts' are fulfilled in operating the machines which produce profits, then indeed the 'evils' of the capitalist system, as the capitalist sees them, would be located and largely solved" (Wells, p. 81). So it is not in fact the "instincts" of the child that take precedence in guiding education after all. It is the Dewey-inspired educator's interpretation of those "instincts" and their indoctrination of the students with that interpretation! *The central complaint of this hard-line leftist thus seems to come down to this: Dewey wanted to undermine tradition by promoting relativism and he wanted to use the schools as a platform for social engineering.*

Perhaps even more remarkably, this view, shared by extremists of left and right, has been echoed by no less formidable an historian of education than Diane Ravitch. Dewey's Marxist critics, suspecting a Trojan horse, had been concerned that "Dewey's pragmatic theory of education would *conceal* the essence of bourgeois education . . . through making bourgeois indoctrination appear as the flowering of the inner being of the child" (Wells, p. 77—emphasis added). For her part, Ravitch, suspecting a Trojan horse, is concerned that Dewey inspired the idea that "the methods of education could be derived from the innate needs and nature of the child" and that "intellectually vacuous courses *were clothed* in the rhetoric of collective social improvement" (There is that word "collective" again.) (Ravitch, p. 308—emphasis added).[8] In other words, *the central complaint advanced by Ravitch seems to come down to this: Dewey inspired and supported those who wanted to undermine tradition by promoting relativism and wanted to use the schools as a platform for social engineering.*

In fairness, it must be admitted that Ravitch's main target is not so much Dewey as what she, as well as Dewey himself, regarded as the excesses of "progressive" educators who claimed Dewey's imprimatur. But the point remains. Given Dewey's emphasis on "severe standards" (MW.9.186), Ravitch's charges appear misdirected: they tend to rely on guilt by association.

I hope that I may be forgiven for pointing out two features of this ubiquitous complaint—one that seems to be so popular among Dewey's critics of left and right alike—that must already appear obvious to everyone who has followed the account this far. First, what comes to mind when one thinks of social engineering is not relativism, but absolutes of one sort or another. Historically, social engineering has been identified with top-down practices in which an elite—perhaps bureaucratic, perhaps technocratic—assesses situations without adequate consultation of the parties or circumstances that will be affected by their decisions. Whether such practices honor ends over means or means at the expense of ends, such situations usually involve a commitment to some sort of absolute.

To accuse Dewey's educational program, therefore, of *both* relativism and social engineering is on its face absurd, unless one or the other of the terms is employed in a Pickwickian sense. Any attempt at social engineering that promoted the type of relativism of which Dewey's critics have accused him would be out of business in short order. It would be self-defeating. Put another way, the type of relativism with which Dewey was charged would not support a program of social engineering.

Second, some of the same critics who fault Dewey with holding *both* the relativism of natural impulses *and* the absolutes of social engineering seem to want to have it both ways. They *also* want to say that what Dewey *really* did was to emphasize one of the extremes—natural impulse *or* social engineering—over the other. It is in this vein, for example, that Ravitch complains in another section of her book that Dewey was "locked in dualisms, the famous 'either-ors' that he so often wrote about." So the real problem, in her view, was that "he never presented them as equally compelling alternatives, so it was scarcely surprising that his followers unfailingly (*sic*) chose society, not the school; the child, not the curriculum; interest, not effort; experience, not subject matter" (Ravitch, p. 309). My own suggestion is that these charges, from left, right, and elsewhere, are supported by little more than caricature. If the analysis that I have provided in the first sections of this chapter is correct, then they exemplify a profound misunderstanding of what Dewey meant by socialization, social efficiency, and social control.

If *Democracy and Education* teaches us anything, it is that social efficiency is an ideal that gives rise to social control as a family of flexible educational methods and activities—that social efficiency and social control in the Deweyan lexicon cannot therefore be reduced to a set program or policy (other than the program of experimentalism, which is, of course, not set but open-ended and self-corrective), educational or otherwise. Furthermore, it is precisely this commitment to the flexible methods and activities of experimentalism that effectively provides the basis for a reconstruction of the false dilemma that says that educators must choose between natural powers, on the one hand, and the "subordination of natural powers to social control," on the other (MW.9.24).

How does Dewey reconstruct this putative dilemma in *Democracy and Education*? He does so in the same way that he had reconstructed the dilemma posed by Thomas Huxley in the latter's Romanes Lecture of 1893, published as *Evolution and Ethics*.[9] As part of his pro-Darwinian polemic, Huxley had sharply separated two things: a natural or "cosmic" order, which he described as replete with struggle and strife ("nature red in tooth and claw"), and ethical progress, which he thought required neither imitating nor fleeing from the cosmic process but instead combating it. For Huxley, social progress meant the substitution of ethical processes for natural processes at every step.

In his response to Huxley, Dewey agreed that we can "never allow things simply to go on of themselves." But he also rejected the separation on which Huxley's argument had hinged. In fact, Dewey wrote, "we do not have . . . a conflict of man as man with his entire natural environment. We have rather the modification by man of one part of the environment with reference to another part" (EW.5.37). On its face, this remark should be sufficient to dispel any suspicion that Dewey's pragmatism was constructed on the dualism that some of his critics claim to have found there. But substitute the term "social control" in this remark—in the sense in which I have argued that Dewey used the term—for "modification" and you get a wonderful statement of Dewey's educational philosophy as well. The teacher is not called on to "combat" what he or she takes to be the struggle and strife of natural instinct, but to utilize one portion of the learning environment as a tool for the modification of another of its parts. This is Dewey's notion of social control as it applies to educational practice.

As he developed the arguments he set out in *Democracy and Education*, Dewey refused to allow the separation that is so often attributed to him by his critics, namely, that of acquiescing to natural impulses on the one side and/or promoting "social engineering" on the other. The error in honoring such a split, he notes, is "in implying that we must adopt measures of subordination rather than of utilization to secure efficiency" (MW.9.125).

In short, education is not a matter of the subordination of natural impulses to absolute values, including those of social engineering (or even the other way around), but rather of socializing natural impulses in ways that reconstruct them as constructive and expansive rather than *reductive*, and far-ranging and comprehensive rather than exclusive. And the test, as I have suggested, is whether such socialization encourages the expansion of the learner's intellectual, emotional, and aesthetic horizons, and whether the learner and the group of which he or she is a member become more comprehensive in terms of their connections and interrelations with other socializing forces. This is the type of social efficiency that leads to the type of increasing control of habits and institutions that Dewey termed "social control."

But what, in terms of our current situation, does this mean? Dewey is clear enough on this point. It means that there can be no social efficiency where there is no social safety net. There can be no social efficiency when children go to school hungry and when catsup is defined as a vegetable. There can be no social efficiency where public school budgets are cut in order to distribute financial favors to rich political contributors. And there can be no social efficiency where the exploration that is a natural part of the educational process is supplanted by preoccupation with test-taking. It means that there can be no social efficiency where "unfair privilege and unfair deprivation" are institutionalized in ways that create homogenized educational settings. It means that there can be no social efficiency where men and women are unable to "judge men and measures wisely and to take a determining part in making as well as obeying laws" because journalism and other forms of public discourse have been corrupted. It means, in short, that there can be no social efficiency in the absence of a socialization of mind that involves "making experiences more communicable [and] breaking down the barriers of social stratification which make individuals impervious to the interests of others" (MW.9.127).

Still more specifically, as I write there are numerous other factors that militate against social efficiency. If we look at state budgets, we find that during the twenty years from 1980 to 2000 spending for education (including higher education) rose only 32%. To see this figure in one perspective, the Consumer Price Index during those two decades rose 109%—thus outstripping rises in spending on education by a factor of more than three to one.[10] To see it in another perspective, it may help to know that during that same period state spending on prisons rose 189%.[11] That comes down to prisons over schools by a factor of six to one. (Of course, some states do better than others. In my home state of Illinois, increases in spending for prisons outpaced increases in spending for education during this period by 217% to 47%, or a factor of 4.62 to 1. In my native state of Texas, the ratio was a remarkable 401% to 37%, or a factor of 11.08 to 1.)

Educators inspired by the work of John Dewey have for years called for more coordination of educational policy at the federal level. More specifically, this has been a call for equalized funding for school districts, renovation of substandard school buildings, better quality free textbooks, better libraries with more librarians, more guidance counselors and school nurses, and more special programs for handicapped and disadvantaged children. These are necessary conditions of social efficiency.

Under pressure from the right wing of its political base, including Christian fundamentalists, the current Bush administration has in fact begun to dramatically increase federal involvement in K–12 education. But it is doing so in ways that are quite different from what the Dewey of *Democracy and Education* had in mind.

Whereas Dewey was a strong advocate of public education, the Bush administration's No Child Left Behind initiative advances on two fronts, legislative and judicial, that seem designed to privatize public education.

Whereas Dewey argued that educational testing should be done retail and with care, for example, much as medical tests are done, the Bush administration's legislative initiative has instituted testing whose results are interpreted at the wholesale level and without regard to the particular challenges of individual students, teachers, and schools. Here is Dewey from *Democracy and Education*: "How one person's abilities compare in quantity with those of another is none of the teacher's business. It is irrelevant to his work. What is required is that every individual shall have opportunities to employ his own powers in activities that have meaning" (MW.9.179–180).

And whereas Dewey held no brief against the existence of religious schools, I am convinced that he would have been a strong and vocal opponent of the judicial initiative of the Bush administration—the decision of the U. S. Supreme Court that legalized the school vouchers that will eventuate in the siphoning of public tax revenues to support private schools that offer or require religious instruction. Dewey argued that public schools have democratizing effects that are paralleled by no other institution. He would have strongly opposed both prongs of the Bush initiative.

Although there is a great deal more to say about these issues, I hope that during the space allotted here I have at least been able to inspire further discussion of Dewey's use of these three terms that play such a prominent role in the message of *Democracy and Education*—socialization, social efficiency, and social control—as well as to indicate some of the ways in which current educational policy in this country seems designed to thwart social efficiency, and therefore social control, rather than promote it.

Notes

1. While writing this chapter I read a remark by Mark Edmundson that seems to capture what Dewey had in mind when he offered his two criteria for evaluating socialization. And it certainly captures Dewey's notion of the well-socialized individual as a work of art that is continually being reconstructed. ("The Risk of Reading," *New York Times Magazine*, August 1, 2004. His essay is at <http://www.nytimes.com/2004/08/01/magazine/01WWLN.html>.)

> Gradually, we are instilled with the common sense that conservative writers like Edmund Burke and Samuel Johnson thought of as a great collective work. To them, common sense is infused with all that has been learned over time through trial and error, human frustration, sorrow and joy. In fact, a well-socialized being is something like a work of art.
>
> Yet for many people, the process of socialization doesn't quite work. The values they acquire from all the well-meaning authorities don't fit them. And it is these people who often become obsessed readers. They don't read for information, and they don't read for beautiful escape. No, they read to remake themselves. They read to be socialized again, not into the ways of their city or village this time but into another world with different values. Such people want to revise, or even to displace, the influence their parents have had on them. They want to adopt values they perceive to be higher or perhaps just better suited to their natures.

2. George Herbert Mead. *Selected Writings*. Edited, with an introduction by Andrew J. Reck (Indianapolis: Bobbs-Merrill,1964). As Mead puts the matter, "the self which consciously stands over against other selves thus becomes an object, an other to himself, through the very fact that he hears himself talk, and replies."

3. "Our thinking is an inner conversation in which we may be taking the roles of specific acquaintances over against ourselves, but usually it is with what I have termed the 'generalized other' that we converse, and so attain to the levels of abstract thinking, and that impersonality, that so-called objectivity that we cherish" (SW 288).

4. Source: www.christianparents.com/jdewey.htm.

5. Source: www.christianparents.com/jdewey2.htm.

6. Source: www.christianparents.com/jdewey.htm.

7. Harry K. Wells. *Pragmatism: Philosophy of Imperialism* (New York: International Publishers, 1954).

8. Diane Ravitch. *Left Back: A Century of Battles Over School Reform* (New York: Touchstone Books, 2000).

9. Thomas H. Huxley. *Evolution and Ethics and Other Essays* (New York: D. Appleton and Co., 1896).

10. Source: Robert Sahr, Department of Political Science, the University of Oregon. "Inflation Conversion Factors for Dollars 1665 to Estimated 2014" <http://oregonstate.edu/dept/pol_sci/fac/sahr/sahr.htm>.

11. These figures are adjusted for inflation and expressed in 1999 dollars. Source: Mother Jones.com Special Report. This report includes a sidebar on methodology. <http://www.motherjones.com/news/special_reports/prisons/atlas.html>.

5

Growth *and* Perfectionism?

Dewey after Emerson and Cavell

Naoko Saito

Introduction: Growth in the Age of Globalization

In contemporary education, the notion of growth, an idea so central to Dewey, has become increasingly unsteady. On the one hand, in the global market economy, growth is associated with free choice, competitive power, and success, often with the image of a differentiated self—an identity developed and extended through acquisition. On the other, there is a counteractive force geared toward standardization, unification, and, worse, assimilation, through which the self is flattened and shrunk. Expansive growth on a global scale ironically narrows the horizon of global awareness, awareness of the foreign, on the part of students. Education in these apparently contradictory directions of growth conspires to deprive students of the independent power of judgment—where to stand in their own judgment and how to trust their own taste. The language of moral and citizenship education paralyzes students' confidence in finding their own language, in connection not only with global affairs, but also with what is going on around themselves, within their familiar, native circumstances. Growth today seems to face a pressing need to be redefined from an alternative perspective—one that helps us to connect our personal ways of life with those of others, with our own culture and the foreign, and to find ways to bridge personal and social moralities. The challenge lies in maintaining the flexibility and mobility of growth in the face of value diversity and concomitant uncertainties, while at the same time not losing a certain sense of direction and hope for attaining some commonality. Is it, however, possible to find a route and language for such growth? Or should we abrogate the very idea of growth?

As one possible standpoint from which to reconsider growth in the contemporary world, John Dewey's idea of growth is examined in this chapter and reconstructed in the light of Ralph Waldo Emerson's moral perfectionism, an idea elaborated by Stanley Cavell. Dewey is well known as a philosopher of growth. His *Democracy and Education* especially represents well the theme of growth. His peculiar view of growth— *growth without fixed ends,* one that is based on his naturalism and prag- matism—has consistently been attacked for its lack of a definite sense of direction and hence its vulnerability to relativism. This is a challenge directed at the process-oriented view of growth in Dewey's pragmatism. In response, I shall argue that Deweyan growth if reconsidered and reinforced in a certain dimension—its Emersonian perfectionist dimen- sion—can provide us with an alternative vision of education and democ- racy in place of those predominant in the age of globalization.

In the following section, I first identify various traits of Dewey's idea of growth as it appears in *Democracy and Education,* and I discuss some of their implications for contemporary education as reflected in David Hansen's interpretation of Dewey. I then examine Nel Noddings's criticism of Dewey. She is a sympathetic supporter of Dewey's philosophy and yet maintains some doubts about it. I argue that the kinds of re- sponses that Dewey might offer are not sufficient as they are, but also that Noddings's own alternative position misses the basic line of his pragmatism. In the section entitled "From Growth to Perfectionism," I introduce an alternative critical standpoint from which to reconstruct Deweyan growth: the standpoint of Emersonian moral perfectionism as advanced by Stanley Cavell. Sharing with Dewey a common stance to- ward democracy and education, and an antifoundationalist, process- oriented view of perfection, Emerson and Cavell reinforce a certain dimension of Deweyan growth. I conclude with a discussion of the educational implications of Deweyan growth reconstructed in the light of Emersonian moral perfectionism, including the role of the teacher in enhancing students' growth and in citizenship education.

Growth without Fixed Ends:
From Dewey to Hansen and Noddings

"Since growth is the characteristic of life, education is all one with growing; it has no end beyond itself" (MW.9.58). Thus Dewey affirms:

growth in the present tense of growing, growth without fixed ends. Growth in itself is "*being* an end" (MW.9.55) and is relative only to "more growth" (MW.9.56). This is derived from Dewey's Darwinian naturalistic view of growth based on "the principle of continuity" (MW.9.5)—the process of continual, reorganization of life. Simultaneously, it epitomizes his pragmatism. Growing is the process of an agent's active involvement with and intelligent control of its environments through the use of things. The agent is responsible for the future consequences in its action and thinking, and hence to resolve problems and conflicts in everyday life. He calls this "the scientific experimental method" (MW.9.348).

Dewey's naturalistic and pragmatist view of growth has social implications; it is closely tied to his idea of democracy. By democracy, Dewey does not simply mean political procedures and mechanisms, but a personal way of life in one's communal relationship with others (LW.14). Growth is not simply a personal matter, but of concern for the whole society. This is not, however, an assimilation of the individual into the whole; rather, his view of democratic community is dynamic and flexible in that people from diverse backgrounds learn from each other. Hence, education is a crucial factor in "creative democracy" (ibid.)—for democracy to be ever growing. Dewey believes that school is a hub of the democratic community from within which his American ideal of democracy is to be gradually created: the "assimilative force of the American public school is eloquent testimony to the efficacy of the common and balanced appeal" (MW.9.26). We might call it Dewey's idea of the *common school*.

The implications of Deweyan growth are developed in the works of contemporary Deweyan philosophers of education. David Hansen inherits and reconfigures Dewey's philosophy of education, and integrates it in his own idea of teaching—an attempt to redeem the "personhood" of the teacher in contemporary education (Hansen, 2001, p. 1). Hansen especially values the moral dimensions of Dewey's philosophy. First, he finds in Dewey's *Democracy and Education* an account of the "moral traits of a growing person": straightforwardness, simplicity, spontaneity, integrity, responsibility, seriousness, open-mindedness, and open heartedness (Hansen, 2001, pp. 41–56). The teacher as a person, Hansen claims, should "influence others for the good rather than for the bad" (p. 40). Indeed, Dewey's consistent claim in *Democracy and Education* is that morality requires personal commitment and should be experienced beyond its verbal articulation. The moral traits that Hansen highlights do not depend on some notions of absolute moral goodness being inculcated in students, but draw attention to "the qualities of mind" that the growing person should acquire (p. 368).

Second, Hansen inherits Dewey's idea that there is no such thing as "the direct influence of one human being on another" (MW.9.33). Hansen claims: "Dewey's perspective helps turn the teacher's gaze away from him- or herself and toward the classroom environment and the diverse factors that figure in its emergence. Teaching indirectly helps the teacher become object- rather than self-conscious" (Hansen, 2001, p. 70). A teacher–student relationship here should maintain both "closeness" and "distance" (p. 155): "a teacher and his or her students should be moving closer and closer *apart* and . . . farther and farther *together*" (p. 156). This is a social aspect of Deweyan growth. In mutual learning, a teacher also grows; as Dewey says, "the teacher is a learner, and the learner is, without knowing it, a teacher" (MW.9.167).

This guides us toward a third implication of Deweyan growth in education: the role of a teacher in initiating the child into "tradition." This does not simply mean a process contributing to the conservation of the past: rather it means an initiation into the common ground for cultivating moral traits in solidarity with humanity *and* for establishing "critical distance" from the past. Though Hansen thinks Dewey's approach to the past is too instrumental to appreciate the inherent value of tradition (Hansen, 2001, p. 139), he shares with Dewey the view that the teacher as a mediator stands at an entrance into humanity. More explicitly than Dewey, Hansen says that the teacher exemplifies her ideal towards humanity—what Hansen calls "tenacious humility" (p. 167).

Like Hansen, Noddings develops Dewey's philosophy of education and his view on growth, but she does this more critically than Hansen. On the one hand, in connection with her own ethics of care, Noddings endorses Dewey's idea of community and the communal self, and its concomitant concept of growth. She argues that Dewey's idea of community presages the contemporary debate between liberalism and communitarianism, if reinforced by an ethics of care, and that education conceived in its terms can contribute to "stability, civility, and personal growth," while not falling into an "illiberal belief system" (Noddings, 2002, pp. 82–83). School as a "community of order" can provide children with a "sense of belonging" (pp. 165, 174). Here she develops Dewey's idea that "democracy must begin at home" (LW.2.368). Since morality, place, and identity are inseparable, Noddings argues, home is a place in which children's identities begin to be cultivated with a sense of being "sheltered" (pp. 150, 154); they "*feel* part of it," of their home community (p. 157). In this regard, she agrees with Dewey that education must begin with "items of familiarity" (p. 174).

However, Noddings goes beyond Dewey: she claims that children should be educated not merely "*from*" home life, but primarily "*for* the centrality of home life" (ibid.). She also values Dewey's idea of growth as not specifying fixed goals or definite criteria and as acknowledging the diversity of goods. The suggestion for the teacher that she draws from this is that each of us must work out "how to reorganize growth" toward better conditions (p. 183). On the other hand, Noddings casts a doubt on Deweyan growth by asking: "what do we mean by 'better,' and how do we decide when conditions are indeed better?" Faced with this question, Noddings claims that Dewey's presentation of "social" criteria is not enough to give us "sound criteria" for making moral judgments. Noddings thinks Dewey does not sufficiently explicitly or adequately provide an account of moral goods because of his evasion of "foundations"; she wishes he had done so. Her alternative ethic, however, does: caring is "a place to stand on," the "foundation" of moral life (pp. 220–223).

While both Hansen and Noddings find implications of Dewey's idea of growth in contemporary education and democracy, they confront us with the need to reconsider and possibly to reconstruct it. Noddings's position is more explicit than Hansen's concerning the need to provide "foundations" for Dewey's idea of growth without fixed ends—those ends expressed in such words as "the best self" (p. 221) and as a well-established ideal (p. 223). Her identification of home as the cultivating ground of morality suggests a drive toward security and stability far stronger than Dewey's original language does. Similarly, though more implicitly, or perhaps unintentionally, Hansen's text gestures toward the need for foundations—in his highlighting of the moral traits that Dewey advanced in *Democracy and Education*, and in his own suggestion that the teacher who embodies humanist ideals should initiate students into the inherent values of tradition (Hansen, 2001, p. 139). In the anxiety over Dewey's antifoundationalism, an anti-antifoundationalist drive reasserts itself. Obviously, this transgresses the basic line of Dewey's antifoundationalist view of growth and his attempt to find the sources of morality in natural life. Is this paradoxical consequence to be attributed to some internal weakness in his idea of growth? Is there anything peculiar in Dewey's language of growth that drives even such sympathetic readers as Hansen and Noddings into a search for foundations? In any case, there is a need to present an alternative and more persuasive language for antifoundationalist growth.

In response to these challenges, it is necessary to reexamine Dewey's language in *Democracy and Education* where he discusses the measures of growth. As Noddings says, it is not the case that Dewey allows *any* choices and preferences (Noddings, 2002, p. 183). He presents alternative concepts and a different language of "criteria," "standard," "aims," and "ends" for growth. These are a part of the activities of the growing self and, therefore, revisable and flexible. As his alternative concept of end most typically shows, the ends and means of growth are inseparable as constituents of the activity of growth, as "ends-in-view" (MW.9.112–113). Likewise "standards" originate in individual experiences depending on contexts: "working as distinct from professed standards depend upon what an individual has himself specifically appreciated to be deeply significant in concrete situations" (MW.9.243). If so, how can a teacher decide whether any individual student meets such conditions in the process of growth? The measure is, in Dewey's language, "a widening and deepening of conscious life—a more intense, disciplined, and expanding realization of meanings" (MW.9.369); it is seen again in the remark that "when pupils are genuinely concerned in learning Latin, that is of itself proof that it possesses value" (MW.9.251). He also discusses the concepts of "democratic criteria" (MW.9.105) and the "democratic ideal" (MW.9.92). An ideal of democratic education is "a freeing of individual capacity in a progressive growth directed to social aims" (MW.9.105). "Democratic criteria" are to be found in the "widening of the area of shared concerns and the liberation of a greater diversity of personal capacities" (MW.9.93) as well as "a continuous reconstruction and reorganizing of experience" (MW.9.332). The measure of "good citizenship" is to "participate more richly in the worthwhile experiences of others" (MW.9.127).

These expressions suggest that Dewey's language concerning the measures of growth is quite general and sometimes prescriptive, to such an extent as to stir among readers a yearning for a foundation—to drive some of its readers to detect in Dewey's text the signs of definite criteria for democratic education. Simultaneously, if the aspects of its principle of continuity and commonality are interpreted even slightly in this foundationalist way and are upheld as *the* aim of democratic education, there immediately occurs the danger of assimilation into totality—the very contradiction of Dewey's principle of growth. Such a danger is detected in Dewey's language itself, for example, when he says: "When the activities of mind set out from customary beliefs and strive to effect transformations of them which will in turn win general conviction, there is no opposition between the individual and the social" (MW.9.306); "The wider or larger self which means inclusion instead of denial of relationships is identical with a self which enlarges in order to assume previously unforeseen ties" (MW.9.362); and "what he gets from living with others balances with what he contributes" (MW.9.369). Here is a sign of the economy of exchange, a tendency to include, and, even worse, to assimilate difference into the same. Or, concerning deviancy in a community, he states: "When others are not doing what we would like them to or are threatening disobedience, we are most conscious of the need of controlling them" (MW.9.31). How can we distinguish these remarks from the assimilating force of control of the teacher confronted with a recalcitrant child in the classroom? Is this only a matter of language or the issue that shakes the very structure of Dewey's thought?

In Dewey's language of continuity, inclusion and the common in *Democracy and Education*, it is hard to find a clue that concretely indicates how one can maintain critical distance from the familiar, despite his call for valuing the uniqueness of individuality. It is then possible, in terms of Deweyan growth, to emphasize, as Noddings does, the aspects of settlement, inclusion, and stability in moral life, and to highlight the significance of home as the place for the cultivation of moral ideals; it is then possible to highlight, as Hansen does, the role of the teacher who initiates children into moral ideals, tradition, and good character; though both Noddings and Hansen, of course, equally value the element of criticism. Dewey's theory and language of growth need to be internally criticized so that they can maintain more thoroughly their antifoundationalist, pragmatist principle, as do his "democratic criteria" in order to sustain unity in diversity—to achieve continuous growth, to resist assimilation into totality, and to avoid the outcome of relativism. His idea of a "growing or active self" (MW.9.362) requires the language that enables us to persevere within the process of transition.

From Growth to Perfectionism: Reconstructing Dewey's Pragmatism in Dialogue with Emerson and Cavell

Emersonian Moral Perfectionism

In order to enhance the potential of Dewey's antifoundationalist view of growth, I shall try to emphasize an aspect that is not evident in Noddings's account and one that is suggested (with reference to Cavell) but not fully developed in Hansen's: the *Emersonian perfectionist strand of Deweyan growth*. Cavell himself resists any facile connection of Dewey's pragmatism with Emersonian moral perfectionism (EMP) (Cavell, 1998). However, because of, and despite, its common ground with Deweyan growth, EMP can constitute a strong standpoint from which to critically reconstruct the latter, while maintaining its antifoundationalist stance.

The presence of Emerson in Dewey's thought is not always perspicuous or constant, and his influence is not necessarily direct. Still, from the early to the later periods of his career, Dewey gradually revealed a latent identity—or, perhaps, a spirit—that he inherited from Emerson. The most explicit early example of this is his essay of 1903, "Emerson—

The Philosopher of Democracy" (MW.3). Dewey's identification with Emerson is sustained in *Democracy and Education*. For example, he explicitly refers to Emerson when he discusses the immaturity of a child as a positive asset for growth (MW.9.57). In other parts of the book, wherever he discusses the native powers of the young and the originality of the individual against the pressures of conformity, Emerson's voice is echoed. Most prominently, in chapter 5, in resistance to the "all-inclusive end of development," Dewey distinguishes his view on growth from the "perfection" of the final, absolute ideal (MW.9.61, 62, 63). He says, "growing is growth, developing is development" (MW.9.63); in *Human Nature and Conduct* (1922) he restates the idea that "perfection means perfecting, fulfillment, fulfilling, and the good is now or never" (MW.14.200). Once one hears the resonance of Emerson's voice in Dewey's text, it is difficult not to read *Democracy and Education* without some sense of an implicit dialogue with Emerson as Dewey's critical interlocutor.

It is in particular this idea of perfection without final perfectibility, with its strong focus on ongoing process in the here and now, that brings Dewey close to Cavell's representation of Emerson's perfectionism. There are four main related characteristics of EMP that Cavell highlights: (1) perfection as perfect*ing* with no fixed ends; (2) the idea of democracy to be ever attained; (3) Emerson's (and Thoreau's) strong focus on the ordinary; and (4) perfection as mutual education through friendship and dialogue. Cavell describes EMP as the endless journey of self-overcoming, where "the self is always attained, as well as *to be* attained" (Cavell, 1990, p. 12); refusing final perfectibility, it is characterized by "goallessness" (p. xxxiv). The process, however, is not merely one of *self*-realization. Illuminating the social dimension of Emerson, Cavell reiterates Emerson's idea of "the criticism of democracy from within" (p. 3) and of an entrance into the "conversation of justice" (p. 28).

EMP treasures the spirit of nonconformity. It resists the nihilism that is internal to democracy, the danger of a "shrinking participation in democracy" (p. 51). Democracy in this sense is ever to be attained; it involves the process of mutual education. The presence of "another" self who is a friend confronts one with the standpoint of perfection (pp. 58–59). Though Cavell consistently refuses to call Dewey an Emersonian moral perfectionist (Cavell, 1990; 1998; 2003), these basic features of EMP have striking similarities to Dewey's idea of growth, to his view of philosophy as education, and to the concomitant idea of democracy—democracy as a way of life, democracy that begins at home with the ordinary, and democracy as a constant process of reconstruction through criticism. Precisely because of this common framework of thinking, and Dewey's identification with Emerson, EMP can constitute a standpoint from which critically and internally to reconstruct and reinforce Deweyan growth.

A point of departure for reconstruction is the metaphysics of EMP—Emerson's idea of circles. This is the view that our lives are "an apprenticeship to the truth, that around every circle, another can be drawn; that there is no end in nature, but every end is a beginning." Emerson calls this "the moral fact of the Unattainable, the flying Perfect" (Emerson, 1990a, p. 166). Taking up this idea of "ever-widening circles" (Cavell, 1992, p. 128), Cavell stresses that its direction is "not up but on" (p. 10). He registers an ambiguity in Emerson's thoughts here "as between what he [Emerson] calls the *generating* and what he calls the *drawing* of the new circle, an ambiguity between the picturing of new circles as forming continuously or disconinuously" (p. 135). But it is this moment of discontinuity that is at the forefront of EMP but is downplayed in Deweyan growth with its focus on continuity and concentricity.[1]

The metaphysics of EMP brings us to its antifoundationalist dimension—the idea of *finding as founding*, which is originally presented in Emerson's essay, "Experience" (Emerson, 1990b), and elaborated by Cavell (Cavell, 1989, pp. 77–118). In "Experience," Emerson's response to the sense of groundlessness when we lose our way is not regret, but the awareness of the futility of regretting. Cavell takes up the idea and presents a view that philosophy begins in loss, with the experience of "the world falling away, the bottom of things dropping out, ourselves foundered, sunk on a stair" (pp. 109, 114). Emerson's philosophical task, however, is not the building of the unified foundation of philosophy as a kind of ground we reach once and for all: "Foundation reaches no farther than each issue of finding" (p. 114). In contrast to Derrida's task of deconstructing the "finished edifice of philosophy," under the weight of its European inheritance, Emerson's, Cavell claims, is "to avert foundation, in advance" through "founding, or deconfounding, American thinking" (Cavell, 1996, p. 65). For Emerson, as exemplified in the "American Scholar," this task of finding as founding is not only a matter of private therapeutic activity, but the perfectionist task of "founding a nation," "this new yet unapproachable America" (Cavell, 1989, pp. 93, 94).

The problem here is that the word "finding" too readily suggests something that is already there. What needs to be emphasized is that the search creates new possibilities. These are then "found." The word "found" is subtly ambiguous between the past participle of "find" and the verb "to found," which means to establish or inaugurate. This means that founding is not to be understood in terms of a source or, in other words, a once-and-for-all foundationalism (which would be tantamount for Emerson to a kind of fixation); it is to be understood in terms of a recurrent finding. The idea of "finding as founding" thus represents the antifoundationalism that is characteristic of EMP, the middle way of living beyond the restrictive, fixed choice between no ground and absolute ground, with a strong focus on process. As Cavell says: "[Emerson's] perception of the moment is taken in hope, as something to be proven only on the way, *by* the way" (Cavell, 1992, p. 137). You attain *a* step in perfecting when you undergo despair over loss [which is not to be "overcome" as "every new finding may incur a new loss" (p. 114)], and then find a new way beyond, drawing a new circle. It is a *continual*, not continuous, process of arriving and leaving. Citing Emerson's phrase, "to find the journey's end in every step of the road," Cavell says: "A finding in every step is the description of a series, perhaps in the form of a proof, or a sentence" (pp. 114–115). This critical moment of undergoing "conversion" and projecting a way beyond itself is a proof—or we might call it a criterion—of perfection (p. 115).

Let us come back to Deweyan growth. Dewey in *Democracy and Education* says that thinking is "prospective," that it is occasioned by an "*un*settlement," and that it aims at "overcoming a disturbance" (MW.9.330). Here again is a striking similarity to, *and* a radical difference from, Emerson and Cavell. Cavell's persistent doubt regarding Dewey is directed at the latter's problem-solving (or overcoming) mode of thinking and language, whereas he finds in Emerson another mode of thinking—of thinking as "thanking" (with its anticipation of Heidegger), as the "reception of being human" (Cavell, 1992, p. 132). Furthermore, in his negation of inner consciousness, Dewey's description of the process of growth avoids the internal landscape of the self as something unreachable, whereas Cavell's and Emerson's language of perfection communicates the sense of the inner, without presupposing the absolute ground of the self. In EMP this sense of the private, internal route of transformation is the necessary condition for public, outward change.

From Growth to Perfection: The Gleam of Light

In finding as founding, the emphasis is on "onwardness," but its fundamental condition is the moment of "leaving." In contrast to Heidegger's drive toward "inhabitation and settlement," Cavell claims that "abandonment," departure, and unsettlement constitute the drive in EMP (Cavell, 1992, p. 138). Along with the moment of discontinuity in expanding circles, the element of "leaving" is perhaps the most representative feature of EMP, the moment when one ventures into the unknown realm beyond old circles—and this is perhaps an aspect of Deweyan growth that needs to be further enhanced in sustaining its antifoundationalism and in resistance to the lure of assimilation into totality. We have seen that Noddings, in her discussion on the connections between place, morality, and identity, puts an emphasis on stability and settlement in the place that is home. Indeed she supports Heidegger's idea of "dwell[ing] in the world" (Noddings, 2002, p. 150) and she discusses the evil of "displacement" and the state of being "im-placed" as "unhappy habituation" (pp. 155, 157, 171). Cavell's thinking may suggest that there is another way of enhancing and reinforcing Deweyan antifoundationalist growth by emphasizing the moment of unsettlement and displacement rather than—or, more correctly, *within*—the process of settlement and placement, and within the familiar. Discussing Thoreau's "experiment in living" at Walden, Cavell in effect deconstructs the concept of home. Walden is a place where Thoreau once found his home, but this is not a permanent home, the place to settle down. It is the place where Thoreau learns "how to sojourn, i. e., spend his day" (Cavell, 1992, p. 52). The teaching of *Walden*, in Cavell's view, is that we must learn how to make the best use of the day here and now. In other words, for Thoreau and Cavell, home is, paradoxically, a place where you learn to reestablish your relationship with the familiar *and* a place that you leave.

To turn again to *Democracy and Education*, there seems to be a need to take a radical departure—from the reiteration of its language toward its reconstruction, this time with a stronger accent on the moment of leaving in continuous growth. Within the structure of his pragmatism and naturalism, we can find a promising direction for thought: the idea of impulse. Dewey's pragmatism is typically associated with intelligence, and hence with the problem-solving method. In *Democracy and Education*, we can detect its various signs. The impulses of the young, however—that is, the "natural, or native, powers," or "natural tendencies"—are equally valued (MW.9.121, 123). By "impulses" Dewey, as a pragmatist, does not, of course, mean any kind of fixed substance or instinct. Impulses are themselves, he says, "neither good nor evil, but become one or the other" (MW.9.121): they can constitute the source of "deviations" (MW.9.124). In *Human Nature and Conduct*, impulse is discussed, along with intelligence, as an ingredient of habits. But we can find its most explicit connection with Emerson in Dewey's later work, *Construction and Criticism* (1930). What Dewey is most concerned with in speaking of impulse is captured by his citation of the idea of the gleam of light in Emerson's essay "Self-Reliance": "A man should learn to detect and watch that gleam of light which flashes across his mind from within" (Emerson, 1990c, p. 131, quoted in LW.5.139). Dewey refers to this idea of the gleam of light in his Emersonian resistance to conformity and his acknowledgment of the uniqueness of the individual. In Emerson's original writing, the gleam of light is a metaphor of one's original sense of being and a driving force of becoming (Emerson, 1990c, pp. 140–141). In Emerson's pragmatic or experimental spirit, it is the prophetic call of "genius" (p. 134), a thrust, in expanding circles, into "a residuum unknown" (Emerson, 1990a, p. 168). Cavell suggests it is "inner impulses from below" (Emerson, 1990c, p. 154), a power that is demonstrated not as the cause, but in the process and result of "leaping the span from one circumference to another," in discontinuous encirclings—and as a source of what Cavell calls Emerson's "onward thinking" (Cavell, 1992, p. 136).

Dewey partially inherits this Emersonian gleam of light. In *Democracy and Education*, it is suggested in his recognition of the power of immaturity as "something fresh, something not capable of being fully anticipated" (MW.9.313). In *Construction and Criticism*, the idea of impulse acquires a more spiritual timber, one that echoes a kind of inner landscape of the self. Dewey concludes with a call for the kind of individual who is a creative and critical force within democracy: "criticism, self-criticism, is the road to its release," the release of creative activity (LW.5.143). The gleam of light in the life of perfection can be a source of deviation in pursuit of connection, the moment of discontinuity in the movement of continuity. Mediating the natural and the social, it symbolizes a spiritual, internal turning point in the perfection of self and society. If the perspective of the gleam of light is more fully integrated in Dewey's idea of intelligence, it can be reconstructed in terms of the more holistic concept of "creative intelligence"—an idea that Dewey presents in his later aesthetic writing (LW.10.351).

Conclusion: Toward an Alternative Rute to Moral Education

Thus, by critically reconstructing and reinforcing Deweyan growth in the light of EMP, we can envision another way of growing without fixed ends, that of the life of perfection without final perfectibility. With a renewed emphasis on the gleam of light, and in the moment of discontinuity in encircling, Dewey's naturalistic growth can be redescribed *and* reconstructed from continuous growth to continual growth through the standpoint of Emersonian *moral* perfectionism. It then points us to an alternative mode and language of moral education.

Morality, for Dewey, is not and should not be "merely symbolic" or "verbal," but must be integrated into personal experience as a "vital personal realization," as "an appreciation of his own" (MW.9.243, 244, 365). Suggesting something of the Emersonian gleam of light, Dewey also claims the significance of "*tastes*—habitual modes of preference and esteem"—as an integral element of the appreciation of values (MW.9.244). Furthermore, open-mindedness and sympathy, as Hansen claims, and the communal quality of human relationships, as Noddings empasizes, may be called moral traits of Deweyan growth. A challenge to Deweyan growth, then, is how we can *live* this moral language by our own light true to our taste, and how this moral language can make us alive; the question is a matter of how to resist being assimilated into the violent, colonizing force of moral rhetoric—the militant language of patriotism and the language of "good character" that tend to suppress individual difference. In the face of these tasks, Dewey's language of "inclusion" and of the "wider or larger self" (MW.9.362) can, as it stands, and despite his intention, be appropriated by those who yearn for foundations.

To resuscitate culture and democracy from within, the standpoint and language of EMP help us and Dewey to realize the force of discontinuity in growth, and so to reconstruct it as continual growing. This is not, however, geared toward relativism or selfish individualism, and it underestimates neither the significance of initiation into tradition and moral ideals (as is Hansen's concern) nor the need to give some sense of stability to children (as is Noddings'). Instead, Cavell's Emersonianism and its antifoundationalist language help us and Dewey to remember, express, and reflect our mutual light with the recognition of the senses of loss, uncertainty, and bottomlessness, and still with the hope of achieving some common ground, for searching for criteria as a matter of "mutual attunement" (Cavell, 1979, p. 32). In contrast to Dewey's language of sharing and continuity, which negates the element of "isolation" as undemocratic (MW.9.363), the emphasis here is on a sharing of our experiences with a keen recognition of the singularity and strangeness of each self; it is the later Dewey, we must acknowledge, who is more conscious of and expressive of this need. This is the process of being initiated into the native and familiar, while at the same time destabilizing, as it were from within, the familiar, the everyday, and the home. This is the essence of Emersonian *self-transcendence*—transcending the familiar framework of one's own, acknowledging the realm beyond one's existing circles. Moral education following Deweyan growth after Emersonian perfectionism encourages us to create a double stance toward our native language, always with some residual space for discontinuity and deviancy from the common. ["Every new relation is a new word" (Emerson, 1990d, p. 204); "In conversation we pluck up the *termini* which bound the common of silence on every side" (Emerson, 1990a, p. 170).]

The teacher's role is to trust the divergent path of the student's gleam of light. She must initiate the student into tradition, into moral ideals and the mother tongue, but within that process the relationship should be thoroughly "indirect," as Hansen, following Dewey, recognizes. The meaning of "indirectness" in Deweyan growth, however, is more to do with the shifting of attention to the environment, as Dewey negates the idea of the mind and the self as objects to be grasped directly. Emersonian moral perfectionism points us to another kind of indirect relationship in order to confront the otherness of the other in acknowledging the ultimate unknowability of the other. This brings us to a paradoxical relationship between the teacher and the student, that of nearness and distance. It is not that the student emulates the persona or the moral traits of a great teacher, or the moral ideals that the teacher espouses. What the student learns is rather the moment of departure through mutual recognition of the singularity of the self, a realization that each of us has to live by his or her own light, and still find his or her own words, in the hope of achievement of the common. In Deweyan education, the emphasis is more on sharing, intimacy and attachment, and as a consequence the moral influence of the teacher as an initiator can be comparatively greater. To resist this direction toward inclusion and, worse, assimilation, EMP reminds us that the teacher must equally be one who demonstrates the location of an exit from *and within* the culture in the very process of the mutual search for criteria. She must be one who teaches students to leave their old selves, to escape from their conformity, and even from the teacher's influence—and, hence, the teacher must always be leaving. In times when schools and teachers are obsessed with quality assurance, reliability, and the avoidance of risk, the courage to trust in the unknown is a promising way of reinforcing the idea of Deweyan growth.

Reconstructing and reinforcing Deweyan growth in the light of EMP is all the more important today, as the force of assimilation does not necessarily take an explicit, clearly identifiable form, but is more subtle and invisible, permeating the moral and political language of education. Emersonian moral perfectionism helps Deweyan growth achieve its ideal of diversity by creating more space for the strange and the foreign within the culture. In times when solidarity and community are catchwords for citizenship education, and cosmopolitanism is emphasized in global citizenship, Deweyan growth after EMP puts the emphasis on hospitality in the sense not so much of accommodating, and indeed welcoming, the different into the same, as of critically confronting the same, of destabilizing the familiar in order to liberate the different, *beyond* familiar frameworks. This requires teachers to cultivate an aesthetic imagination and a sensibility to the unknown, to the invisible, and to the silenced voice of students as strangers within the culture. As

Cavell says of Thoreau, citizenship education must then involve "embracing the immigrant in yourself" (Cavell, 1992, p. 158). This is a crucial way of enhancing global awareness and perfecting humanity, of a perfectionism without perfectibility.[2]

Note

1. In his later writing, "Time and Individuality" (1940), Dewey discusses the moment of *discontinuity*. He introduces the idea of "genuine qualitative changes," "genuine transformations," when "unpredictable novelties" break into a stream of time. This he calls "genuine time," which he understands as "breaches" or "breaks" in continuity, or the moments of "critical junctures." Based on this concept of time, Dewey introduces the notion of genuine individuality—"individuality pregnant with new developments." The *quality* of change to produce genuine time hinges on unpredictable novelties that "individuals as individuals" can produce (LW.14.108–109.111–112).

2. The argument of this chapter is drawn in part from my *The Gleam of Light: Moral Perfectionism and Education in Dewey and Emerson* (New York: Fordham University Press, 2005).

References

Cavell, Stanley. (1979). *The claim of reason: Wittgenstein, skepticism, morality, and tragedy*. Oxford: Oxford University Press.

Cavell, Stanley. (1984). The politics of interpretation (politics as opposed to what?). In *Themes out of school: Effects and causes*. Chicago: University of Chicago Press.

Cavell, Stanley. (1989). *This new yet unapproachable America: Lectures after Emerson after Wittgenstein*. Albuquerque, NM: Living Batch Press.

Cavell, Stanley. (1990). *Conditions handsome and unhandsome: The constitution of Emersonian perfectionism*. La Salle, IL: Open Court.

Cavell, Stanley. (1992). *The senses of Walden*. Chicago: University of Chicago Press.

Cavell, Stanley. (1996). *Contesting tears: The Hollywood melodrama of the unknown woman*. Chicago: Chicago: University of Chicago Press.

Cavell, Stanley. (1998). What's the use of calling Emerson a pragmatist?. In Morris Dickstein (Ed.), *The revival of pragmatism: New essays on social thought, law, and culture*. Durham: Duke University Press.

Cavell, Stanley. (2003). *Emerson's transcendental etudes*. Stanford: Stanford University Press.

Dewey, John. (1977). Emerson—The Philosopher of Democracy. In J. A. Boydston (Ed.), *The middle works of John Dewey. Vol. 3*. Carbondale: Southern Illinois University Press.

Dewey, John. (1980). *Democracy and education*. In J. A. Boydston (Ed.), *The middle works of John Dewey. Vol. 9*. Carbondale: Southern Illinois University Press.

Dewey, John. (1983). *Human nature and conduct.* In J. A. Boydston (Ed.), *The middle works of John Dewey. Vol. 14.* Carbondale: Southern Illinois University Press.

Dewey, John. (1984a). *The public and its problems.* In J. A. Boydston (Ed.), *The later works of John Dewey. Vol. 2.* Carbondale: Southern Illinois University Press.

Dewey, John. (1984b). *Construction and criticism.* In J. A. Boydston (Ed.), *The later works of John Dewey. Vol. 5.* Carbondale: Southern Illinois University Press.

Dewey, John. (1987). *Art as Experience.* In J. A. Boydston (Ed.), *The later works of John Dewey. Vol. 10.* Carbondale: Southern Illinois University Press.

Dewey, John. (1988a). Creative democracy—The task before us. In J. A. Boydston (Ed.), *The later works of John Dewey. Vol. 14.* Carbondale: Southern Illinois University Press.

Dewey, John. (1988b). Time and individuality. In J. A. Boydston (Ed.), *The later works of John Dewey. Vol. 14.* Carbondale: Southern Illinois University Press.

Emerson, Ralph Waldo. (1990a). Circles. In Richard Poirier (Ed.), *Ralph Waldo Emerson.* Oxford: Oxford University Press.

Emerson, Ralph Waldo. (1990b). Experience. In Richard Poirier (Ed.), *Ralph Waldo Emerson.* Oxford: Oxford: Oxford University Press.

Emerson, Ralph Waldo. (1990c). Self-Reliance. In Richard Poirier (Ed.), *Ralph Waldo Emerson.* Oxford: Oxford University Press.

Emerson, Ralph Waldo. (1990d). The Poet. In Richard Poirier (Ed.), *Ralph Waldo Emerson.* Oxford: Oxford University Press.

Hansen, David T. (2001). *Exploring the moral heart of teaching: Toward a teacher's creed.* New York: Teachers College Press.

Noddings, Nel. (2002). *Starting at home: Caring and social policy.* Berkeley: University of California Press.

6

Rediscovering the Student
in *Democracy and Education*

GARY D FENSTERMACHER

Consideration of the student has all but disappeared from a good deal of the contemporary discussion about education. It is true that the student remains the *object* of this discussion, but he or she is left out of it nonetheless. I do not mean by this claim that students are not consulted, although they certainly are not. Rather, they are simply assumed or taken for granted. It is as if the current crop of policy analysts, law makers, researchers, and regulators is saying, "we are deeply concerned for students and care deeply about what is happening to them," while at the same time paying little if any heed to what these same students bring to the educational setting, and what they desire, care about, consider important, and plan for. Students are the object of the discourse, but not its *subject*. This is a state of affairs that is impossible to imagine in the context of John Dewey's *Democracy and Education*.

One cannot read *Democracy and Education*—indeed most of the Dewey corpus—without encountering the student as a person, deserving of the deepest and most profound consideration in the processes of education. Students as intentional, independently capable, autonomy-deserving persons are at the core of Dewey's work. Yet not only is consideration of the student as person seldom encountered in much of the current educational rhetoric, it is also often absent in discussions of Dewey, particularly with regard to his landmark educational work, *Democracy and Education*. This chapter is an attempt to redress the loss of the student in our discourse about education and in our discussions of *Democracy and Education*. It explores the place of the student in Dewey's text and examines how Dewey's conception of the student would reconfigure contemporary discussions of teaching and learning in the setting of the school.

The Student as Agent

When David T. Hansen, first as organizer of a symposium at the 2005 annual meeting of the American Educational Research Association, then as editor of this book, asked if I would write about what happened when I returned most recently to *Democracy and Education*, I was quick to reply in the affirmative. It had been more than five years since my last careful engagement with Dewey's classic work and I was looking forward to rereading it to see if I might find connections with the work I was doing on democratic theory and forms of schooling. This work involves such matters as the contested relationship between pluralism and the formation of the commons in the democratic state, and how private alternatives to the public school effect this relationship. I thus began reading the text with every intention of exploring how Dewey's work might connect with my current interests.

I set out in much the same manner as I would guess Saul did when he departed for Damascus, without a clue that I was soon to be struck by an idea that was both unexpected and mind-altering. I do not know quite where I was in the book when this idea began to form. It was chapter 3, I think. Recall that the chapter is titled "Education as Direction" and explores the meaning and uses of three important ideas: direction, control, and guidance. While reading this chapter, an idea crept into the basement window of my consciousness: The student is the point of origin for Dewey's argument for the interconnectedness of democracy and education. Consider this quotation from the early pages of chapter 3:

> It is sometimes assumed, explicitly or unconsciously, that an individual's tendencies are naturally purely individualistic or ego-tistic, and thus antisocial. Control then denotes the process by which he is brought to subordinate his natural impulses to public or common ends. Since, by conception, his own nature is quite alien to this process and opposes it rather than helps it, control has in this view a flavor of coercion or compulsion about it. Systems of government and theories of the state have been built upon this notion, and it has seriously affected educational ideas and practices. But there is no ground for any such view. (MW.9.28)

About whom is Dewey speaking here? Clearly it is about a human being engaged in the process of maturation. Certain conceptions of control, Dewey argues, engender a tension between the individual and society. This tension is moderated by "systems of government and theories of the state" that make demands on the individual to restrain himself or herself on behalf of common interests. Dewey impugns this conception when he asserts that while individuals are at times interested in having their own way, "they are also interested, and chiefly interested upon the whole, in entering into activities of others and taking part in conjoint and cooperative doings. Otherwise, no such thing as community would be possible" (MW.9.28).

With these words, Dewey makes an initial foray into explicating the nature of the student as learner. It is with this exploration of the notions of control, direction, and guidance that he fashions a concept of the student as an engaged, purposive agent, desirous of exploring and gaining facility with his or her surroundings. A careful reading of how Dewey develops the concepts of control, direction, and guidance makes clear that he is not in favor of allowing students free rein in pursuit of their desire to become more fully acquainted with their surroundings. Nor, on the other hand, is the tutor or teacher to have free rein in determining what students will do and how they will do it. What is noteworthy about Dewey's analysis is that, while it appears from our usual discourse that there is a tension, perhaps even opposition, between the interests of the student and those of the teacher, it is possible to construct the relationship so that their interests are in harmony. As readers familiar with Dewey know, moves of this kind are common in his work. In this particular case, he argues that student and teacher need not be in opposition, that the demands of the teacher for mastery of subjects need not be in conflict with the interests of students for mastery of their settings.

On reading chapter 3 and appreciating the philosophical groundwork that supports the nuanced meanings Dewey imparts to the everyday usage of the terms "control," "guidance," and "direction," one does not stretch his logic in the least by asserting the fundamental position of the student in the larger text of *Democracy and* Education. This position becomes even more evident as one reads on. A bit later in chapter 3, Dewey notes that although the "customs and rules of adults" do indeed influence the young, "the young, after all, participate in the direction which their actions finally take" (MW.9.30).

In the strict sense, nothing can be forced upon them or into them. To overlook this fact means to distort and pervert human nature. To take into account the contributions made by the existing instincts and habits of those directed is to direct them economically and wisely. Speaking accurately, all direction is but *re*direction. . . . (MW.9.30, emphasis in original)

By the time I reached chapter 6, I was enjoying the pursuit of the student as learner in this work that so many others (myself included) have turned to for far more abstract and theoretical notions. Chapter 6 opens with both praise and criticism of Herbart's contributions to education. In praise of Herbart, Dewey writes: "He brought [teaching] into the sphere of conscious method; it became a conscious business with a definite aim and procedure, instead of being a compound of casual inspiration and subservience to tradition" (MW.9.76–77). These words resonate grandly today, for teachers and their methods of instruction are the focus of a great many educational policy initiatives before the American public. But consider Dewey's objections to Herbart's contributions:

[Herbart's] theory represents the Schoolmaster come to his own. This fact expresses at once its strength and its weakness. . . . The philosophy is eloquent about the duty of the teacher in instructing pupils; it is almost silent regarding his privilege of learning. It emphasizes the influence of intellectual environment upon the mind; it slurs over the fact that the environment involves a personal sharing in common experience. It exaggerates beyond reason the possibilities of consciously formulated and used methods, and underestimates the role of vital, unconscious attitudes. It insists upon the old, the past, and passes lightly over the operation of the genuinely novel and unforeseeable. It takes, in brief, everything educational into account save its essence—vital energy seeking opportunity for effective exercise. (MW.9.77)

While praising Herbart for explicating the relationship between teaching method and subject matter, Dewey takes him to task for ignoring the learner, for failing to attend to the attitudes, interests, and purposes that the student brings to the teaching–learning relationship. For Dewey, it is not simply a matter of effectively imparting subject matter to the learner; rather, it is the value of this subject matter for reconstruction. Dewey concludes his discussion of Herbart with words that have a function similar to the leitmotif in Wagnerian opera—they recur again and again, calling us back to what is foundational to the endeavor: "All education," Dewey writes, "forms character, mental and moral, but formation consists in the selection and coordination of native activities so that they may utilize the subject matter of the social environment. Moreover, the formation is not only formation *of* native activities, but it takes place *through* them. It is a process of reconstruction, reorganiza-tion" (MW.9.77–78, emphasis in original).

That inchoate thought that sneaked through the basement window of my consciousness somewhere in chapter 3 now occupied a prominent position on the main floor. It now seemed obvious that the child as learner in the setting of the school is a central concept in Dewey's inquiry into democracy and education. On reading chapter 8, "Aims in Education," and then again in chapter 13, "The Nature of Method," followed by the several chapters on subject matter, the salience of the student as learner is not only unavoidable, it is a remarkable vantage point from which to reread these chapters. My prior readings of these chapters were through the lens of the teacher, or as a theoretician con-cerned with democracy and its relationship to education, but never be-fore from the point of view of the student—from the point of view of the one who is, in a profound sense, the occasion, the purpose, the object and the subject of Dewey's quite remarkable exegesis of the in-tersection of democracy with education. I began to sense that in my prior readings I had made what Dewey might call "Herbart's Error"; I viewed the educational landscape solely through the lens of the teacher or scholar, not through that of the student. In short, I made the student disappear as active agent in his or her own learning.

What is it that makes this fairly simple, perhaps even obvious, point worthwhile? I believe it is this: Too many of us today commit "Herbart's Error," placing so much of the emphasis on what teachers do to ensure the acquisition of subject matter by students that we lose sight of how and why students learn. What may be more egregious than losing sight of how and why students learn in the setting of the school is improperly identifying the principle reasons we provide the young with an education in the first place. Dewey speaks directly and forcefully to the how and the why, as well as to the proper ends for education. The how and the why are discussed in many different places in *Democracy and Education*, typi-cally in words such as these:

> Children doubtless go to school to learn, but it has yet to be proved that learning occurs most adequately when it is made a separate conscious business. When treating it as a business of this sort tends to preclude the social sense which comes from sharing in an activity of common concern and value, the effort at iso-lated intellectual learning contradicts its own aim. (MW.9.44)

With regard to the proper ends for learning, Dewey reminds us repeatedly of the point and purpose of the educative endeavor. In the chapter on educational values (chapter 18), he asks this poignant question: "How shall the individual be rendered executive *in* his intelligence instead of at the cost of his intelligence?" (MW.9.257, emphasis in original). Reading the text from this perspective, one senses that democracy and education form the ground, while the student forms the figure. It is because democracy and education open so much space and opportunity for the extension of human possibility and human flourishing that they can be connected in the fashion that Dewey describes.

On this view, any decrement in the agency of the student, in the freedom and the capacity of the student to actively engage his or her intelligence, diminishes human flourishing and thereby reduces such advantage as is obtained by the synergy that exists between democracy and education. As Dewey puts the point, "The very existence of the social medium in which an individual lives, moves, and has his being is the standing effective agency of directing his activity" (MW.9.32). Any approach to teaching and learning that diminishes the interests of the learner, that distances the learner from the social community, that values one form of subject matter over another form, corrodes the potential to be gained from a life lived where democracy and education are in harmony.

Student and/or Learner?

Dewey's conception of the student as learner forestalls a differentiation that has become all to common in contemporary schooling. It is the difference between being a student and being a learner. As this distinction may strike many as strange, if not counterintuitive, it is here developed in some detail. The distinction rests on the difference between the social role of being a student in school and the active mental processes of learning that may occur in or out of the school setting.

Imagine, for purposes of argument, that the term "student" might function as noun or verb. That is, one can be a student, and one can also student. To student is to be engaged in a series of performances whose form and substance are primarily shaped by the institutional and organizational properties of the school setting. Thus, the term "student," employed as a verb, may be distinguished from the term "learn," where this latter term might be defined as a series of performances that are, in considerable part, formed by the properties of a discipline or subject matter as well as the methods of inquiry appropriate to that subject matter. Given these definitions, one "students" when his or her performances in school settings are determined more by the institutional dynamics of the setting (what I here call systemics) than by the demands of the content area under consideration.

Many of us think that the task and the achievement of being a student are to learn. Consider, however, the possibility that what a student (noun) does is not learn, but instead students (verb). That is, the student becomes proficient in doing the kinds of things that students do, such as "psyching out" teachers, figuring out how to get certain grades or "beat the system," dealing with boredom so that it is not obvious to teachers, negotiating the best deals on reading and writing assignments, threading the right line between curricular and extracurricular activities, and determining what is likely to be on the test and what is not.

All of us are familiar with these aspects of student conduct. Though we are often put off by them, they are typically accepted as a part of what it means to be a student. Seldom, however, do we ponder the prospect that learning to student may occupy as much or more of the student's time, energy, and attention than either learning the subject matter being taught or even learning to learn. While teachers presume that they are engaged in assisting, enabling, or empowering students to learn, what students may perceive is that teachers, administrators, parents, employers, and college admissions officers are more interested in the number and types of subjects completed, grades and test scores attained, diplomas and honors received. To earn these artifacts of the system of schooling, students may acquire understanding and skills that are quite different from those that teachers believe they are teaching.

This problem is exacerbated when the student cannot ascertain the relationship between what takes place in school and what is meaningful and important for the student outside the school (a point often made in *Democracy and Education,* and in most other of Dewey's writings on education). Unable to make a clear connection between experiences in and out of school, the student constructs, if you will, a separate mental "space" for schoolwork. That is, what takes place at school, at least in many academic subjects, may be so discontinuous with other aspects of the student's life that he or she cannot usefully employ inside-the-school experience to explore, corroborate, falsify, extend, or illuminate outside-the-school experience. Given such discontinuities, the student quickly comes to understand that it is better to "wall off" the academic world of school, learning its language, rules, and customs as a separate undertaking.

There is a useful analogy here to games. Take the game of chess as an example. In chess, the rules are said to constitute the game. Without the rules, there simply is no game. Thus, to the student, school may be a kind of game, constituted entirely by its rules. To learn these rules and to follow them is a necessary condition for success in the game. Mastery and proficiency in the rules often brings high scores, as well as other rewards. Failure to learn the rules and follow them bring low scores and few, if any, rewards.

It is intriguing to note that one likely masters the studenting game while also learning academic and other school subjects. That is, the fact that the student may be studenting does not mean that the student is not learning. Rather, the distinction between studenting and learning has value insofar as it illuminates how the two may be discontinuous with one another. There is no logically necessary opposition between studenting and learning, as our senses are testimony to the fact that one can learn academic content and also play the role of the student. Though there is no logical opposition here, there is an empirical or practical one; that is, it may turn out that students attend more to "studenting" their way through courses and academic content than they do to learning their way through this content.

Consider this quotation from a provocative work titled *Selling Students Short* (Sedlak, Wheeler, Pullin, & Cusick, 1986):

> In most high schools there exists a complex, tacit conspiracy to avoid sustained, rigorous, demanding academic inquiry. A "bargain" of sorts is struck that demands little academically of either teachers or students. Many organizational policies protect and reinforce this arrangement, which governs classroom interaction, determines what teachers can require of their students, and shapes prevailing academic standards. (p. 5)

The authors go on to state that the bargain is "principally an adaptation that teachers and students make to the institutions which they occupy together" (p. 5). This startling observation—that what happens between teachers and students is not the result of the intellectual demands of the discipline or content studied, not the result of some noble theory of education, not the result of an enlightened pedagogy, but an adaptation to the institution that teachers and students occupy together—is a more contemporary version of what Dewey stated seventy years earlier. If you separate the child in school from his or her experiences out of school, the result is not authentic growth but some parody of growth. Studenting is a form of parody wherein the learner is directed more to mastering the rules of the game of school than to the mastery of subjects that enhance his or her power to be and to act in the world.

A similar perspective is offered in *The Shopping Mall High School* (Powell, Farrar, & Cohen, 1985). Here the authors contend that students and teachers engage in the making of treaties for the purpose of negotiating the degree of approach or avoidance to academic work. These treaties may be public and explicit (as when a syllabus is discussed at the beginning of a course), or they may be tacit, with both parties unaware of the deal they have struck with one another. Treaties are most frequently formed around considerations of time, relationship, and intensity. When a treaty is based on time, it might, for example, take the form of a student pondering to what extent doing the work assigned in some course interferes with other activities perceived as more desirable. When relationship is the basis for a treaty, teacher and student negotiate what is required to effect a tolerable or acceptable relationship between them. Treaties dealing with intensity occur, for example, when students deliberate on how seriously to take the material in a course or how deeply to engage that material. These examples of treaties provide excellent illustrations of what is involved in studenting.

In *Teachers for Our Nation's Schools*, John Goodlad (1990) writes of another characteristic common to the activity of studenting. Students, he states,

> are largely passive and, at least by the time they reach the upper elementary and secondary school grades, appear to assume that passivity is what best fits the nature of the school. They even come to dislike disturbances of their passivity. This ethos seems to accommodate well the flaccid curriculum of homogenized classroom topics and textbooks. (p. 24)

In a complementary way, the work of Walter Doyle (1979, 1983) on the topic of academic task structures is also pertinent to the notion of studenting. Doyle argues that the processes of teaching and learning may insightfully be understood as an exchange of performance for grades, wherein students make highly rational moves to manage their work, including negotiating the complexity and ambiguity out of academic tasks (by, for example, asking such questions as how many pages an assignment requires, whether references are necessary, what criteria will be used for grading, and whether some topic or problem will appear on the test). Doyle views much of this negotiation as an attempt by students to reduce their tasks to the most simple and manageable form, so that they can predict what level and type of performance will result in which grade.

When teachers hear students asking whether something will be on the test, how many pages an assignment must be, or if considerations of grammar and style will impact their grade, they often dismiss these queries as peripheral to the point of the activity. What is often unrecognized is that these questions are often *the* point of the activity for the student. The student seeks a sense of how the teacher will establish the grade for an assignment, so that the student may then turn to deciding what grade *is possible* under the circumstances, as well as what grade *is to be sought* in this particular instance. Thus, the student expends no small amount of energy on attempts to remove as much ambiguity as possible from the task. Students who have not learned to do this are typically at a disadvantage in playing the game of school.

The upshot of treating 'student' as a verb is to call attention to the possibility that what students may learn best in school is to do school, to understand how the system works, and to how to get from it what one wants. They also learn academic content, of course, but such learning may be subsidiary to learning this content in the context of the systemics of schooling. These contentions are not far removed from what Dewey sought to argue in much of his educational writing. The point is driven home in the chapter on method in *Democracy and Education*:

> When the subject matter is not used in carrying forward impulses and habits to significant results, it is just something to be learned. The pupil's attitude to it is just that of having to learn it. Conditions more unfavorable to an alert and concentrated response would be hard to devise. Frontal attacks are even more wasteful in learning than in war. (MW.9.176)

For Dewey, teaching and learning can and should be undertaken so that the differences between studenting and learning are minimal or entirely absent. To take Dewey seriously is to diminish the gap between the role of student and the activity of learning. It would be more accommodating to Dewey's views to think of the "learner as student." That is, assuming that the young are learning virtually all the time, learning in the setting of the school becomes a special case of learning. In the context of the school, learning has purpose and directionality; it is not random or accidental, but intentional for both the learner and the teacher. It is fostered through the explicit guidance of the teacher, while it remains connected to both the experiences of the child and the larger world beyond the school. In the Deweyan context, one could not student in ways that inhibited genuine learning; there would simply be no need to do that.

Reading *Democracy and Education* from the vantage point of the student as learner places it in opposition to much of the current discourse on educational policy and reform. One of today's most actively discussed educational policy initiatives pertains to notions of teacher effectiveness and teacher quality. The next section examines this particular policy context in order to illustrate how the learner as student has been separated from, then ignored by, current considerations on teaching and schooling.

The Eclipse of the Student

A large number of current conceptions of educational research and policy emphasize the teacher and the school, treating the student, not as an agent in his or her own learning, but as passive recipient. Consider a recent report prepared for the Carnegie Corporation by a Rand research team (McCaffrey, Lockwood, Koretz, & Hamilton, 2003). The subject of the report is what has become known as value-added models of teaching, or VAM. The first two paragraphs of this report are quoted in full to provide a greater sense of how many researchers and policymakers are thinking about making education better.

> Value-added modeling (VAM), a collection of complex statistical techniques that use multiple years of students' test score data to estimate the effects of individual schools or teachers, has recently garnered a great deal of attention among both policy makers and researchers. For example, a recent bill drafted by the General Assembly of Pennsylvania proposes using student achievement results and value-added models to evaluate and reward administrators and teachers. In this bill, VAM-based estimates of teacher and school effects would affect salaries and career ladder stages as well as contract renewal for teachers and administrators.
>
> There are at least two reasons why VAM has attracted growing interest. One reason is that VAM holds out the promise of separating the effects of teachers and schools from the powerful effects of such noneducational factors as family background, and this isolation of the effects of teachers and schools is critical for accountability systems to work as intended. The second is that early VAM studies purport to show very large differences in effectiveness among teachers. If these differences can be substantiated and causally linked to specific characteristics of teachers, the potential for improvement of education could be great. (p. xi)

The student as agent, as even semiautonomous person, is nowhere to be found in discourse of this kind. Perhaps that is not surprising, given that this work is not about students, but about how to improve teaching. Thus, it may be unfair to hold the work accountable to the criterion of giving the learner as student a central place in the analysis. On the other hand, what is it that permits us to discuss teaching without any reference to the nature and interests of students, their social settings, their experiences and backgrounds? Perhaps the answer is that students as intentional agents in their own learning are not considered relevant to the improvement of teaching, that instead the objective is to develop conceptions of teaching that can improve the achievement of any student, regardless of experience, interest, or community. Though a noble goal in some ways, the consequence is that the intentionality of the student, his or her interests, voice, and experiences are neither sought nor heard.

The disappearance of the student as an intentional agent in his or her own learning is increasingly evident in the renewed demand for producing solid gains in student achievement. From the regulatory demands of No Child Left Behind to calls for unblemished empirical studies that yield clear evidence to show which instructional treatments work and which do not, the interests and purposes of the student are ignored or subordinated to those of other stakeholders. The following quotation from a recent article on the effects of teachers on student achievement provides another illustration of this point:

> We reasoned that what would matter most to student achievement was not the amount of time teachers spent on instruction nor even how teachers distributed their time across active teaching behaviors. Instead, we hypothesized that the important variable would be how much active teaching occurred. . . . What would matter most, we reasoned, was the extent to which the teacher was operating as an active agent of instruction. (Rowan, Correnti, & Miller, 2002, p. 1545)

Once again, it would be unfair to judge the merits of these contentions outside the context in which they were made. In this case, the authors were specifically examining the topic of teacher effects, so it is not inappropriate for them to ignore considerations of the student. Yet there is something incongruous about discussing student achievement without any consideration of students—without student voice, student characteristics, student interests, or student intentions. Returning to the first few words of the quotation, "we reasoned that what would matter most to student achievement," is it not reasonable to argue that students themselves should be a part of what would matter most to student achievement?

There is a puzzling lack of concern on the part of many educational researchers and policymakers for the constant erosion of student agency in deliberations about educational reform. Instead, the focus of the researchers and reformers seems increasingly on all that Dewey railed against, from supposedly preparing them for some future life to denying their legitimate interests in the name of our knowing better than they what will be required of them. Reading *Democracy and Education* from the perspective of the learner as student, then situating it alongside so much of the contemporary discourse on educational policy and research, suggests that we are not really much interested in the student's experiences, interests, and purposes. In their stead, we substitute what it is we think they must know to be prosperous and what we believe will keep the nation competitive.

If I have that right, then there is one more insight we can gain from *Democracy and Education*. Failing to educate the young in ways that treat them as active agents in their own growth and development, that respects and incorporates their experiences and interests, places democracy itself in jeopardy. It does this by signaling that the game itself is more important than what the game is about; that figuring out the system and bending it to personal advantage are objectives more vital than advancing the welfare and potential of the species. If the student does not hold a position of regard in our studies of or policies for schooling, the lesson learned by students seems obvious. They are invisible, except as mere objects of our attention and recipients of our plans. To treat them so is to ill prepare them to inherit and advance a democratic nation.

These are troubling conclusions, stirred by a particular way of reading *Democracy and Education*. As they took shape during my reading of the text, I wondered how I missed them on prior readings of the book. One answer, of course, is that good educational theory offers fresh insights with every new era in which it is studied. But, in this case, I suspect that my missing these insights on prior readings had more to do with the somewhat troubled history between John Dewey and me. That history adds some flavor to the interpretation of text provided here.

Rediscovering Dewey

I purchased my first copy of *Democracy and Education* on 3 August 1964. I know that because I like to write such things on the inside covers of the books I buy. Sometimes I also enter the city where I made the purchase, an idiosyncrasy that most likely springs from my seeking out bookstores in new cities and towns the way others search for cathedrals or museums. And, very rarely, I make a short note about why I bought the book. Such a notation appears on the inside cover of my copy of *Democracy and Education*. It reads, "felt I should have it." It seems that back then, more than forty years ago, this was a reluctant purchase. A book I thought I ought to own, but not one I believed I needed or desired. What would explain such an entry?

The answer to that question comes easily, as my memory of events surrounding the purchase of the book are still quite vivid. At the time I acquired *Democracy and Education*, I was in the early phase of my doctoral studies. Although nominally admitted to a program in philosophy of education within the School of Education, a condition of that admission was that I would take most of my courses in the department of philosophy. Dutiful and compliant student that I was, I began a series of philosophy courses that endured without interruption for three years. The faculty with whom I identified most closely were not the education faculty, but members of the philosophy department.

Inasmuch as this was Cornell University in the 1960s, I was situated practically at the inner core of analytical philosophy in America. My mentor at the time was Norman Malcolm, justifiably famous in his own right, but often more discussed among the graduate students because of his personal relationship with Ludwig Wittgenstein. For those of you familiar with the place and the times, my short entry on the inside cover of *Democracy and Education* comes as no surprise. Some time early in my studies I recall asking Malcolm if the work of John Dewey might be relevant to a problem we were pursuing in his seminar. He responded that he tried many times to read Dewey, but always got discouraged by philosophical differences with him and by the lack of clarity in Dewey's writing. Good graduate student that I was, I acquired a comparable capacity for discrimination. I thought that I, too, could get along fine without reading more than a few pages of this reigning star of philosophy of education. But I could not entirely dismiss him, hence my entry in the book: "felt I should have it."

This history has haunted me in a number of ways. Perhaps the most obvious is that Dewey's work has seldom been the foundation for my own. Instead I pursue his writing for other purposes. Sometimes for solace, sometimes for confirmation, and at other times, to spark my imagination. I am not a Dewey scholar; indeed I would barely credit myself with being a Dewey student. A good bit of my standoffish relationship with Dewey has to do with my history, of course. But a not inconsiderable part is also due to the immensity of Dewey's corpus, which I find intimidating. When I read something of his that is provocative or useful, my temptation to elaborate on it in my own work is always hindered by such questions as, did he have a different position in his earlier (or his later) writing, am I interpreting him correctly, does he state the point better in another work, what will my colleagues who have spent decades exploring Dewey make of my use of this idea from his work? These questions trouble me enough to keep me from systematically engaging Dewey in much of my own work.

Alas, the AERA symposium and the book containing this chapter require that I suspend this isolation with Dewey. Still, I venture my interpretation of the text in *Democracy and Education* with some trepidation given my checkered association with Dewey's work. I was heartened, however, to come across Reginald Archambault's (1964) discussion of Dewey's educational writings. Archambault describes four central concepts in Dewey's educational theory: (1) the aim of the activity; (2) the means employed to pursue the activity, including content and method; (3) the teacher; and (4) the student. In prose that is most apt for our discussion here, Archambault writes of the student (who is most often referred to as the "pupil"):

> He is the purpose for which the educational enterprise exists. Since democracy receives its impetus from creative individuals, the contribution of education to the society consists in the development of free, imaginative, and creative individuals. Analogously, the educative process is fired and sustained by the impulse that comes from the desires, interests, and purposes of the pupil. (p. xxvi)

Just a few pages prior to these words, Archambault examines notions of curriculum and method (means), indicating that even here the pupil is central: "The teacher should be considered a guide who should help the pupil achieve his own purposes. The subject matter of instruction should be completely redefined in terms of those facts, ideas, and objects that are helpful in fulfilling pupil purposes" (p. xxiv).

Given this affirmation of some of the positions taken in this chapter, it may be that Dewey would not be disturbed by my interpretations of his text. Perhaps he would even find them congenial. And were he to observe the current educational scene, he might even applaud the contention that the student has nearly disappeared from much of the policy and research discourse (although he would likely want to remind us that consideration of the student must go hand in hand with careful development of the subject matter to be learned). Whether he would accept my implication that this has occurred because we are not so much interested in the student as an autonomy-seeking, capacity-building, identity-striving person as we are in readying that student for a world that adults believe will be there when the student inherits it is another matter. There is enough in *Democracy and Education* to suggest that though he might not give ready assent to this implication, it would earn his serious consideration.

I would like to close with words penned by Dewey some twelve years before the publication of *Democracy and Education*. Two sentences in Dewey's 1904 article, "The Relation of Theory to Practice in the Education," foreshadow a theme that appears often in *Democracy and Education*. They are: "The greatest asset in the student's possession—the greatest, moreover, that ever will be in his possession—[is] his own direct and personal experience. There is every presumption (since the student is not an imbecile) that he has been learning all the days of his life, and that he is still learning from day to day" (MW.3.258). These words leave little doubt about the place of the learner as student and the role he or she ought to play in the educational process. They connect well to words from *Democracy and Education* quoted earlier, when Dewey states that the problem before us is "how shall the individual be rendered executive *in* his intelligence instead of at the cost of his intelligence" (MW.9.257).

One cannot read these words, and so many others in a similar vein, without gaining a renewed and robust understanding of the place and importance of the student. *Democracy and Education* is a work that makes the student both visible and vital, the holder of a central place in educational theory, research, policy, and practice. Dewey's text permits us to rediscover the student, to restore the student to a place of importance and high regard in the several discourses of education. Until the student is understood and treated as an intentional agent in his or her learning, it should not surprise us that he or she often lacks both the will to excel as a learner in the setting of the school and the willingness to accept much, if any, responsibility for this harmful state of affairs.

References

Archambault, R. D. (Ed.). (1964). *John Dewey on education*. Chicago: University of Chicago Press.

Doyle, W. (1979). Classroom tasks and students' abilities. In P. Peterson & H. J. Walberg (Eds.), *Research on teaching: Concepts, finding and implications* (pp. 183–209). Berkeley, CA: McCutchan.

Doyle, W. (1983). Academic work. *Review of Educational Research*, 53, 159–199.

Goodlad, J. I. (1990). *Teachers for our nation's schools*. San Francisco: Jossey-Bass.

McCaffrey, D. F., Lockwood, J. R., Koretz, D. M., & Hamilton, L. S. (2003). *Evaluating value-added models for teacher accountability*. Santa Monica, CA: Rand Corporation.

Powell, A. G., Farrar, E., & Cohen, D. K. (1985). *The shopping mall high school*. Boston: Houghton-Mifflin.

Rowan, B., Correnti, R., & Miller, R. J. (2002). What large-scale, survey research tells us about teacher effects on student achievement: Insights from the Prospect Study. *Teachers College Record*, 104, 1525–1567.

Sedlak, M. W., Wheeler, C. W., Pullin, D. C., & Cusick, P. A. (1986). *Selling students short: Classroom bargains and academic reform in the American high school*. New York: Teachers College Press.

7

Dewey's Reconstruction of the Curriculum

From Occupation to Disciplined Knowledge

Herbert M. Kliebard

With the publication of *Democracy and Education* in 1916, John Dewey brought to near fruition his long-standing inquiry into the deceptively simply question: what should we teach? That question was brought into Dewey's consciousness with a certain urgency once he had undertaken to found and run the Laboratory School at the University of Chicago between 1896 and 1904. Most of Dewey's creative work on the curriculum was undertaken in those years. For Dewey at the time, tackling the question was no arcane intellectual puzzle; it was a matter of practical necessity. No school has ever existed without something to teach, and during the period of the Laboratory School, Dewey turned first to existing turn-of-the-century answers to the "what to teach" question. He was satisfied with none of them, but, like so many of Dewey's other philosophical undertakings, his analysis and criticism of those extant positions became the basis for forging his own, and during that time he published freely on the subject, most notably *The Child and the Curriculum* and *The School and Society* (1902). By the time *Democracy and Education* was in the works, he articulated a version of his own distinctive theory of curriculum and integrated it into a framework encompassing social aspects of education including the role that organized knowledge plays in human affairs and the nature of democracy, not only as a political system, but as a way of living, thinking, and intelligently acting.

There is a sense, of course, in which much of *Democracy and Education* is about "what to teach," but in the interest of a focused discussion, I will concentrate on the three consecutive chapters in the book that deal most directly with the curriculum: "The Nature of Method," "The Nature of Subject Matter," and "Play and Work in the Curriculum" (chapters 13 through 15). In approaching those chapters, I will endeavor to extract what I believe to be the main themes that Dewey explores. I will quote liberally from the text, and then comment on those themes with reference to their genesis. I will also refer to previous or subsequent works of Dewey's in which themes are also expounded. This approach is particularly pertinent to the concept of occupations with which Dewey opens the chapter on play and work in the curriculum. "Occupations" is a deceptively complex idea and, from Dewey's treatment of it in *Democracy and Education* alone, it may be difficult to apprehend just how it is to supposed to function in his theory of curriculum.

In exploring these themes, I am also concerned with the broad question of Dewey's influence on American education in general and the curriculum in particular. A widespread belief exists that Dewey's ideas had a profound influence on what is taught in schools, a belief that is so often repeated that it has become conventional wisdom. As I hope will become clear, my own view on this matter is that Dewey's actual influence on American schooling has been negligible not only with respect to practice but even with regard to dominant beliefs over time within the professional curriculum field. In fact, many of his ideas on the curriculum actually run contrary not only to conventional practice but to what many of the leading reformers in the curriculum world tried to promote. Dewey's philosophy of education ought to be studied, and studied seriously, but not because of some vague sense that he was a powerful mover and shaker in the world of education or that he somehow anticipated what American education would become but because of the integrity of his ideas and because they present a formidable challenge to how education is conventionally conceptualized and practiced, not simply in Dewey's time but in ours.

The Nature of Method

Dewey's devotes a chapter, "The Nature of Method," as well as the subsequent chapter, "The Nature of Subject Matter," to establishing the unity of method and subject matter. His position here is an extension of a lifelong effort to create unity out of what are long-standing divisions and false dichotomies—the theoretical and the practical, experience and nature, schooling and life. In this case, the dualism takes for granted that subject matter, "a ready-made systematized classification of . . . facts and principles" and method, "the ways in which this antecedent subject matter may best be presented to and impressed upon the mind" (MW.9.171), are two more or less independent provinces. Dewey seeks to make the case, however, that the orderly arrangement of subject matter in any given discipline is itself method. Method does not exist independent of subject matter. He takes zoology as an example. Zoology as a discipline is not simply an odd collection of facts about animals. It is a systematic arrangement of those facts organized in such a way as to put them within a framework that not only aids memory and observation but moves the discipline in the direction of further inquiry. The very way in which the subject matter of the discipline of zoology is arranged becomes its methodology.

"Method," Dewey says, "means that arrangement *of* subject matter which makes it most effective in use. Never is method something outside of the material" (MW.9.172). When human beings eat, they do not eat in general, they eat food. They do not simply play an instrument, they play something on that instrument. When human beings love, they do not love in general; they love someone. Dewey hopes to persuade his readers that just as the unity of acts such as these is destroyed when we divide them and treat them as separate entities, so the unity of teaching and the subject matter of instruction are undermined when they are artificially set apart.

But what harm can there be in separating, say, for purposes of teacher education, one area that concentrates on the actual subject matter of study and another on how that subject matter should be taught? Perhaps anticipating such a reaction, Dewey enumerates four "evils" that flow from such a separation. First, in the area of teacher education, Dewey says, "'methods' have been authoritatively recommended to teachers instead of being an expression of their own intelligent observations" (MW.9.175). Here Dewey is not just assigning to the teacher an active role in creating the methodology. He is calling attention to a commonly ignored fact of school life. Schooling is supremely *contextual.* No two things happen in school in the same way or under the same conditions. The prevailing tendency in educational research and hence in teacher education, however, is to seek to establish generalized rules of practice. There are presumed to be rules of action for teachers that have been abstracted from the particular circumstances in which they occurred. In this respect, the method of doing something develops an independent existence from the subject matter of experience. Obviously, there is nothing inherently wrong in constructing generalizations. In terms of actual practice, however, a generalized rule of action needs to be employed by a sentient human being who is intellectually in command of the conditions and circumstances of the unique situation in which that action takes place and is capable of making the necessary adaptations to those conditions. The method, in other words, cannot be applied willy-nilly to a wide variety of situations. It is an instrumentality that teachers can use to deal intelligently with the particular circumstances and conditions they face.

A second "evil" resulting from the separation of method from subject matter that Dewey touches upon is that artificial means tend to be employed to compensate for the absence of an authentic relationship. Teachers often resort to excitement—the "shock of pleasure" or "tickling the palate." Interest, Dewey contends, cannot be created by sprinkling an artificial methodological sweetener on distasteful subject matter. Attaching painful consequences for inattention is of the same order. Authentic interest can best be achieved when the teacher is able to find within the child's own experience something that can lead to the experience of the human race as expressed in the subject matter of study. It is not something added to the mix; it is part of the process of choosing what to teach,

The third "evil" is compellingly reminiscent not only of much current practice but of the kind of sage advice that has for years been passed on to novice teachers. "Learning," Dewey says of this evil, "is made a direct and conscious end in itself" (MW.9.176), whereas learning under less artificial circumstances takes place as a consequence of playful activities. Dewey is thus challenging the widespread assumption that learning proceeds best when its outcomes are directly identified and specified at the outset. When a specific fact is to be learned, so the conventional wisdom goes, it is best to state what it is and then to make sure it is accomplished. The alternative that Dewey proposes here is that a student be engaged in an activity, and "in the process of engagement he learns" (MW.9.176). This sounds awfully vague. What Dewey is proposing, though, is that we take the process of learning as it usually goes forward, such as, say, the process in which a toddler learns to walk or talk, and make that the model for how learning takes place in schools. Learning in those instances is a by-product of largely playful activities in which the exact outcome is for the most part only dimly anticipated. Under those circumstances, learning in school becomes just as natural as the learning that children are constantly engaged in the world outside of school. To be sure, the wise guidance of the teacher is absolutely required to give some direction to those activities, and Dewey indicates in previous chapters the role that broad and tentative aims play in lending direction to activity. However, teaching does not take the form of relentlessly steering the learning process to a prespecified end.

Anyone who has carefully observed preschool children will testify that they are primarily learning organisms. Their play and their social interactions become the medium for that learning without overt conscious intent. Learning can be said to be their principal activity, and, unless unduly inhibited and restrained by adverse conditions, they are mostly very good at it. Yet, when children arrive in school, we are urged to impose on their natural learning proclivities an artificial model that demands that what is to be learned must be carefully specified at the outset of an educational activity and then that the activity be carefully designed to achieve the predetermined outcome. Something specifically to be learned is substituted for devising a rich and benevolent setting where all sorts of indirect and even unanticipated learning can take place.

The approach Dewey advocated was not merely a matter of providing a more humane environment for learning to take place. It was actually for the purpose of the school's becoming a more effective environment in which learning can be effectively achieved. Dewey was able to provide an especially powerful metaphor for expressing that idea. "Frontal attacks," he said, "are even more wasteful in learning than in war" (MW.9.176). Here again, prevailing wisdom runs contrary to Dewey's thinking on this subject. Modern teachers are continually urged to state specifically what it is that must be learned and then to charge straight up the hill—to resolutely pursue achievement of the designated objective. Dewey recognizes that an indirect approach—winding paths, so to speak—may ultimately be far more effective in getting up the hill.

In articulating the fourth and final "evil" associated with the divorce of "method and material," Dewey challenges the widespread assumption, in his time and our own, that learning takes place through a prescribed series of "certain preordained verbal formulae" rather than through direct experience with problems at hand and with the children learning to assess for themselves the consequences that accrue from that engagement. Insofar as teacher education is concerned, that problem takes the form of providing future teachers with carefully laid out prescriptions for how to conduct an educational activity. Those prescriptions may provide a false sense of efficacy in the form of presenting the "best" way to do something, but, in the end, Dewey says, "nothing has brought pedagogical theory into greater disrepute than the belief that it is identified with handing out to teachers recipes and models to be followed in teaching" (MW.9.177). Undoubtedly, one source of the persistence of that identification is that the public and novice teachers (and sometimes even policymakers) believe that such recipes and models are precisely what educational research and theory and hence teacher education are all about.

Immediately following the articulation of these four "evils," in a section called "Method as General and Individual," Dewey proceeds to elaborate on the last evil by making the case for teaching not as the following of a set of carefully laid out rules of action but as the practice of an art form. He is careful to say, however, that "the practice of a fine art is far from a matter of extemporized inspirations" (MW.9.177). Rather than merely following some mysterious inner inclination, a fine artist must employ an intimate knowledge of the materials of the art form and possess a deep understanding of the evolution of that art form, its successes as well as its failures. As Dewey puts it, "The assumption that there are no alternatives between following ready-made rules and trusting to natural gifts, the inspiration of the moment and undirected 'hard work' is contracted by the procedures of every art" (MW.9.177). To be sure, natural gifts play a part in all the arts, including teaching, but those gifts need to be subjected to the discipline of *general* procedures, that is, procedures that do not specify exactly what needs to be done but suggest a course of action to be mediated both by the artist's own gifts and the constraints imposed by the art form itself as well as the artistic conventions of the period and other contextual factors.

When Dewey refers in this regard to "a cumulative body of fairly stable methods for teaching results" under the banner of general method, he is most likely referring to a feature in American Herbartian theory that by the time *Democracy and Education* was published had established itself pretty firmly in some normal schools. Interestingly, Dewey's first exposure to serious pedagogical theory was to the theories American Herbartians were promulgating in the late nineteenth century and, for the most part, he was intrigued by them. In fact, in 1892, at the annual meeting of the National Education Association in Saratoga Springs, New York, he became a founding member of the National Herbart Society. After eight years as a faculty member at the University of Michigan, his interest in Herbartianism was the clearest sign that Dewey had developed a strong interest in education. He was probably attracted to the reputation that Herbartians had established as pedagogical reformers who had undertaken to challenge the status quo in American education. Almost all of the other founding members, like Charles DeGarmo and Charles McMurry, had studied Herbartian theory under disciples of Herbart who held key posts in German universities. Although drawn to some of their ideas, Dewey was anything but an orthodox Herbartian, and some of his very early writings on education were critiques of Herbartian doctrine.

His references to the shortcomings of general method in "The Nature of Method" were most likely to what Herbartians were advocating as the "five formal steps." This was a series of invariant steps that teachers were urged to follow in introducing a topic irrespective of the subject. The steps were as follows: (1), preparation—soliciting from the children what they already know about the topic to be introduced; (2) presentation—actually presenting the new material in the form of lecture, demonstration, pictures, and so on; (3) comparison and contrast—comparing and contrasting the new thing to learned with other things that may resemble the new material; (4) generalization—forming a generalization related to the topic; and (5) application—applying the new material. Dewey devoted much of the last of his lectures in his philosophy of education course at the University of Chicago in 1899 to a critique of those five formal steps. His position was that the prescribed sequence was unnecessarily rigid and that one could make the case of scrambling that sequence under the right circumstances. In the end, he refers to the sequence of the five steps as a "superstition" (Dewey, 1899/1966, p. 333).

Dewey doesn't actually reject the idea of general method, providing, of course, that he can define general method in his own way. In this regard, he rejects the idea of general method as a rule or set of rules that must be followed and proposes instead that general method serve as a guideline that needs to be intelligently interpreted. For Dewey, the main difference between general method as he sees it and a prescribed rule is that "the latter is a *direct* guide to action; the former operates indirectly through the enlightenment it supplies as to ends and means" (MW.9.178). In other words, a prescribed rule is something that can be carried out without the intervention of human intelligence whereas general method, as Dewey sees it, requires the creative engagement of the teacher. That engagement is not simply desirable; it is made necessary by the vagaries of classroom life, including the contextual differences that inevitably present themselves from one teaching situation to the next. Method, in Dewey's sense, becomes an invaluable aid to intelligent functioning in the classroom. As such, it contrasts with a factitious formula like the five formal steps that must be strictly adhered to, and with a template that fraudulently is presumed to guarantee success.

The Nature of Subject Matter

At first, the opening lines of this chapter seem a bit disappointing. Dewey declares that, in relation to the previous chapter, "there is nothing to add to what has been said" (MW.9.188). He then defines subject matter as

"the facts observed, recalled, read, and talked about, and the ideas suggested, in the course of a development of a situation having a purpose"
(MW.9.188). But, as it turns out, there is quite a bit to be said if only
by way of elaboration of points made in the previous chapter. For one
thing, if context is so critically important, then it is fair to say, as Dewey
does, that "obviously studies or the subject matter of the curriculum
have intimately to do with this business of supplying the environment."
This subject matter, after all, "represent[s] the stock of meanings which
have precipitated out of previous experience" (MW.9.188). This is not,
however, how subject matter is conventionally understood. For the most
part, subject matter is seen simply as the content of school subjects—
mathematics, history, literature, science, and the like. Yet from a Deweyan
perspective, those disciplines are advanced, refined, and logically organized forms of knowledge that had their genesis in ordinary experience.
They are the experience of the human race as recorded, interpreted, and
set down. In this respect, subject matter is not a breed apart from the
kind of experience that makes up individual human life. The job of the
teacher and indeed the curriculum is to establish the connection between
the relatively inchoate but immediate and vital experience of the child
and the logically organized but rather remote and abstracted experience
of the human race. Whatever the differences between these two forms of
experience, in Dewey's view, they remain organically connected.

Subject matter in Deweyan terms is also instrumental to accomplishing human purpose. It is a resource rather than a possession. It may
not be the case that all subject matter must therefore appear in the
curriculum in the context of human purpose, but if knowledge is presented to the child principally as something that simply needs to be
learned without any relationship to its origins in human experience,
knowledge, particularly school knowledge, as perceived by the learner
becomes an inert assemblage of facts that bears no relevance to life as it
is lived. Under those circumstances, it should come as no surprise that
even when the more compliant students are able to reproduce such
knowledge as part of a recitation or on a test, they promptly abandon it
once the defined period of schooling is past. What makes that situation
more than simply wasteful is that knowledge perceived in this way is so
artificially contrived. It is an aberrant form of knowledge that finds a
home only in the bizarre world of schools. Dewey makes this point,
rather poetically, "Only in education, never in the life of farmer, sailor,
merchant, physician, or laboratory experimenter, does knowledge mean
primarily a store of information aloof from doing" (MW.9.193). Under
those circumstances, "the sole problem of the student is to learn, for
school purposes, for purposes of recitations and promotions, the con-

stituent parts of this strange world" (MW.9.194–195). That characterization of the way subject matter was conventionally regarded at the time *Democracy and Education* was being written is not substantially different from the prevailing way subject matter is understood in today's schools.

One thing that makes this Deweyan perspective difficult to absorb is that subject matter is so ingrained in our consciousness as something rarefied and abstract without any bearing on life situations. Our own schooling has served to socialize us into that view. Whatever subject matter is, it finds its home in schools—not in the way we live our lives. What is most notably missing from that perspective is that subject matter, whatever its lofty status, is simply a distilled and elaborated form of what human beings during earlier periods of their existence experienced in the course of growing, preparing food, building shelter, creating clothing, and the like. What was once directly useful—indeed necessary for human survival—has become ever more remote from existence. For Dewey, that connection between subject matter and human purpose needed to be reestablished in a school setting—not because those activities are still necessary for individual survival, but because they provide an avenue for reestablishing the taut connection between knowledge and human affairs.

As a result, subject matter is conventionally presented in schools as something simply set out to be learned, and it should not be surprising that many students, although they may engage with that subject matter temporarily and may even be able to provide correct answers during class recitations and on tests, ultimately find the subject matter as presented in schools to be remote from their genuine interests. When contemporary surveys of the knowledge that adolescents and young adults possess reveal abysmal ignorance in science, government, and history, for example, it is generally not because the basic knowledge in those fields has been ignored in schools. It is because those adolescents and young adults have ultimately come to reject the school knowledge that is taught largely because of what Dewey calls the school's "gradgrind preoccupation with facts" while at the same time ignoring the bearings that such knowledge has on the experience of the learner (MW.9.195).[1]

Not surprisingly, Dewey chooses science—at least an idealized from of science—to illustrate the virtues of subject matter properly considered. Here, however, Dewey elects to emphasize not the continuities of science with ordinary human experience, but with the ways it serves to correct certain widespread human tendencies. Human beings by nature seek certainty. "The undisciplined mind," Dewey says, "is averse to suspense and intellectual hesitation; it is prone to assertion" (MW.9.196). Science, however, "is born of doubting." Truth in science, even when it is the result of experimental testing, is "tentative and provisional" (MW.9.197). Part of the value of science as a discipline, Dewey argues, is precisely because it is "artificial," that is, it runs contrary to the common natural tendency to "cling to our conceptions irrespective of their actual consequences." In this respect, the value of science as a school subject lies not in its outcomes but in that it offers the prospect of initiating young persons into the "scientific spirit," a spirit that in this case, rather than interpreting the consequences of our actions as "hard luck and the hostility of circumstances" or even an "untoward fate," serves to direct reflection toward the objective consequences of our actions. "Science," Dewey concludes, "represents the safeguard of the race against . . . natural propensities and the evils that flow from them" (MW.9.197). Science, in other words, does not merely extend and refine certain natural human tendencies; at least in part, it serves as a corrective to those tendencies.

Play and Work in the Curriculum

In the opening section of chapter 15, "The Place of Active Occupations in Education," Dewey returns to a theme that has been central to his theory of the curriculum. When he undertook the founding of the Laboratory School at the University of Chicago in 1896, Dewey rejected both of the major alternatives that were available at that time—a curriculum based on the interests of learners (as advocated by the likes of G. Stanley Hall) and one based on the disciplines of knowledge (as advocated by the likes of William Torrey Harris). What he sought was a curriculum that somehow reconciled the seeming opposition between these two not by taking an eclectic approach to the problem but by reconstructing the problem so that their seeming opposition would disappear. For about the first two years of the school's existence, Dewey settled for something like a Herbartian curriculum. The subject matter in the early grades tended to be drawn from earlier stages in human history and gradually progressed toward more modern times. It had a roughly chronological organization.

Herbartian curriculum theory was based on what was then a widely accepted scientific principle, namely, that ontogeny recapitulates phylogeny (i.e., the development of the individual follows the development of the human race). If one could identify a historical stage of the development of the human race, in other words, one could find a parallel state in the development of the individual child. On its face, this had little to do with the school curriculum, but, out of that presumably scientific truth, Herbartians constructed their theory of culture epochs, which, in their view, provided a scientific basis for deciding what to teach. If, for example, one could identify a period of human history like the so-called savage stage, then that provided the basis for identifying a comparable stage in the child's psychological development in which the child exhibits what might be called savages tendencies or ways of thinking or interests. In practice, the work selected for study in this early stage was often Longfellow's *Hiawatha*, a poem about a so-called savage, thus ensuring some affinity between the child's natural tendencies and propensities and the subject matter of what was studied in school. The same would be true of such other so-called culture epochs as the nomadic stage and the agricultural stage. The presumed correspondence between the historical epoch and the developmental stage in the child was believed to provide the key to choosing the subject matter of instruction. (In practice, the works selected for study tended to be literary representations rather than actual artifacts of the period.)

To the modern ear, culture epochs as a theory of curriculum sounds quaint at best and absurd at worst, and, in some of his early work, Dewey undertook to challenge some of its assumptions. Nonetheless, it is clear that he was also intrigued by its possibilities. Presumably, it appealed to Dewey's effort to tie the experiences of the human race in the form of subject matter with the individual experiences that the child brought to school. In his 1899 lectures, for example, Dewey begins his discussion of culture epochs by accepting the general notion of a parallelism between historical stages and developmental psychology stages (Dewey, 1899/1966, p. 202). What he objected to most strongly was that the parallelism between historical periods and the stages of the development of the child was being taken far too literally. Dewey says, for example, that "the mere fact that the race has gone through a certain stage of development does not seem to be an adequate basis for inferring that the child not only does go though it, but that we should emphasize or prolong his passing through it" (p. 203). Instead of assuming that a direct counterpart to a historical epoch exists in the child's mind, "we should carefully watch the development of the child and then hunt through literature and history and science in order to furnish the material that is most appropriate to the child at that stage of development" (p. 211). The rest, so far as Dewey was concerned, was a lot of useless baggage.

In the end, Dewey rejected the idea that historical epochs hold the key to connecting the experience of the human race as embodied in the disciplines of knowledge with the experience of the learner, but he never gave up the idea of making that connection. While repudiating culture epochs per se, Dewey's resolution of the problem retained something of a historical time line. What was ultimately being reconstructed in Dewey's curriculum was the way knowledge gradually became organized and refined out of the fundamental activities that he called occupations. In other words, *Dewey substituted a reconstruction of the evolution of organized knowledge for the recapitulation of human history in the form of culture epochs.*

Here Dewey's concept of occupations became crucial because it was by injecting these occupations into the curriculum that the origins of organized knowledge could be reconstructed. The occupations he introduced into the Laboratory School were activities such as gardening, cooking, building a clubhouse, and making clothing. These occupations, despite the vocational connotations sometimes associated with the term, were not introduced into the curriculum for their potential monetary value or even for practical purposes. Taking gardening as his example in *Democracy and Education*, Dewey argues that it "need not be taught either for the sake of preparing future gardeners, or as an agreeable way of passing time. It affords an avenue of approach to knowledge of the place farming and horticulture have had *in the history of the race* and which they occupy in present social organization" (MW.9.208, emphasis added). Such knowledge is thus liberated from its rarefied and abstract setting and reconnected with its human roots. "Instead of subject matter belonging to a peculiar study called botany," Dewey says, " it will then belong to life and will find, moreover, its natural correlations with the facts of soil, animal life, and human relations" (MW.9.208).

What applies to gardening applies equally to such other occupations as "wood-working, cooking, and on through the list" (MW.9.208). Dewey goes to great length to disassociate these activities from the idea that their introduction into the curriculum is primarily for the purpose of making education more practical or simply to provide amusement. "The problem of the educator," he says, "is to engage pupils in these activities in such ways that while manual skill and technical efficiency are gained and immediate satisfaction found in the work, together with preparation for later usefulness, these things shall be subordinated to *education*—that is, to intellectual results and the forming of socialized dispositions" (MW.9.204). His protestations notwithstanding, Dewey's introduction of these activities into the curriculum continues to be associated, at least in the popular mind, with mere play or, at the least, a desire to cater to the immediate interests of children.

Some of this misunderstanding of Dewey's intention may stem from his effort to vitiate the notion that work and play are somehow antithetical. There are differences of course, but the gulf between the two is not nearly as wide as is sometimes imagined. In fact, in Dewey's mind, their similarities are striking. "Both involve ends consciously entertained and the selection and adaptations of material and processes designed to effect the desired ends" (MW.9.210). The principal difference seems to be that, in play, interest operates more directly; it is in the forefront. Nevertheless, play, much like work, does entail an element of looking ahead and perceiving the consequences of an action. Hunting, for example, an adult form of play, surely exhibits that characteristic. "The point," Dewey says, "is that play has an end in the sense of a directing idea which gives point to successive acts" (MW.9.211). The antagonism between play and work is just one of many mischievous divisions and dualisms that Dewey, over the course of his lifetime, sought to dispel both within and outside of the education sphere. In this case, however, the reconciliation of play and work required the abandonment of commonsensical distinctions that most people found difficult to relinquish. As a result, Dewey's effort to introduce active occupations into the curriculum continues to be interpreted, especially by his detractors, as his attempt merely to make school fun rather than to make it more authentically intellectual by demonstrating in the curriculum how knowledge can function instrumentally in anticipating and successfully carrying forward a course of action.

What is perhaps insufficiently articulated in *Democracy and Education* is that occupations provide the starting point, not the end point, of Dewey's curriculum. The end point is mastery of the organized disciplines of knowledge. As the child moves through the grades and matures intellectually, less attention is given to direct participation in active occupations and more emphasis is given to the organized intellectual resources of the culture. A much clearer exposition of that aspect of Dewey's curriculum theory appears in his last book on education, *Experience and Education* (1938) There, Dewey actually gives his theory a name, "the progressive organization of subject matter." "Progressive" in this sense has nothing to do with so-called progressive education. It refers to the fact that, over the course of schooling, Dewey's curriculum becomes ever more systematized so that in the end it closely comes to resemble the refined and logically organized knowledge embodied in the academic disciplines.

Implementing Dewey's Theory of Curriculum

One of the problems Dewey faced in establishing his theory of curriculum in American schools is that so much of what he sought to accomplish ran directly contrary to long-standing ideas about what the curriculum was and what it should aim at. Whatever the intellectual rigor of his analysis and the international stature he ultimately achieved during his lifetime, evidence of the implementation of those ideas in American schools remains extremely sparse. Conventional notions about method, subject matter, and the curriculum generally remain as firmly entrenched as ever. Method in the context of teacher education, for the most part, consists of prescribed ways for teachers to behave, subject matter is still for all intents and purposes a compilation of facts derived from the disciplines of knowledge, and the curriculum remains as much as ever a body of prescribed school knowledge remote from human experience.

There is no easy explanation for this, but certain factors are hard to ignore. First, Dewey's ideas on education are far more radical than is sometimes imagined. They are not as radical perhaps in the political sense as they are in terms of how Americans typically conceptualize the process of schooling. In the first half of the twentieth century, when Dewey was most active, educational reforms of a sort were indeed successfully introduced, but they tended to reflect established values as well as growing anxieties about the relationship between school and life rather than Dewey's reaction to them. Vocational education, probably the most successful of the twentieth century's educational innovations, appealed to the long-standing belief, still held by most Americans, that schooling exists primarily, almost exclusively, to get jobs. In *Democracy and Education*, however, Dewey devotes the chapter on vocational aspects of education to a serious critique of that assumption. Paradoxically, the philosopher who on some level is regarded as quintessentially American found himself constantly swimming against the tide of prevailing American public opinion.

A second factor that cannot be ignored is that many of the educational ideas that Dewey set forth in *Democracy and Education* and elsewhere were profoundly incompatible with existing structures of schooling. Dewey understood this. He articulated this point in an early essay in which he made the case that the structural features of schools such as "the grouping of children in classes, the arrangement of grades, the machinery by which the course of study is made out and laid down, the method by which it is carried into effect" and so on "really control the whole system, even on its distinctly educational side" (Dewey, 1901, pp. 337–338). Even the best of ideas, it appears, cannot be implemented successfully when the machinery of the system has been built to sustain something else entirely. Nothing like the kind of curriculum that Dewey proposed, for example, stood much of a chance when the system of rewards and punishments for both teachers and students was keyed to reproducing factual knowledge on tests. Dewey's ideas, in other words, were done in on a genuinely national scale by the fact that schools were organized and operated for a purpose radically different from the one he proposed. The system was geared to make the existing social order operate more efficiently, not to produce citizens who would challenge prevailing social norms.

Note

1. Dewey's reference to Mr. Gradgrind, the memorable schoolmaster satirized in Charles Dickens's *Hard Times*, evokes Gradgrind's famous speech at the opening of his school that begins with a impassioned endorsement of the teaching of facts: "Now all I want is facts. Teach these boys and girls nothing but facts. Facts alone are wanted in life. Plant nothing else, and root out everything else." E. D. Hirsch Jr. (1987) in his best-seller, *Cultural Literacy: What Every American Needs to Know*, dismisses arguments like Dewey's as "an old prejudice" (p. 133).

References

Dewey, J. (1899/1966). In R. D. Archambault (Ed.), Lectures in the philosophy of education: 1899. New York: Random House.

Dewey, J. (1901). The situation as regards the course of study. *Journal of the Proceedings and Addresses of the Fortieth Annual Meeting of the National Education Association.*

Dewey J. (1902). *The child and the curriculum.* Chicago: University of Chicago Press.

Dewey, J. (1938). *Experience and education.* New York: Macmillan.

Hirsch, E. D., Jr. (1987). *Cultural literacy: What every American needs to know.* (New York: Houghton Mifflin.

8

A Teacher Educator Looks at
Democracy and Education

SHARON FEIMAN-NEMSER

I have always taken quiet pleasure in the fact that I studied at three of the universities where John Dewey taught,[1] that I began my teaching career at the University of Chicago Laboratory School that he founded, and that I started my career as a teacher educator in the Department of Education at Chicago that he established. In three decades as a scholar and practitioner of teacher education, no semester has passed without my reading something by Dewey with my students, first at Chicago, then at Michigan State, and now at Brandeis. *School and Society, The Child and the Curriculum, How We Think, Experience and Education,* and an essay called "The Relation of Theory to Practice in Education" have been staples in my undergraduate and graduate classes.

Yet I never read *Democracy and Education.* It felt too daunting to tackle on my own. I accepted David T. Hansen's invitation to write this chapter, in part, because I felt that I *should* read this Dewey classic.[2] I read it as a teacher educator interested in how people learn to teach and how professional education contributes to the process. More specifically, I read it as a teacher educator much influenced by Dewey's ideas.

Writing about philosophy of education in *Democracy and Education,* Dewey refers to education as "the laboratory in which philosophic distinctions become concrete and are tested" (MW.9.339). Over the years, my programmatic experiments and research have been opportunities to clarify some of Dewey's distinctions and test their usefulness in overcoming some of the pervasive dualisms in teacher education such as theory and practice, subject matter and method, and knowing and doing (see, e.g., Feiman, 1979; Feiman-Nemser, 1980; Feiman-Nemser & Buchmann, 1985; Norman & Feiman-Nemser, 2005).

Democracy and Education has a lot to say about how people learn in general and how they should be taught in school. While Dewey does not write directly about teacher education, I found myself transposing ideas about learning and teaching to the contexts of teacher learning and teacher education. In particular, I tried to figure out what Dewey means by education as the reconstruction of experience and how this idea relates to the education of teachers. I also looked for expressions of this idea in two proposals for the reform of teacher education, one by Dewey himself (1904) and one by Deborah Ball and David Cohen (1999).

In the opening chapters of *Democracy and Education*, Dewey argues that "the educative process is a continuous process of growth, having as its aim at every stage an added capacity of growth" (MW.9.59). He contrasts his view of education as the reconstruction of experience with other conceptions of education—education as preparation, development, formation, and training. Reading these early chapters, it struck me that these ideas are quite pervasive in the discourse of teacher education.

Before turning to Dewey's conception of education as the reconstruction of experience and what it could mean for teacher education, I want to examine his critique of preparation and development as it bears on the work of teacher educators.

(Teacher) Education as Preparation

Since Dewey is mainly writing about the education of children, his critique centers on how focusing on a distant future diverts the attention of both teacher and taught from "the needs and possibilities of the immediate present." Dewey identifies three evils that flow from basing education on future requirements. Children live in the present. The future lacks urgency. So one negative consequence is that teachers have to use reward and punishment to get children to do work whose only justification is its usefulness in the future. A second problem is substituting a vague standard for what young people may be expected in general to become in some more or less remote future for a keen assessment of students' present strengths and weaknesses. A third is the way such a view encourages procrastination and the postponement of serious work since the present offers many temptations and the future is far away. The resulting education is less effective than it would be if educators had focused on making present conditions as educative as possible.

It isn't such a stretch to think about teacher education as preparation for teaching. In fact, it seems quite logical to assume that the learning opportunities provided by teacher educators are intended to prepare teachers for their future work. Surely the schools that hire teachers and the states that certify them want some assurance that teachers are prepared to teach.

Nor are we talking about an extended gap in time between teacher education and future teaching since teacher education is a relatively brief affair. In fact, the prospect of being a teacher of record in the not too distant future often intensifies the teacher candidate's desire to learn how to teach and serves as a strong incentive. So what's wrong with thinking about teacher education as preparation for future teaching?

One problem is the narrowing effects on the curriculum. Feeling the pressure to get teacher candidates ready for teaching may lead teacher educators to focus mainly on the practical skills of teaching. Certainly this is what many prospective teachers expect to learn from their education classes and why they value student teaching and other "real world" learning opportunities. Learning a discrete set of practical skills, however, may not enable teachers to use those skills with flexibility and judgment. Dewey makes this point in his 1904 essay on the education of teachers that I review later in this chapter.

A second problem with the conception of teacher education as preparation for teaching is that it promotes a view of preservice education as an end in itself. This gives teacher educators the feeling that they should try to cover as much as possible in their courses since this could be their one and only chance to influence future teachers. Seeing teacher preparation as self-contained rather than as part of a continuum of learning opportunities prevents teacher educators from thinking through what can best be taught and learned before someone begins teaching and what can more appropriately be learned later on (Feiman-Nemser, 2001).

Finally, the idea of preparing individuals to teach by equipping them with all that they need to know is, on the face of it, impossible. Teaching happens in particular situations with particular students around particular content. No amount of preparation can equip teachers with the knowledge they need to respond to the particulars of their teaching situation. Teachers can certainly learn subject matter and acquire knowledge of children, learning, and pedagogy in a variety of settings, but learning to use such knowledge in teaching depends on knowing things that cannot be learned in advance or outside practice. This idea is central to the argument that Ball and Cohen (1999) make in their essay on teacher education.

(Teacher) Education as Development

Dewey also criticizes the view of education as development or the unfolding of latent powers. Such a view values growth only as a step toward the attainment of some ideal state remote from what exists in the present. It means movement toward an alleged final maturity. Since the goal is completing the process, anything along the way is transitory. Dewey sums up his criticism as follows: "An abstract and indefinite future is in control with all which that connotes in depreciation of present power and opportunity" (MW.9.61–62).

A distant standard of development cannot provide guidance for the present. So educators must work out criteria for determining whether or not children's present attitudes or actions represent the so-called unfolding of latent powers. Without such guidance, the only alternative is to avoid intervening in what is regarded as a natural process. In practice, developmental educators sometimes pay lip service to the ideal of development while using indirect means to elicit what they regard as desirable responses in the learner.

Those who believe that teachers are born not made may embrace a view of learning to teach as the unfolding of natural powers. At various times in the history of teacher education, this view has had some standing and traces of it are visible in the language of teacher development.[3] Like the belief that teachers must find their own style and figure out "what works" for them, a view of learning to teach as a developmental process tends to promote a reactive (some would say responsive) stance on the part of teacher educators.

One example of an empirically constructed theory of teacher development comes from the work of Frances Fuller and her colleagues at the University of Texas at Austin. They posit that teachers go through stages of concern in learning to teach. At first, teachers are preoccupied with their own adequacy. As self-oriented concerns get resolved, teachers become preoccupied with their teaching performance. Only later do they move on to concerns about student learning (Fuller, 1969; Fuller & Bown, 1975). The implication that pupil-oriented concerns are more desirable than self-oriented concerns is clear. Researchers speculate that these later concerns cannot emerge until earlier concerns are resolved. Furthermore, they recommend that teacher educators "match" their efforts to developing teachers present concerns rather than "teaching against the tide."

This advice confuses description (what student teachers are concerned about) with prescription (what teacher educators ought to do about it). It diminishes the role of teacher education to cultivate dispositions and enlarge and enrich teachers' experiences. It leaves to chance the likelihood that teachers will develop the capacity and commitment to help all children to reach their fullest potential.

Education as the Reconstruction of Experience

In contrast to these "one-sided" views of education, Dewey advances the idea of education as the constant reconstruction of experience. It is "that reconstruction or reorganization of experience which adds to the meaning of experience and which increases the ability to direct the course of subsequent experiences" (MW.9.82). Such a view of education connects ends and means, unifies thought and action, and links past, present, and future. It is a continuous interplay of actions and ideas that lead to increased understanding and personal agency over time.

Central to this conception of education is Dewey's definition of experience, which, according to Israel Scheffler (1974), has three elements: (1) the biological emphasis on experience as the outcome of an interaction between objective conditions and organic energies; (2) the scientific notion of experiment as the deliberate alteration of environment by inquirers leading to new knowledge; and (3) the Peircean doctrine of meaning in which ideas are analyzed in terms of their consequences for action and function in the reflective regulation of conduct (p. 197).

For Dewey, experience is not mere activity. It involves an interaction between a person and his or her environment in which both are changed. It is a process in which a person attends to or acts on something and then undergoes or suffers the consequences. Learning from experience involves a backward and forward connection between what we do to things and what they do to us. "Doing becomes a trying, an experiment with the world to find out what it is like; the undergoing becomes instruction—discovery of the connection of things" (MW.9.147).

For Dewey, the key to acquiring knowledge is seeing relationships between actions and their consequences. By perceiving these connections and retaining the lessons of experience, we expand our understanding and our control of future experiences. Meaning and control are the criteria for judging the educative quality of experience. Meaning comes from increased perception of connections and continuities in the activities we engage in. Control comes from increased ability to predict, anticipate, and prepare for subsequent experiences.

Thinking gives meaning to experience. As Dewey puts it, "it is an explicit rendering of the intelligent element in our experience" (MW.9.152). Thinking is a process of investigating, looking into, figuring something out. It is activated by doubt, uncertainty, or confusion—a condition that invites inquiry. The basic pattern is the same whether the example is a child exploring his or her environment or a scientist conducting an experiment in the laboratory. It includes sensing a problem, observing conditions, forming and elaborating suggestions, and active, experimental testing (MW.9.158). Scientific thinking is a variety of intelligent thinking and intelligent thinking promotes responsible actions in the world.

Within a conception of education as the reconstruction of experience, ends and means are continuous. The end is enlarged meaning and power; the means, a process of enlarging meaning and increasing power. In a democratic community, education should "enable individuals to continue their education . . . the object or reward of learning is continued capacity for growth" (MW.9.107). Knowledge and conduct are unified.

Dewey develops these ideas across a number of chapters before turning to formal education or schooling. He offers suggestions to educators about how to foster intelligent learning in the service of developing good habits of thinking animated by social concern. This is the fundamental imperative for democracy and the main task of education.

Dewey's suggestions flow from his conceptions of education and experience. To foster the ability to think, schools must create conditions that "exact, promote and test thinking" (MW.9.159). This recommendation means creating situations that give students something to do that demands thinking and the intentional noticing of connections. What is needed is not ready-made subject matter, but an actual empirical situation that presents something new and therefore uncertain or problematic, but sufficiently connected to existing habits to call out an effective response. In a remarkable passage, Dewey characterizes the pedagogical task of framing problems with the right kind of challenge, a task that depends on knowledge of students and subject matter: "A large part of the art of instruction lies in making the difficulty of new problems large enough to challenge thought, and small enough so that, in addition to the confusion naturally attending the novel elements, there shall be luminous familiar spots from which helpful suggestions may spring" (MW.9.164).

Teacher Education as the Reconstruction of Experience

What would it mean to think about teacher education as the reconstruction of experience? How does the idea of education of, by, and for experience relate to learning to teach? One might assume that Dewey's ideas relate mostly to the practical side of teacher education where learning by doing prevails. Writing about this misinterpretation of Dewey, Joseph Schwab (1959) points out that "to learn by doing was neither to learn only by doing nor to learn only how to do. Doing was to go hand in hand with reading, reflecting and remembering" (p. 158).

Dewey does not write directly about teacher education in *Democracy and Education*. Some connections may be drawn from the chapter on "Vocational Aspects of Education" where he argues against narrow, technical trade education that perpetuates social divisions in favor of cultivating workers' practical intelligence in the service of understanding and improving social and economic conditions. Dewey's conception of vocation as a motivating force for learning and an intellectual framework for organizing knowledge seems relevant to teaching as vocation. Imagine inserting "teacher" into the following passage about the power of a "calling":

> The lawyer, the physician, the laboratory investigator, the parent, the citizen has a constant working stimulus to note and relate whatever has to do with his concern. He unconsciously, from the motivation of his occupation, reaches out for all relevant information and holds to it. The vocation acts as both magnet and as glue to hold. Such organization of knowledge is vital because it has reference to needs; it is so expressed and readjusted in action that it never becomes stagnant. No classification, no selection and arrangement of facts which is worked out for purely abstract ends, can ever compare in solidity or effectiveness with that knit under the stress of an occupation. (MW.9.319)

But a reader seeking more explicit connections to teacher education from *Democracy and Education* may be disappointed. The best he or she can do is extrapolate general principles about curriculum or pedagogy or the purposes of teacher education from Dewey's discussion of formal education. Such extensions presume a parallel between the work of teachers and the work of teacher educators in terms of both ends and means. A Deweyan teacher educator would want to prepare teachers who are committed to creating democratic classrooms where students engage in active, meaningful learning and who know how to learn well from experience. The teacher educator would also want to proceed in a manner consistent with an understanding of education as the reconstruction of experience.

Dewey insists on the necessity of an actual empirical situation as the initiating phase of thought. A genuine situation arouses thinking by confronting the learner with something new and therefore uncertain or problematic and yet sufficiently connected to existing knowledge and skills to call out an effective response. For Dewey the pragmatist, an effective response means a perceptible result. It follows that teacher educators would need to think about the design of learning opportunities for teachers in terms of their power to arouse thinking and initiate some kind of meaningful problem solving on the part of teacher candidates.

This relates to the Deweyan principle that one educates indirectly, not directly. It follows that teacher educators cannot "give" teacher candidates experience or ideas. Like all teachers, they can only educate by creating the conditions through which teacher candidates will have fruitful experiences. In a chapter, "Thinking in Education," Dewey draws the educational moral and I have inserted "teacher educator" into the passage: "When the parent or teacher (or teacher educator) has provided the conditions which stimulate thinking and has taken a sympathetic attitude toward the activities of the learner by entering into a common or conjoint experience, all has been done which a second party can to instigate learning. The rest lies with the one directly concerned" (MW.9.167).

Other principles bear on the aims of teacher education. Actually, Dewey would probably object to the implication that teacher education has aims. As he points out, "education as such has no aims. Only persons, parents, and teachers have aims, not an abstract idea like education" (MW.9.114). Dewey is critical of aims imposed from the outside or based on some remote accomplishment or responsibility. We saw this in his critique of education as preparation. In his view, worthwhile educational aims grow out of the situation at hand. They take into account the needs, interests, and powers of the persons being educated. "A good aim," writes Dewey, "surveys the present state of experience of pupils, and forming a tentative plan of treatment keeps the plan constantly in view, yet modifies it as conditions develop." Aims help educators observe, plan, and pursue a course of action. They are guides to present actions that get evaluated by their consequences. Here is a reminder to teacher educators that they must adopt an experimental stance toward their own practice, judging its success by monitoring effects on students.

Given Dewey's formulation of habits as expressions of growth, one would expect him to favor intellectual and emotional habits or dispositions as aims in teacher education. "Where there is a habit," Dewey writes, "there is acquaintance with the materials and equipment to which action is applied. There is a definite way of understanding the situation in which the habit operates" (MW.9.53). What prevents a habit from becoming fixed, what gives it flexibility, is the intellectual element of judgment and reasoning. "Modes of thought, of observation and reflection, enter as forms of skill and of desire into the habits that make a man an engineer, an architect, a physician, or a merchant" (MW.9.53) and, I would add, a teacher.

While these general principles provide some direction, they do not go very far in painting a picture of what teacher education should be like. Fortunately, Dewey has outlined a position on teacher education in an essay published in 1904, twelve years before the appearance of *Democracy and Education*. Called "The Relation of Theory and Practice in Education," it offers a concrete proposal regarding the purposes and the curriculum of teacher education. It can help us imagine what teacher education as the reconstruction of experience might be like.

Dewey on Teacher Education

Inspired by the rise of the research university with its faith in experimental science, Dewey (1904) favors a laboratory approach over the more traditional approach of apprenticeship learning. He proposes a curriculum designed to develop teachers' powers of observation and interpretation and to help them bring subject matter and educational principles to bear in decisions about what and how to teach.

Dewey recognizes that learning to teach requires a certain amount of practical work, but he believes that plunging student teachers prematurely into the complexities of classroom teaching precludes achieving the most important goal of teacher education—turning out "students of teaching" rather than "masters of the craft." Teachers must be educated and socialized so that they develop the habit of directing their attention to the intellectual and motivational processes of the child. Such teachers are disposed to the critical examination of their teaching and their students' learning.

Dewey recognizes that new teachers face two challenges in learning to teach. They must master skills of classroom management and instruction and they must master subject matter and educational principles in relation to one another. While both are necessary, making mastery of technical skills the aim "puts the attention of the student teacher in the wrong place and tends to fix it in the wrong direction"—not wrong absolutely but relative to more immediate needs and opportunities (MW.3.253).

If student teachers are plunged prematurely into the pressing business of managing a class before they learn how to observe psychologically, they will develop their teaching habits on the basis of "what works" to maintain order rather than what pupils need to move their learning forward. Only teachers who are students of subject matter and "mind activity" have the "power to go on growing" (MW.3.256). Although

Dewey's language may be a bit quaint, he is arguing for a kind of teacher education that fosters an experimental, inquiry-oriented stance toward teaching. Teachers with such habits can think for themselves. They know how to learn well from experience.

It's worth looking at the sequence of learning opportunities that Dewey lays out in order to imagine how a spirit of inquiry can animate what seems like a very conventional structure—foundations and methods courses followed by student teaching. Even though Dewey privileges theory in the education of teachers, he situates the study of theory in contexts designed to provoke thought, reminding me of the following passage in *Democracy and Education*:

> An ounce of experience is better than a ton of theory simply because it is only in experience that any theory has vital and verifiable significance. An experience, a very humble experience, is capable of generating and carrying any amount of theory (or intellectual content), but a theory apart from an experience cannot be definitely grasped even as theory. (MW.9.151)

The principle of situating the study of theory in practice informs his approach to the teaching of psychology. Since student teachers have been "learning all the days of their lives," Dewey observes, they have in their own experiences "plenty of practical material by which to illuminate and vitalize theoretical principles and laws of mental growth in the process of learning" (MW.3.258). This includes cases of successful learning as well as cases of arrested development. So teacher educators should tap the power and interest attached to the personal experiences of student teachers as learners in and out of school as a basis for generating hypotheses about laws and theories of learning.

The next step is designed to transform new understandings of learning theory into lens for observing how good teachers create classroom conditions that promote learning. Instead of observing the teacher's strategies and techniques, the student teacher is supposed to observe psychologically, to see "what is going on in the minds of a group of persons who are in intellectual contact with one another" (MW.3.259). Unless student teachers develop the "habit of psychological observation," they are likely to rely more on imitating what other teachers do rather than figuring out for themselves what pupils need based on what they can observe.

Once student teachers have acquired "power in psychological observation and interpretation," they are ready to observe the methods and materials that good teachers use to teach subject matter. If a proper foundation has been laid, Dewey argues, they will be able to translate these methods and materials into their psychological equivalent. This means figuring out why and how they work and exercising judgment in determining proper uses and adaptations in their own teaching.

The goal is to secure the critical mental habit of a teacher—"that habit which looks upon the internal, not upon the external; which sees that the important function of the teacher is direction of the mental movement of the student, and that the mental movement must be known before it can be directed" (MW.3.262). Such a habit enables teachers to discern relationships between the intellectual and social conditions they create to promote learning and their effects on students.

Dewey outlines a parallel sequence for learning subject matter that avoids the harmful divorce between scholarship and method that he discusses in chapters 13 and 14 in *Democracy and Education*. The approach turns on teaching subject matter to student teachers in ways that make visible their origins in natural attitudes, impulses, and intellectual methods. Having learned subject matter in this way, student teachers are ready to think about how to organize subject matter for purposes of teaching it to others.

Before they focus on individual lessons, however, Dewey wants student teachers to get a picture of the educational movement of the school—how the same subject develops not only day to day in a given grade but year to year across the grades. What does it mean for children of different ages to learn mathematics or geography or science? How are ideas and skills situated in tasks and learning activities that fit the needs and interests of learners at different ages? As the student teacher constructs a broad understanding of subject matter learning over time, he or she is ready to begin designing and teaching sequences of lessons for particular age groups. Here is a chance to frame ends, implement plans, and make adjustment in response to the effects on individual learners.

Even at the stage of practical work, Dewey cautions against too close supervision and critique lest it undermine the student teacher's developing sense of independence and intellectual authority. As Dewey writes: "Students should be given to understand that they not only are *permitted* to act upon their own intellectual initiative, but that they are *expected* to do so, and that their ability to take hold of situations for themselves would be a more important factor in judging them than their following any particular set method or scheme" (MW.3.269). Of course, there would be critical discussion with expert teachers, but the emphasis should be on getting student teachers to judge their own work critically, to find out for themselves the extent to which they have succeeded or failed and the probable causes for both results. Such critical discussion should be directed toward "making the professional student thoughtful about his work in the light of principles, rather than to induce in him a recognition that certain special methods are good and certain other special methods bad" (MW.3.270).

Dewey concludes with the observation that the principles he has just outlined are hardly "utopian" and should not be that difficult to institute. What is most needed, he writes, is leadership to improve the quality of education "not by turning out teachers who can do better the things that are now necessary to do, but rather by changing the conception of what constitutes education" (MW.3.272. More than one hundred years later we may conclude that Dewey's ideas were more utopian than he thought.

Centering Teacher Education "in" Practice

In an essay called "Developing Practice, Developing Practitioners," Deborah Ball and David Cohen (1999) outline a contemporary proposal for the reform of teacher education. Written nearly a century after Dewey's essay, it situates the professional education of teachers in the intellectual tasks of teaching. Like Dewey, Ball and Cohen want teaching and learning in schools to be substantially different from the norm. Like Dewey, they believe that professional education should foster the habit of inquiry so that teachers will know how to learn in and from their practice. Unlike Dewey, however, they take practice, not theory, as the starting point.

Ball and Cohen frame their argument around answers to three questions: (1) What do teachers need to know and be able to do to offer more powerful instruction to students? (2) What kind of professional education would help them learn that? (3) What does this imply for the content, method, and structure of professional education?

After outlining what teachers need to know about subject matter, learners, learning, and pedagogy, they argue that even if teachers knew all these things, they would still not know enough to teach in ways that reformers advocate because "much of what teachers need to know must be known and learned in context and in the moment" (p. 11). Their elaboration of skills or capacities that teachers need to be "actively learning as they teach" extends Dewey's notion of teachers as students of "mind activity" and leads to a similar conclusion—that "a stance of inquiry should be central to the role of teacher" (p. 11).

Teachers must be able to "size up situations" from moment to moment, eliciting students' ideas and interpreting them in the context of their teaching. They must be able to frame and reframe questions and problems in response to what is happening. They must be able to study and analyze their practice with some detachment, asking themselves, What is and is not working and for whom? These requirements for assessment, improvisation, experimentation in the context of teaching lead Ball and Cohen to their main recommendation—that professional education should be centered "in" practice and framed around investigations of practice.

Situating professional education "in" practice does not mean locating it in real classrooms in real time. Rather, it means grounding professional learning opportunities in the study and analysis of materials taken from real classrooms that present salient problems of practice. Copies of student work, videotapes of classroom lessons, curriculum materials, written cases about teaching, teacher journals are examples of the kind of documentation and artifacts that Ball and Cohen have in mind.

Imagine a group of teacher candidates studying student work on two-digit multiplication along with the relevant curriculum materials and a videotape of the class when that mathematical topic was taught. They could investigate what students seemed to have learned and how that fit with what the teacher was trying to teach. In the course of analyzing student learning, they could also consider other related issues such as what it means to know two-digit multiplication and what other mathematical ideas are related to this topic. If the documentation included different approaches to teaching the same topic, teachers could explore the teaching and learning of two-digit multiplication from a comparative perspective (cf. Lampert and Ball, 1998).

This example not only suggests the kinds of materials needed to implement such a professional curriculum, it also highlights the process—studying and analyzing teaching and learning. Simply looking at student work would not be enough. To examine student thinking and assess student learning (which are core activities in teaching), teachers and teacher educators would have to "develop and debate ideas about what to look at, ways to describe what is observed, and conceptions of what is sufficient evidence for any given claim" (p. 16). Developing the requisite analytic skills and communicative norms shifts the focus of teacher talk from answers and quick fixes to alternative possibilities, methods of reasoning, and supportive evidence and arguments.

A third element in Ball and Cohen's proposal involves making professional learning more of a collective endeavor. Besides breaking down the traditional isolation of teachers, the joint study of teaching and learning pushes teachers to develop more precise descriptive and analytic language for talking about teaching and learning and grappling with standards of practice. "What is good teaching? What is a good enough paper? Which response to this question shows that students understand?

Where do we agree? Where do we disagree and why? Such discussions make public the bases of knowing in and about teaching and learning," contributing to the development of teachers and the improvement of teaching (p. 18).

This proposal also helps us imagine what teacher education as the reconstruction of experience could be like. The nature of the goals, the continuity of ends and means, the linking of thought and action, the emphasis on inquiry—all these are part of Dewey's conception of education as the reorganization of experience. In addition, Ball and Cohen appreciate that even the most compelling materials are not self-enacting. They require well-framed tasks and skillful guidance by teacher educators who are insightful students of teaching, who understand teachers as learners, and who have a repertoire for engaging them in productive learning.

The ultimate goal of the professional curriculum that Ball and Cohen outline is improving teaching by developing teachers. A central aim is "to help teachers learn the intellectual and professional stance of inquiry" (p. 27). Ball and Cohen name some of the dispositions that contribute to such a stance—not leaping to conclusions, framing interpretations as conjectures, seeking and weighing evidence. Such dispositions contribute to more complex understandings of teaching and learning and more defensible courses of action.

A professional curriculum focused on core activities of teaching and situated in authentic records of practice promises to engage teachers' interests and purposes. Still, the likelihood of productive learning depends on the quality of thinking and engagement. Some disequilibrium is inevitable. The point is not to confirm what teachers already believe but to stimulate doubt, challenge assumptions, open up new possibilities. The ends become the means—engaging teachers in the study and analysis of teaching and learning so that they become active learners in their teaching.

Recognizing the power of technology to overcome the limitations of firsthand experience, Cohen (1998) summarizes the way the proposed curriculum supports the reconstruction of experience:

> We can now steal experience from real life, violating the rules of time, place, relations and access that constrain learning in real classrooms. . . . Educators can turn vivid and complex records of instructional experience into curriculum. . . . We can reconstruct experience so that it fits intending teachers' puzzles and schedules, rather than the demands of real-time instructional performance. (p. 180)

Reconstruction, Not Reproduction, of Experience

Written one hundred years apart, the two proposals for the reform of teacher education embrace the reconstruction, not the reproduction, of experience. Aware of the problems associated with learning from "live" experience, the authors outline a curriculum that prepares teachers to learn in and from teaching. Dewey emphasizes the study of theory-in-practice; Ball and Cohen emphasize the study and analysis of practice (see Figure 1). Despite their different starting points, both proposals share the goal of fostering an experimental, inquiry-oriented stance toward teaching.

Optimistic about the promises of experimental science and university-based professional education, Dewey focuses on laying an intellectual foundation in psychology and subject matter as preparation for practice work in teaching. His preferred sequence begins with an analysis of the intending teacher's own experiences as learners, then moves on to the study of how students respond to classroom learning opportunities. Dewey emphasizes that teachers need to think for themselves rather than imitate what they see other teachers doing. Developing the habit of psychological observation and insight and learning subject matter from a pedagogical perspective prepares teachers to learn how to teach themselves.

	Dewey	*Ball and Cohen*
Aims	Educating "students of teaching" Developing the disposition to focus on "mind activity"	Educating teachers who are actively learning in teaching Fostering an inquiry stance
Starting point	Educational theory and subject matter knowledge from a pedagogical perspective	Professional performance— tasks and ways of thinking that teaching entails
Curricular focus	Theory-in-practice	Core activities of teaching (practice)
Pedagogy	Guided reflection and observation in the service of illustrating theoretical principles	Study and analysis of "records of practice" that embody problems of practice; professional discourse

Figure 1: Teacher Education as the Reconstruction of Experience

Ball and Cohen place greater emphasis on learning in a professional community. Their curriculum for teachers imports classroom experience in the form of records of teaching and learning that serve as the basis for joint study and analysis. Dewey rejects apprenticeship learning because it favors imitation. Using new technologies, Ball and Cohen find a way for teachers to learn from the work of master teachers without being under their direct supervision. They also improve on Dewey's guided observations by enabling teachers to visit and revisit records of teachers' and students' experiences. Their professional curriculum is not intended as a substitute for practice. Rather it is designed to broaden teachers' understanding of teaching and its relationship to learning and to foster the habits and skills teachers need to learn in and from practice.

In his recommendations to educators in *Democracy and Education,* Dewey stresses the importance of creating conditions that provoke thought, elicit the learner's own purposes, and activate intentional, intelligent learning. He comments on the instructional art of framing problems with the "right" kind of challenge. One unique feature of the two proposals is the serious attention they give to the organization of learning opportunities for teachers. Ball and Cohen suggest what a "pedagogy of investigation" would entail. They acknowledge the need for skillful teacher educators to frame appropriate tasks and guide the study and analysis of records of practice. Dewey helps us imagine how to activate teacher candidates' purposes and interests in the study of educational theory and subject matter and the observation and interpretation of teacher–student interaction. In these ways, they help us imagine how teacher educators can substitute the reconstruction of experience for the reproduction of experience.

Notes

An earlier version of this chapter was presented at the annual meeting of the John Dewey Society in Montreal, April 2005.

1. University of Michigan, University of Chicago, and Teachers College, Columbia University

2. I did prevail on Professor Israel Scheffler, eminent philosopher of education and currently scholar in residence at the Mandel Center at Brandeis University, to lead a small study group on *Democracy and Education* that my colleagues Jon Levisohn, Dirck Roosevelt, and Susan Kardos participated in.

3. For a critical analysis of teacher development as a metaphor for teacher education, see Feiman-Nemser & Floden, 1981.

References

Ball, D. L., & Cohen, D. K (1999). Developing practice, developing practitioners: Toward a practice-based theory of professional education. In L. Darling-Hammond & G. Sykes (Eds.), *Teaching as the learning profession: Handbook of policy and practice* (pp. 3–32). San Francisco: Jossey-Bass.

Cohen, D. K. (1998). Afterword. In M. Lampert and D. Ball, *Teaching, multimedia and mathematics: Investigations of real practice* (pp. 167–187). New York: Teachers College Press.

Feiman, S. (1979). Inquiry and technique in teacher education: A curricular case study. *Curriculum Inquiry, 9*(1), 63–79.

Feiman-Nemser, S. (1980). Growth and reflection as aims in teacher education: Directions for research. In G. E. Hall, S. M. Hord, & G. Brown (Eds.), *Exploring issues in teacher education: Questions for future research* (pp. 133–152). Austin: Research and Development Center for Teacher Education.

Feiman-Nemser, S. (1998). Teachers as teacher educators. *European Journal of Teacher Education, 21*(1), 63–74.

Feiman-Nemser, S. (2001). From preparation to practice: Designing a continuum to strengthen and sustain teaching. *Teacher College Record, 103*(6), 1013–1055.

Feiman-Nemser, S., & Buchmann, M. (1985). The pitfalls of experience in teacher preparation. *Teacher College Record, 87*(1), 54–65.

Feiman-Nemser, S., & Floden, R. (1981). A critique of developmental approaches in teacher education. *Action in Teacher Education, 3*(1), 35–38.

Fuller, F. F. (1969). Concerns of teachers: A developmental conceptualization. *American Educational Research Journal, 6*(2), 207–226.

Fuller, F., & Brown, O. (1975). On becoming a teacher. In K. Ryan (Ed.), *Teacher education (the 74th national society for the study of education yearbook)*. Chicago: University of Chicago Press.

Lampert, M., & Ball, D. (1998). *Teaching, multimedia and mathematics: Investigations of real practice*. New York: Teachers College Press.

Norman, P., & Feiman-Nemser, S. (2005). Mind activity in teaching and mentoring. *Teaching and Teacher Education, 21*, 679–697.

Scheffler, I. (1974). *Four pragmatists: A critical introduction to Peirce, James, Mead, and Dewey*. Atlantic Highlands, NJ: Humanities Press.

Schwab, J. J. (1959). The "impossible" role of the teacher in progressive education. *The School Review, 67*(2), 139–159.

9

Dewey's Philosophy of Life

ELIZABETH MINNICH

Overview: A Philosopher of Life

Democracy is once again being claimed as value and virtue not solely for a form of governance, but as a way of life. That way of life is once again being taken as cause for which to die, and as justification to kill. Surely this calls us, as it did John Dewey in his times (1859–1952), to reflect on democracy's relation to life, to the living of our physical, material lives; our biographical lives; our historical social, political, associative lives. I will, then, revisit *Democracy and Education* to see what this remarkable book may still have to offer us not just as an American classic, but as an expression of Dewey's radical quest for an understanding of life and living by and for which to inform a morally aspirational ideal true to both democracy and education.

Focusing on life, we remember with Dewey the given that, as living organisms, we are creatures and creators of mutual interchange, always in transactional relations with our environments that are physically essential. For Dewey, this physical condition of life is not something to be overcome, to "rise above," to transcend. On the contrary: it is both the sine qua non of and a picture, or analog, for processes of co-creative relationality with which moral, social, political thinking and action as well as art and faith can and should correspond. For Dewey, this correspondence entails recognizing that all human possibilities and problems are problems and possibilities of relevance to the informal and formal education by which societies adapt and renew themselves.

That the nature of life is dynamically relational does not, of course, tell us all we need to know.[1] It does not tell us *what* we should be and do. It does, however, suggest *how* we are and should be who we are, *how* we should do what we do, and it reminds us of *why* the *how* of it all matters so much. Life is always vulnerable: individuals can fail to sustain themselves, to develop, to thrive; so can species, and societies, and polities. Individuals can die; so can collectivities. However, Dewey always remembers birth as well as death, youth and development as well as adults and senescence. He writes, "If a plague carried off the members of a society all at once, it is obvious that the group would be permanently done for. Yet the death of each of its constituent members is as certain as if an epidemic took them all at once. But the graded difference in age, the fact that some are born as some die, makes possible through transmission of ideas and practices the constant reweaving of the social process" (MW.9.6).

Thus, Dewey remembers that life continues and evolves—that reproduction, birth, nurturance, development as well as death are part of life's ongoing story. Remembering life's recurrently new beginnings, he is moved to focus not, as so many philosophers and theologians have, on how individual "Man" might overcome his own physical death, but on how living continues. "Continuity of life," he writes, "means continual readaptation of the environment to the needs of living organisms" (MW.9.5). Such successful transactional relations not only preserve life, but we could say that they *are* life, that life *is* living transitively. Dewey thus finds crucial lessons not only in individual entities' survival, but in the evolution of physical life forms that must also continuously "readapt" to (always also changing) environments. Just so, he believes, must conscious life forms be adapative, that is, transmitted not just as they once were, but as they are ongoingly co-created through successfully transactional adjustments. He writes, "Society exists through a process of transmission quite as much as biological life" (MW.9.6). This observation brings forward a relation of society and biological life that links them also with education: all three have the intrinsic aim of transmission.

This is why I believe we may understand Dewey most richly if we read him as a philosopher of life who turned to education as the most expressive practice of the confluence of his ontological, moral and political views. He wrote, "[P]hilosophy is . . . an explicit formulation of the various interests of life. . . . Since education is the process through which the needed transformation [of interests into fruitful relations] may be accomplished . . . we reach a justification of the statement that philosophy is the theory of education as a deliberately conducted practice" (MW.9.341–342).

As a conscious project of cultures to renew and improve themselves, education transmits and so conserves specifically human life. The
idea that education involves cultural conservation was, of course, hardly
new, but Dewey's regrounding of philosophy in lessons to be learned
with as well as from life (already quite radical) also, and to thoroughgo-
ing transformative effect, entailed his radical democratic egalitarianism. It
was his conviction that *all* people—females as well as males; all racialized,
ethnic, national groups; all classes—are essentially equal, and I believe he
located that equality not just at birth, when we enter human society as
individuals who may or may not be equalized by prevailing custom and
law, but by the birthing that culminates one phase of reproductive renewal even as it initiates its next individual, social, evolutionary phases.

I am stressing the significance of reproduction for Dewey not only
because it is a transactional co-creative relation that serves the continuity
of life in its various forms, but because it does not do so by mere
replication. Reproduction enables the process of improvement through
evolution. I am aware that Dewey himself stressed evolution. However,
not only does evolution depend on reproduction, but what Dewey writes
of evolution can be read as pertaining more aptly to reproduction issuing
in birth as transition into the human species' world. To wit: "For the
doctrine of organic development means that the living creature is a part
of the world, sharing its vicissitudes and fortunes, and making itself
secure in its precious independence only as it intellectually identifies itself
with the things about it, and, forecasting the future consequences of
what is going on, shapes its own activities accordingly" (MW.9.347).

Successful physical, intellectual, individual, species, and social life *is*
adaptively, co-creatively, communicatively reproductive. Its development,
or evolution, conserves through and by successfully relational change;
education, to fulfill its conservationist purpose, should then be designed
with a related aim in view. Dewey writes, "Society not only continues to
exist *by* transmission, *by* communication, but it may fairly be said to exist
in transmission, *in* communication" (MW.9.7). Further, "Not only is all
social life identical with communication, but all communication (and
hence all genuine social life) is educative" (MW.9.8). And here again
Dewey finds grounds for insisting on a radical equality. Unequal relations
such as the "[g]iving and taking of orders," the use of some by others
"without reference to the emotional and intellectual disposition and
consent of those used," "does not . . . effect a sharing of purposes, a
communication of interests" (MW.9.8). Dominance, then, works against
conservation by lessening the ongoing co-creative, communicative transactions that *are* living, whether of individual organisms or social and
political forms. Choosing to lessen the possibilities of vitally multiple,

mutually engaging relations of life in social, political associations that correspond with healthy ecosystems, those who would dominate have chosen stagnation that leads to devolution—the processes of dying rather than living.

Dewey undertook to rethink education not as a limited transmission of the highest achievements of the past from a few to a few, but as discipline of and practice in creative adaptation through solving problems in living for the good of each and for all. Thus, education also became, for him, a process of enhancing living, rather than preparation for life, as if living were something that could be deferred until we, some of us, have been trained and made ready for it. This, Dewey thought, was as absurd as it is pernicious.[2]

Strikingly for Dewey, consciousness, mind, intellect, and the learning they enable remain related to physical life, neither as 'lower' nor 'higher,' nor as 'purer,' but as source of lessons in thriving in concert, beyond mere survival, that may inform our highest ideals and projects, our moralities, arts, and politics. He chose life over death as what we are born to. In so doing, Dewey has disavowed "two-world" schematisms by which humans are divided from and exhorted to elevate themselves above the rest of life as its supposed "masters," a relation of dominance that thereby also divided "Man" (who sometimes reminded himself that he was "of woman born" only to remind himself of shame, and sin) into a mind that was to transcend and master a body. This hierarchy also, of course, underwrote social orders in which those who are educated to live "the life of the mind" are to rule those who are forced to labor productively and reproductively for them. But Dewey wrote, "It is the aim of progressive education to take part in correcting unfair privileges and unfair deprivation, not to perpetuate them" (MW.9.126).

Renewing Language, Thinking, Meanings

Dewey, who is not infrequently charged (always, I confess, to my astonishment) with being a poor writer, is in fact writing very carefully indeed in *Democracy and Education*. If we find the writing awkward, it is because he is trying to renew our thinking by refreshing, shifting, transfiguring meanings. That is, he is himself practicing what he is preaching as he centers his pregnant definitions of life, of experience, of democracy and education in the interesting renewal of meanings that he takes to be the gift of democracy, the essence of morality, and so the proper practice of education that should not undermine but enhance them.

Democracy and Education opens with a line that would seem odd indeed if we had not recognized that Dewey is, at heart, a philosopher of life: "The most notable distinction between living and inanimate things is that the former maintain themselves by renewal" (MW.9.4). This opening is reaffirmed in its transfigured meaning three hundred and fifty-nine pages later with the book's concluding line: "Interest in learning from all the contacts of life is the essential moral interest" (MW.9.370). There we have in a nutshell Dewey's philosophy of life as it may inform a morally aspirational democratic practice of philosophy through education.

Beginning with *life* as a physical process that must "maintain" itself through "renewal," he ends with *life* in the sense of conscious individual and social processes for which the transactions of physical renewal transfigure into renewal through learning. He links such renewing learning with morality, not as a creed, a set of do's and don'ts, but as an egalitarian ("all the contacts of life") "interest." With that word—*interest*—he translates the ongoing physical exchanges with our environment that keep us alive into a virtue we could call respectful attentiveness that is not only actively receptive but dynamically motivated as authentic curiousity (we might say that, for Dewey, curiousity is precisely not "idle"). This is, again, radically, democratically egalitarian. Dewey writes, " 'Life' [which refers also to "a physical thing"] covers customs, institutions, beliefs, victories and defeats, recreations and occupations" (MW.9.5). That is, it "covers"—gathers democratically under a large, open-sided tent—the activities and meanings of our diversely associational lives with which morality must be concerned.

Life is not, then, something we do or do not have (as in that odd phrase, "He lost his life"): living is how we are in the world as it is for us among others. And that, for Dewey, connects life and morality with one of his most familiar and elusive terms, *experience*, which, he also says early in *Democracy and Education*, he uses "in the same pregnant sense" (MW.9.5) as he is using "life." That is, "with [not from: *with*] the renewal of physical existence goes, in the case of human beings, the re-creation of beliefs, ideals, hopes, happiness, misery, and practices" (MW.9.5). We can and should make distinctions among all these terms—life and experience; ideals and hopes; happiness and misery; and between these and practices—but for Dewey we should not confuse these distinctions with divisions to be found in life, which recurrently begins anew. We distinguish but should not divide individual lives from social life: "Every one of the constituent elements of a social group . . . is born immature, helpless, without language, beliefs, ideas, or social standards. Each individual, each unit who is the carrier of the life-experience of his [her] group, in time passes away. Yet the life of the group goes on" (MW.9.5).

Here we encounter reproduction and birth again. Dewey is employing "the word 'experience' in the same pregnant sense" (MW.9.5) as he 'employed' "life." Why "pregnant"? Because "pregnant" is coherent with an emphasis on life, and specifically with its continuity through renewal enabled by co-creative relation. Philosophers and others have long used "pregnant" as a trope, of course: for example, a pregnant silence; a poem pregnant with meaning; a pregnant suggestion, as well as that philosopher's ideal, an impregnable argument (which suggests both resistance to renewal and the male body). Dewey is invoking the physical reproduction of life to remind us of its significance for all humans, and all of human experience. He is also, and thereby, as always radically egalitarian: he is not appropriating pregnancy as a figure for 'higher,' long definitionally masculine, rational, and/or imaginative creation. This is a philosopher of life writing against the grain of traditions that took mortality, or death, rather than natality, or birth, to be "man's" definitive issue ("Man, who is mortal").

Despite the fact that Hannah Arendt later focused her study of the vita activa (the life of action) on the human condition of *natality*, the given that humans are born, recognition of the full human significance of reproduction remains rare (and Dewey himself slid by it en route to evolution). This weird omission is finally changing as feminist works transfigure the old masculinist traditions. But it is striking that Dewey, like feminist moral theorists of care (cf. Ruddick, Gilligan, Tronto, Noddings, and of course Dewey's good friend Jane Addams), remembers that relation precedes individuation; that dependence precedes independence; that the relational needs and obligations of care and nurturance precede individual rights. ("Precede" developmentally, not necessarily by the logic of an ethics—but a philosopher of life will not trump development by any absolutized logic.)

Dewey's choice of the word "renewal" also has, then, a newly "pregnant" sense. We are to hear the "re" and the "new": to realize that the novel does not cancel and replace what was but, rather, recurrently ("re") sustains by revitalizing it (making it "new" again). What is revealed with and through an individual newborn, or "reborn" adult, is the possibility and promise of beginning not again, but anew. Reproduction is not replication. And this, of course, is why Dewey wrote so much about education—not to find ways to control the unruliness of life, the ongoing threat of change from newcomers, but, rather, to connect with and cooperatively direct life's dynamic processes, to renew societies as birth renews the species, as adults may be recurrently reborn through inter/esting, pregnant experiences.

Thus accepting both the challenge and the gift of ongoing development as a philosopher of life who embraces renewal as the ongoing problem and possibility of birth/natality and death/mortality, of beginnings and endings, Dewey saw that necessity turns around to underwrite freedom. We can decide, not to persist in being as individuals (being mortal, that is finally not ours to choose), but to choose life while we can, and to care and provide for social continuity beyond our life span. To do so entails choices: What is to be passed on to the newcomers? By whom? To all, or only to some? In what ways? For what purposes?

Accepting the responsibility that is the gift and burden of such indeterminate choices, Dewey does not turn his attention away from life and experience to seek some transcendent, 'higher' moral guide. He chooses to remain in the space of freedom within which we must judge, choose, and act, the space of life's vulnerable relational indeterminacy within which both moral and political issues arise, and call us together to seek their meanings. He closes *Democracy and Education,* as we have seen, with this: "Interest in learning from all the contacts of life is the essential moral interest" (MW.9.370). He is practicing us in hearing "interest" in its root meaning: *inter* = between, among; *est* = is. *Being among* is how we have our human lives, how we *are*: we live between and among other sustaining as well as threatening experiences; between and among diverse people; between and among richly multiple possible meanings and actions. That is life as it is given to us, as we may choose more or less fully to live it.

What is given for us as developmental physical and social beings informs, but does not dictate, what we can and morally should make of it. The givens of our being, like the past, are prologue, but the play we enact with others will shape them anew while we live, surprising and interesting us ever again like an emerging work of art.

Being true (not submitted) to living life for humans requires that we reject ways of being that are modeled on what is not living. It is not being true to life to seek guidance for living that requires replication rather than renewal; predictability that seeks the warrant not of future efficacy but of control that must reject novelty; singularity rather than plurality; rigid hierarchies of worth that are imposed on the egalitarianism of life's ongoing recreation of new beings. Thus, Dewey uses the term "machine-like" (MW.9.8) simultaneously to characterize and to dismiss moralities, politics, and educational practices he holds to be morally and politically wrong. He writes, "A large number of human relationships in any social group are still upon the machine-like plane," that is, they are "not yet social." "Individuals [on this plane] use one another so as to get desired results. . . . So far as the relations of parent and child, teacher and pupil, employer and employee, governor and governed, remain upon this level, they form no true social group" (MW.9.8).

Dewey is calling us, by his use of language as well as his propositions, to relinquish a static, mechanistic picture of atomistic entities, of individuals abstracted from development, and so definitionally and definitively divided from each other such that they can only be related externally, like the parts of a machine (or the citizens of Hobbes' *Leviathan*). It is for him morally and politically significant that living calls us not to force things, or each other, out of lively relation into divisive orderings, or to treat anyone as no more than a means to a supposedly higher end or purpose (as a part has no value except as it serves to make the machine work).

We should notice, then, that Dewey's philosophy of life rejects the notion that "self-interest" is essentially competitive, entailing struggle, even unto death, among aggressive individuals, societies, or states, over scarce (or even abundant) resources. Instead, he takes the dynamic motivation of our interests, our natural and social interbeing and inter-dependence, to be his dynamic principle. It is "conjoint activity" in which we make our own "the purpose which actuates it" (MW.9.26) that makes life in all its meanings sustainable and fruitful for each as for all. His morality and politics, and the education that transmits and renews them, need not, then, pit themselves against, or embrace, a "natural" drive to compete, each against all. Instead, they can and should enhance vitally co-creative renewal—the rebirthing by which death is not staved off, but transfigured. Just as we saw the interactive relationality of physi-ological life transfigured into Dewey's "essential moral interest," that is, "interest in learning from all the contacts of life," we may see physical death transfigured by a "common faith" that recognizes that "the things in civilization we most prize are not of ourselves. They exist by grace of the doings and sufferings of the continuous human community in which we are a link." And here again is Dewey's deep egalitarianism informing his turn to the principle of pregnant, life-enhancing cooperation. "Ours," he writes, "is the responsibility of conserving, transmitting, rectifying and expanding the heritage of values we have received," not just as we have them, not just for ourselves and our own, but for "those who come after us ... not ... confined to sect, class, or race" (LW.9.57). Need I add that he did not mean that we should transmit even our rectified, ex-panded heritage through domination? Here he was perhaps fiercest of all, railing against a competitive individualism that can become "a cancer in the blind social body; [add] up into the destructive ego-nation, the passive herd or the regimented egomaniac hord," with their "arrogance and complacence" turning "finally into that supreme symbol of our dis-ease; the armaments which are fast becoming the total modern nations."[3] Here his use of "the machine" as figure of non-life reaches its apotheosis in the machinery of killing.

Picturing Dewey's Philosophy of Life in Practice

To be Deweyan, we should reconnect all these rather abstract reflections on what Dewey is about and has to offer us with experiential realities that express ongoing problems of living. I suggest that we picture, first, two classrooms, followed by two ways of relating morally, and then two ways of relating politically. In the first of each of these paired pictures, we will imagine people relating to each other in ways that derive from trying to solve problems of teaching/learning, being moral, or being political posed within an ontology that takes us to be atomistic individuals who can only be related by some externally imposed order—a mechanistic, nonliving model.

In the second pair of pictures, we will imagine people relating as Dewey holds that we both can and should if we understand physical and conscious, cultural life processes as recurrently renewing themselves through mutually sustaining and enhancing relations. In the former set of pictures, the problem that seems to have been solved by those who follow its model is one of maintaining order among divided, discrete entities. In the latter, the problem is how to inform and direct ongoing relations modeled on a Deweyan philosophy of life.

I do recognize that thus pairing alternative pictures may suggest that I am reducing Dewey's organic complexities to a simplistic dualism. That, of course, would be ironic or worse; Dewey was one of history's most trenchant critics of dualistic thinking. Antidualistic thinking does not, however, require us not to make clear distinctions, or to avoid discerning important differences between and among real alternatives. Dewey himself was a passionate advocate of some educational, political, and moral choices over others, so, yes, he did take positions for and against, and invite us to do so, too. Being willing to choose, and even to be in opposition as necessary in the course of things, is not at all the same as being a dualist.

Picturing Classrooms

In our first picture, students sit still at identical desks arranged in neatly ordered rows looking at the same page in the same book under the watchful eye of one teacher, who is proud of having established such good order in this class. These students, the teacher hopes, will do well on the standardized test soon to be given them. "Doing well" means that as many as possible will put down the same correct answers to the same questions. Their reward for doing so will come from the teacher, from their parents, from their society: they will earn the currency of a good grade. When the class ends, the students stand immediately and file quietly out the door, into the hallway, where, if there were not (but there will be) a hall monitor, they would burst into talk and rowdy behavior. Here we have, Dewey says, "the pedagogue's view of life," and we may hear an echo of "the demagogue's view of life." Plurality, the lively differences among the students, is considered a problem. It is to be reduced to sameness. Activity, the expressed liveliness of physical and social beings experiencing the world in which they are naturally interested, is also considered a problem. It is to be reduced to stillness. All the generative energy is to come from the teacher; the students are to receive, to take in, to store, to replicate.

In this class, not thinking but, rather, as Dewey puts it, a "perfected" form of knowledge that has been reduced by professionals in the field to "topics according to the order of the specialty," then simplified by textbook writers, and perhaps still further simplified and ordered by experts in learning and age-appropriate curricula, is presented to students who are to "copy at long range and second hand the results which [such experts] have reached" (MW.9.228). Memorization of results obtained by others has replaced the activity of original discovery. The reward for learning is not inherent in the quest and satisfaction of successful inquiry, but added on in the form of extrinsic reward, backed by threat of equally extrinsic punishment, creating a situation Dewey bluntly calls "corrupting" of character. Why "corrupting"? Because what the students are learning is to seek a reward from people who are in power regardless of their own judgment of the intrinsic merit and satisfaction, or lack thereof, of what they must do to earn that reward. They are being trained to work for bribes.

In the second classroom, students stand and sit and move around, and the teacher moves among them, now with this cluster of students cooperating on their project, now with that one. The students are trying to solve a problem designed by the teacher to be of genuine personal interest to them because it connects with their ongoing lives. They are helping each other figure out what to do, looking in their books for help, using the materials—from scissors to computers to theories—the teacher has provided. When the class period ends, they do not want to stop, so engaged, so interested, are they. The problem that has been solved in this classroom is not how to control lively, differing students so that learning can be put into their minds despite their lack of intrinsic interest in it. It is how to connect with and enhance their lively natural, social interests by helping them learn how to pursue them effectively.

Picturing Moral Relations

Then shift to two analogous pictures of people being moral (I know: that seems odd, but let's try it). In the first, people are behaving in disciplined ways, controlling themselves to keep from deviating from moral dicta specifying what "good people" do. When they do well, they all do pretty much the same things in the same ways, and their reward, should they receive any, comes after the fact (like a bribe). They are praised by an authority, and perhaps given some authority over "less good" people—or they are punished for their failure to measure up, and submitted to tighter controls. Few make it; most fall all too often into loose talk and rowdy behavior that infuriates The Good who are struggling to contain their own "animal" energy. This we might call the dogmatist's view of life. Here, as in the pedagogue's view, people are to copy "at long range and second hand" a 'perfected' creed created in the past. They, too, are to become more alike: differences, after all, can only be deviance and deficit when the right way to behave is already known.

In the second picture, people are trying to cooperate with each other in finding creative ways to solve problems of living that are afflicting some among them. Each recognizes that such problems also limit them. They are concerned, too, with problems that efforts among differing people to cooperate entail. Those who do well are those who see beyond prevailing definitions of any immediate problem, and whose thinking and empathy and imagination are neither blocked nor deformed by prevailing socioeconomic systems that rank and divide people. They can imagine solutions, locate resources, make effective plans, and think through far-reaching consequences not only of the problem but also of possible solutions that they know will and should never be final. The reward for those who thus engage fully with meliorative efforts is intrinsic to what they do and how they are doing it with others. A good person, Dewey says, both "gets and gives . . . not external possessions but a widening and deepening of conscious life—a more intense, disciplined, and expanding realization of meanings" (MW.9.369). "And education," he underscores, "is not a mere means to such a life. Education is such a life" (MW.9.369). Or, it is such a life when and insofar as it enhances our interest in all the contacts of life, and thereby realizes what we have already heard Dewey calling "the essential moral interest."

Political Pictures

I should not need to connect these pictures to public, political life: the translation is obvious and, for Dewey, always already made, if sometimes for good, sometimes for ill. Nevertheless, because education has for so long protected itself against being "politicized," we should make the translation explicit. It is central to the book Dewey called, after all, *Democracy and Education.*

Our first political picture is of people reduced to sameness and silence by externally imposed, forcibly maintained order that reaches into all corners of their lives. They do not gather to communicate with each other: we see them as faceless members of mass rallies reduced to cheering and chanting on cue. They do not join together to act; we see them marching in lockstep or scuttling down streets as anonymously as possible. We can call this picture, as Dewey did, the totalitarian, or demagogue's, view of life.

On the other hand, we have the picture Dewey paints in "Creative Democracy—The Task Before Us." In it, we see "free gatherings of neighbors on the street corner to discuss back and forth what is read in uncensored news of the day, and in gatherings of friends in the living rooms of houses and apartments to converse freely with one another" (LW.14.227). Of this picture, Dewey says, "I am inclined to believe that [it is] the heart and final guarantee of democracy." It is also the heart and guarantee of education. Dewey writes, "The measure and worth of the administration, curriculum, and methods of instruction of the school is the extent to which they are animated by a social spirit" such that "intercourse, communication, and cooperation—all [extend] the perception of connections" (MW.9.368). And this, which comes at the end of *Democracy and Education,* also refers us back to his beginning, where he wrote, "Society exists through a process of transmission quite as much as biological life" (MW.9.6). Here, we notice his careful word choices again: Dewey does not say, society uses, or must have, a "process of transmission." He says, "Society exists through" such a renewing process. It *is as* that process, and each society has its identity and is more or less enlivened intellectually, morally, and politically in the degree to which its characteristic formal and informal education is democratically communicative.

Connecting with Experience: A Teaching Story

I recently convened an interdisciplinary graduate seminar called "Thinking and Moral Considerations" that I designed to facilitate a shareable experience of thinking *with* as well as *about* the highly engaged political philosopher Hannah Arendt. (Arendt's biographer, Elisabeth Young-Bruehl, aptly titled her book, *For Love of the World.*) I was blessed to have an extraordinary group of participants in the seminar, but there was one—I'll call him Max—who troubled me from the first day. Fortunately,

I remembered that Dewey says, "Thinking includes . . . the sense of a problem" (MW.9.148). Well, I had one in Max.

Max is a doctoral student with an M.A. in psychology who is presently employed as a business consultant on consumer behavior. Early on, he informed us that he *knows* "how we think," and so found what Arendt (and Plato, Shakespeare, and Kant, among others Arendt cites) has to say about thinking to be uninformed, sloppy, and wrong. "Who," asked a woman who teaches theater and was clearly thinking also of her community work with the homeless, "is the 'we' you have in mind when you say you know how 'we think'?" Max was puzzled. "I mean," she said, "who was studied by your experts? Was everybody in the world studied? If not, who was in the sample?" Max, despite claiming to be a good empiricist, waved away the question: "It doesn't matter anymore," he said. "This is known; it's been known for maybe seventeen years now. It's true."

For most of the seminar, Max appeared to remain in what Plato, whom Arendt quotes prominently, called a "dream of certainty" that left Max puzzled, at best, that we so evidently were not going to submit to his truths. Dewey would have seen Max's certainty that he knew how "we" think both as indication of his limited experiences with people unlike himself and as a confusion of the proper relation of thinking and knowledge. "While all thinking results in knowledge," Dewey writes, "ultimately the value of knowledge is subordinate to its use in thinking. For we live not in a settled and finished world, but in one which is going on, and where our main task is prospective" (MW.9.148).

Dewey characterizes what appears to be the teaching principle in Max's approach this way: it "emphasizes the unique role of subject matter. . . . According to it, education is . . . instruction taken in a strictly literal sense, a building into the mind from without" (MW.9.75). Notice that Dewey is renewing meanings again: we are to experience afresh the difference between "in/struction" and "inter/esting." Dewey then observes that this unidirectional relationship (for him, as we have seen, a presocial one), in which a designing teacher seeks to shape a moldable mind, is "the pedagogue's view of life" we saw in our first picture of a classroom because it "is almost silent regarding [the student's] privilege of learning" (MW.9.77). In disregarding the present experience of learning, it focuses instead "upon the old, the past," and so "passes lightly over the operation of the genuinely novel and unforeseeable" (MW.9.77). Dewey, by contrast, suggests that we learn to practice with our students an artful, free (rather than submissive) "grace of intelligence" (MW.9.159) that can aim to renew and ameliorate a transitive present. And he holds that such intelligence is both needed to guide, and is enlarged and enlivened by, the ongoing engagement of many minds genuinely cooperating with each other in "conjoint," or mutually engaging activity. Nothing static or unidirectional in this picture.

True to his own method, however, Dewey does not simply dismiss theories of education that he disagrees with. In *Democracy and Education,* he conserves influential past theories by discerning what was once apt but now needs to be renewed. In this spirit, I tried to draw Max into thinking with us by asking him to tell us his 'truths,' and then asking questions I hoped would engage him in thinking with us about, and not only from within, them—questions such as, "What kind of thinking were you doing when you tried just now to communicate what you know to us?" It didn't work: Max retreated behind his laptop. He knew how to tell us things, and he knew how to take in what we told him, but he didn't know how to engage with us in thinking.

Our problem seemed to be getting worse. If Dewey would see it as deriving from Max's training in "retrospective" knowledge and his consequent lack of interest in the "prospective" thinking that engages us across social and other barriers, and, indeed, with "all the contacts of life," Arendt—the subject of the seminar—might have seen it as "thoughtlessness." In her essay "On Thinking and Moral Considerations," and in *Eichmann in Jerusalem: A Report on the Banality of Evil,* which we also discussed at length (before and after we had the troubling, and so thought-provoking, experience of viewing a video of Eichmann's trial), Arendt depicts thoughtlessness as being enclosed inside accepted conceptualizations, clichés, conventions such that we admit of no challenges to them, whether from experience, from other people, from other ideas and other fields, or from the questioning activity of thinking itself. It is this lack of the reflective, representative, prospective thinking that holds us open to engagement with others and the worlds we share, Arendt concluded, that enables "the banality of evil."

You can see, I'm sure, why Max was troubling to me. He gave no indication that he could or would explore the connections among thinking, engagement with others and the world, knowledge, and morality the others found so interesting. Perhaps this was because he took *his*—but, as he could well have assumed, not Eichmann's—authoritative truths and closed language games to be *scientific.* But we discussed that, too. A lab scientist, a physiologist, who was also at the seminar, described the scientific method in good Deweyan terms as a way *not* to achieve thereafter irrefuteable knowledge, but, on the contrary, as a way to keep inquiry going—to keep it "prospective," as Dewey put it. This practicing scientist spoke also of the anomalies, the novelties, for which he is always on the lookout, and of how important they are. Max shrugged; no anomalies, no startling challenges, left in his field; "trust me," he said, "it works every time."

Need I say that by this point I was having some trouble seeing Max as the unique individual he is, rather than as an exemplar of the kind of unthinking against which both Arendt and Dewey were trying to warn us? But I did find Max interesting—how could I not, given the focus of this seminar?—so I didn't give up.

I started worrying about whether I, and we, were failing to communicate in ways that took the real individual Max adequately into account such that he could engage more openly and fully with us. That is, the problem of Max called me back to the real heart of *Democracy and Education*, in which, as I have noted, Dewey reflects on processes of transmission, and especially the experience of communicating. He writes:

> Try the experiment of communicating, with fullness and accuracy, some experience to another, especially if it be somewhat complicated, and you will find your own attitude toward your experience changing. . . . The experience has to be formulated in order to be communicated. To formulate requires getting outside of it, seeing it as another would see it, considering what points of contact it has with the life of another. . . . Except in dealing with commonplaces and catch phrases, one has to assimilate, imaginatively, something of another's experience in order to tell him [or her] intelligently of one's own experience. (MW.9.8)

Notice that Dewey refers us to an experience recast as a thought experiment so that we may discover afresh and for ourselves what it means. The equalizing mutuality of thinking involved in such experiences and thought experiments is crucial to Dewey, I believe, because it continually revitalizes the practices of communicative transmission without which there is no renewing continuity.

It is because, and when, we experience our ability to question, to see from differing perspectives, to step outside of and reflect on our own thinking and knowledge and conventions that we become able to be morally responsible. Thinking, I will then say, is the gift we have that underlies and realizes an experience of the freedom of mind without which no other kind of freedom is literally conceivable. This is why, for Dewey, classrooms in which differing people gather to learn are also pictures of moral and political relations as they are, and in the making.

Hannah Arendt, the subject of our seminar, had had far more dramatic occasions than having Max as a student to experience failures of engaged thinking, but she knew them to be not uncommon. Sounding increasingly like John Dewey to me as, fretting about Max, I held him in mind, she wrote:

> We see how unwilling the human mind is to face realities which . . . contradict . . . its framework of reference. Unfortunately, it seems to be much easier to condition human behavior than it is to persuade anybody to learn from experience . . . that is, to start thinking and judging instead of applying categories and formulas which are deeply ingrained in our mind, but whose basis of experience has long been forgotten [i.e., which are, as Dewey says all knowledge is, retrospective] and whose plausibility resides in their intellectual consistency rather than in their adequacy to actual events. (2003, p. 37)

Should I have despaired? There are grounds for despair, as history and our own contemporary experiences in these times of renewed efforts to enforce the kinds of educational, moral, and political relations we saw in the non-Deweyan pictures we earlier explored. But I realized that John Dewey, as if in response, wrote of his faith not in any actual government, or in any one method of teaching, but in the aspirational moral ideal of a democracy of thinking people of all ages engaging in ongoing free communication with each other. It is this vision, I believe, that informs all his work:

> Democracy is belief in the ability of human experience to generate the aims and methods by which further experience will grow in ordered richness. Every other form of moral and social [and educational] faith rests upon the idea that experience must be subjected at some point or other to some form of external control; to some 'authority' alleged to exist outside the processes of experience. . . . Since the process of experience is capable of being educative, faith in democracy is all one with faith in experience and education. . . . The task of democracy is forever that of creation of a freer and more humane experience in which all share and to which all contribute. (LW.14.229)

With Dewey in mind, faced with Max, I was (well, mostly) able to keep the faith by treating him with interest and respect just as the other participants did. We all talked and listened in turn, questioning each other and the materials we drew on—books and papers, videos and poems, cartoons, drawings, and newspaper articles I and others brought for our own, daily growing, library. We also regularly drew on our differing political and moral values as well as our differing professions and academic fields as we practiced thinking about thinking as it is, and enables, engagement with the world.

On our last day, Max said to me, "I'm sorry if I was too opposi-
tional. I still don't know about all this, but I've never heard so many
different perspectives and I'll think about them." He also told me that
he realized he needed to renew the history he had studied. "I thought
I knew about World War II," he said, "but I didn't know anything about
what we talked about here." And recently, an artist and teacher of art in
the seminar told me that Max said to her, before he left, "Will you help
me understand art? I need to become more imaginative."

Whether he understood our subject or not, Max, I now dare to
think, had experienced it through what we did together and how we did
it because he had found us odd enough to startle him back into thought:
we interested him. And, as I have thought further, I have been startled
to realize that what Max had finally discerned from behind his laptop was
strikingly apt, and true to what Dewey taught. Let me close with the
renewed insight Max left us with, first in the words of John Dewey in
Art as Experience, then of the theater teacher. The last word I will give
to *Democracy and Education*.

The Dewey quote is from *Art as Experience*, which, as Max reminded me, is an important complement to *Democracy and Education*:

> The first intimations of wide and large redirections of desire and
> purpose are of necessity imaginative. Art is a mode of prediction
> not found in charts and statistics, and it insinuates possibilities
> of human relations not to be found in rule and precept, admo-
> nition and administration ... "Art may tell a truth/ Obliquely,
> do the deed shall breed the thought." (LW.10.351–352)

Drawing on her own lively interests, knowledge, imagination, and experiences as she engaged with the miniature society of our seminar, the
theater teacher came to her own original understanding. She wrote:

> On day one of the seminar ... after introductions, the seminar
> convenor ... read aloud from three poems by Auden—"The
> Unknown Citzen," "September 1, 1939," and "#48 (Law is)."
> I realized then how valuable it can be to begin adult learning
> experiences with the reading and discussing of poetry. It stimu-
> lates imaginative activity, evokes experiences, and exposes mul-
> tiple dimensions of meaning ... I could feel how it opened a
> space for me to search for my own associations and relevance.
> This was not only a valuable exercise in making distinctions and
> proliferating meanings but an exhilarating way to begin a group
> adventure into thinking about thinking.

I believe her understanding would have pleased Dewey. Had he been with us in our class, I can imagine him saying, in response and recognition, something he once wrote that I think clarifies how, for a philosopher of life, learning, imagination, and significance are indeed mutually creative, sustaining, renewing:

> Only a personal response involving imagination can possibly pro-cure realization even of pure 'facts.' The imagination is the medium of appreciation in every field. The engagement of the imagination is the only thing that makes any activity more than mechanical. . . . In so far as any study has a unique or irre-placeable function in experience, in so far as it marks a charac-teristic enrichment of life, its worth is intrinsic or incomparable. Since education is not a means to living, but is identical with the operation of living a life which is fruitful and inherently signifi-cant, the only ultimate value which can be set up is just the process of living itself. . . . And what has been said about appre-ciation means that every study . . . ought to have just such ulti-mate significance. (MW.9.224, 9.248)

Notes

1. Dewey is at pains to be clear in *Democracy and Education* that he is not a "back to nature" philosopher of life. Discussing Rousseau, for a key ex-ample, he writes, "The natural, or native, powers furnish the initiating and lim-iting forces in all education; they do not furnish its ends or aims. There is no learning except from a beginning in unlearned powers, but learning is not a matter of the spontaneous overflow of the unlearned powers" (MW.9.121).

2. Compare chapter 5 of *Democracy and Education*, "Preparation, Un-folding, and Formal Discipline," in which we find, for example, "Specific evil effects . . . result from" the educational aim of "getting ready for some future duty or privilege," which, Dewey argues, "defeats its own professed purpose" (MW.9.73).

3. John Dewey, *The Political Writings*, edited by Debra Morris and Ian Shapiro. Indianapolis/Cambridge: Hackett, 1993, p. 23)

References

Dewey, John. (1993). In Debra Morris and Ian Shapiro (Eds.), *The political writings*. Indianapolis/Cambridge: Hackett Publishing Company.

Arendt, Hannah. (1971). Thinking and moral considerations: A lecture, *Social Research, 38*(3), 417–446.

Arendt, Hannah. (2003). In Jerome Kohn (Ed.), *Responsibility and Judgment*. New York: Schocken Books.

10

Dewey's Book of the Moral Self

DAVID T. HANSEN

Dewey closes *Democracy and Education* with this penultimate statement: "Interest in learning from all the contacts of life is the essential moral interest" (p. 370[1]). The fact that Dewey bookends the sentence with the term "interest" symbolizes its dynamic place in his wide-ranging inquiry. For Dewey, interest and self boil down to two names for the same fact: "The kind and amount of interest actively taken in a thing reveals and measures the quality of selfhood which exists" (pp. 361–362). It is equally noteworthy that the phrase, "the contacts of life," resides at the center of his closing words. That feature mirrors Dewey's focus throughout the text on the quality of human interaction: how it is conducted, perceived, expanded, and enriched. The sentence as a whole summarizes Dewey's vision of the finest outcome of education, namely, a human being willing and able to engage intelligently and ethically with a changing world.

Dewey's concluding words may be inspirational, but they are not easy to live by. As he surely knows, his final sentence constitutes a sentence of another sort. Dewey implies that if persons are to realize their full humanity, and if they are to support others in that process, they must be in close contact with the world. They must be willing to address "all the contacts of life" whether these be pleasant or painful, happy or sad, fulfilling or frustrating, joyful or tragic. Posed differently, "contacts" often lead to conflicts, and Dewey contends that people must be willing to learn from *all* of them, which means engaging *all* of them, which means not withdrawing or fleeing from *any* of them. That "interest,"

Dewey concludes, is "essential." To enact their full humanity, people have no alternative, or so it seems, but to accept the sentence.

Why does Dewey place such weight on this viewpoint? Why does he close his book with an urgent claim whose commanding tone echoes Kant's categorical imperative? (Dewey retained a lifelong respect for Kant's philosophy—he wrote his doctoral dissertation on Kant's ethics—even though he differed sharply with its underlying premises.) In a famous formulation of the imperative, it states that, in all that we do, we should treat others as ends in themselves, never merely as means to our own ends (Kant, 1985/1785, p. 45). That ideal mirrors Dewey's notion of *learning* from all our contacts with others, a posture that seems to presume treating them as ends. After all, Dewey does not speak of interest in *using* all our contacts to serve our purposes, and it is striking that he refers to learning from others as a "moral" interest.

Dewey selects his terms with care. The initial chapter titles in the book feature "as" rather than "is"—for example, "Education as a Necessity" rather than "Education is a Necessity." The difference is more than semantic. Dewey wants to avoid preachy, hard-and-fast definitions of education, hoping instead to draw readers into an inquiry. However, his final words in the book pivot around the emphatic verb "is." That verb choice is paired with the equally insistent term "essential" with all its connotations of both necessity and significance. Dewey bears down on readers with a powerful normative message: to live fully, we are sentenced to a particular mode of education. Our education resides "in" learning from all the contacts of life; Dewey intends the preposition literally. If we succeed in that, or at least attempt to do so, then we can be said to be leading not just a life but a moral life. We can be said to have become moral selves.

To rephrase the questions posed earlier, Why does Dewey conclude his long inquiry by underscoring the ideas of interest, learning, and the moral, especially since other concepts such as growth, experience, and democracy loom large in the book? Why does he bequeath us, as his parting act, with an image of the moral self? In responding to these questions, I will approach *Democracy and Education* as falling within a long-standing philosophical and educational tradition centered around what various writers have called "the art of living" (see, e.g., Nehamas, 1998). That term highlights the quest to fashion a life rich in meaning (but not necessarily in material goods), substantive in accomplishment (but not necessarily in fashionable or popular ways), and worthy of esteem (but not necessarily with respect to visible rewards or public praise). Dewey believes the art of living and the art of democracy are symbiotic.

Neither is fully realizable without the other. As we will see, perhaps it is art rather than prescription that is at play in his final sentence.

To interpret Dewey's image of the moral self, I begin by locating its origins in Ralph Waldo Emerson's idea of reception. Emerson describes an educational orientation through which people learn to "receive" life's gifts. With this background in view, I turn next to an analysis of how and why Dewey fuses the concepts of interest and self. He roots his philosophical anthropology in an ecological vision of human experience. The fusion of self and interest mirrors his familiar rejection of dualisms such as those between mind and body, person and world, and the like. In the final section, I examine how Dewey's merger of self and interest metamorphoses into an image of the moral self. The qualifier moral becomes decisive for Dewey as he tackles the question of what kind of education, and what kind of selves, both emerge from and make possible a democratic way of life. I conclude the chapter by reconsidering briefly the demanding quality of Dewey's ideal and whether it is inhabitable.

An Emersonian Origin of Dewey's Conception of the Self

Dewey's final chapter in *Democracy and Education* is entitled "Theories of Morals." The previous two chapters center, respectively, on "Philosophy of Education" and "Theories of Knowledge." Together, the three chapters both sum up the book and generate a platform from which Dewey surveys historic claims about the nature of philosophy, knowledge, and the moral. He argues that philosophy, or the pursuit and love of wisdom, is another name for the general theory of education. That is, philosophy fundamentally springs from questions regarding human and societal formation. Dewey argues a pragmatist view of knowledge, suggesting that knowledge in actual life functions as a verb rather than as a noun. It has nothing to do with so-called ultimate reality, and everything to do with the quality of life. Knowledge describes human conduct *in* the world rather than what is stored inertly, whether in encyclopedias or in the head. The latter would be better described as information and facts, which for Dewey differ functionally from knowledge. Information and facts are meaningless, if not also confusing and distracting, unless they operate within knowing and doing.

In keeping with these down-to-earth perspectives, Dewey argues in his final chapter that the idea of the moral points to an associative mode of human interaction. I employ the qualifier associative mindful that he conceives democracy as "more than a form of government; it is primarily a mode of associated living, of conjoint communicated experience" (p. 93). The associative mode supports in every way possible each human being's growth, while it also draws from each human being the best that he or she can provide to others. Communication and expressivity, or personal style, characterize the mode of interaction. In the way of life Dewey envisions, persons do not exchange merely physical materials, including their labor, as much as that will always be a part of any functioning society. Rather, individuals leading a moral life give their best imagination, their best hopes, their best creativity, their best listening, their best responsiveness, to "all the contacts of life." What they take in the course of such a life constitutes more than just goods and services. It transcends that everyday market image of human interaction. From "all the contacts of life," persons take inspiration, courage, ideas, determination, hope, delight, humility, dedication, resolve, strength, and more. As Dewey puts it, people give and take not just "external possessions, but a widening and deepening of conscious life—a more intense, disciplined, and expanding realization of meanings" (p. 369).

Thus, for Dewey communication and expressivity literally constitute the associative mode of interaction. Human beings give their best and take the best from others through all their ways of doing in work and in play. In Dewey's idealistic vision, the latter are transformed from mere customary or habituated activity into artful communication and contribution. In that process, conscious rather than thoughtless life expands. Deliberate rather than routine or casual life widens and deepens. Experience becomes more intense rather than more shallow; it becomes more disciplined, or focused, rather than distracted; and it grows rather than diminishes in meaning.

In crafting this outlook, Dewey took inspiration from—in the sense of being in-spirited by—a writer whom he described as "the philosopher of democracy," Ralph Waldo Emerson (MW.3.184–192). In essays such as "Experience" and "The Over-Soul," Emerson describes a mode of being marked by what he calls reception. In that mode, a person is neither a mere spectator of life, as if he or she were a passive receptacle, nor a mere tool or cog in nature's inexorable wheel of time. In the receptive mode, a person does not grasp experience as a consumable item, nor treat it as a series of discrete events to be categorized or logged according to some conventional accounting system, as if living was reducible to a resume or curriculum vitae. To be receptive means taking in from others and from experience all that was referred to in the previous paragraphs: courage, heart, inventiveness, ideas, hope, and faith in possibilities. Emerson says such things are not "gotten" as if they were goods off a shelf. They cannot be purchased or borrowed. They are received if people learn to listen, to heed, to be open, and to believe there is a *quality* that life can have rather than being formed solely by various quantities (this home, that car, these clothes, that city, this college degree, that job, etc.). "All I know is reception," writes Emerson; "I am and I have: but I do not get, and when I have fancied I had gotten anything, I found I did not" (1983/1844, p. 491).

For Emerson, the impulse to want to grasp the world and keep it still may feel natural, but it is a will-o-the-wisp. That which we "clutch hardest" will most swiftly slip out of our hands (p. 473). Experience is not a program through which to grasp and hold the world. Posed differently, experience is not a means for coming to know things and other people in a clairvoyant sense. Human beings are not constituted with a god-like insight (if they were, their humanity would instantly disappear). What people can come to know with assurance is reception. They can know that they are in debt to life for life itself, and for bringing in its train all that we name nature, love, family, community, art, and more. They may "have" all these and more if they dwell in a receptive mode. More strongly, they may *become* all these things and more. Rather than "getting" love, they can be love; rather than "getting" art, they can be artful; rather than "getting" an education, they can be educated. Emerson's verb choice "is"—"all I know is reception"—fuses knowing and being.

Emerson's viewpoint foreshadows Dewey's emphasis on learning from "all the contacts of life" as contrasted with merely using them strategically. The idea of experience as receptivity also anticipates Dewey's emphasis on what he calls "readiness to learn." That capacity marks a person poised to engage all the contacts of life. In *How We Think*, a book addressed primarily to teachers, Dewey writes:

> No one can think about everything, [and] no one can think about *any*thing without experience and information about it. Nevertheless, there is such a thing as *readiness* to consider in a thoughtful way the subjects that do come within the range of experience—a readiness that contrasts strongly with the disposition to pass judgment on the basis of mere custom, tradition, prejudice, etc., and thus shun the task of thinking. (LW.8.139)

Dewey adds that the "essential constituents" of this general readiness are open-mindedness, wholeheartedness, and responsibility, which he describes in that book as "personal attitudes" and "moral traits." In *Democracy and Education*, he continues to call these same attitudes—to which he adds a fourth named directness—moral traits (pp. 366–367), but he also dubs them "traits of method" (pp. 180–187). They define readiness to learn. They grease the doorways and paths of reception.

Open-mindedness denotes the willingness to consider the new and the unfamiliar. Dewey underscores its active quality; to be open-minded does not mean to be empty-minded or a merely passive receptacle. On the contrary, an open-minded person merges curiosity, wonder, and respect into an active receptivity to new points of view, to new outlooks, and to new ways of thinking and knowing. Wholeheartedness describes the willingness and desire to engage fully in a task or activity. Where a halfhearted person may give up quickly in the face of challenge, a wholehearted individual remains absorbed, immersed, engrossed, and as best as possible sees the activity or task through to completion. Responsibility points to the willingness to accept the consequences of thought and inquiry. That attitude does not entail agreeing with or blindly acting on whatever those consequences may be. However, a responsible person does face up to them, and takes action accordingly rather than ignoring them. Dewey suggests that responsible persons consider the *meaning* of what has been learned, with regards to "what difference it makes to the rest of their beliefs and to their actions" (LW.8.138). Finally, directness implies faith in human action. This faith does not mean confidence per se (much less hubris), but rather an attitude that it is worthwhile addressing problems rather than being resigned to them. Moreover, directness means tackling problems with "sureness" (p. 181), with all the energies, resources, and focus at one's disposal, and not letting oneself be easily sidetracked or diverted. "Taking an attitude is by no means identical with being conscious of one's attitude," Dewey writes. "The former is spontaneous, naive, and simple. It is a sign of whole-souled relationship between a person and what he is dealing with" (p. 181).

Dewey describes these qualities as both traits of method and as moral traits because he regards them as aspects of both intellect and character. The qualities position a person to inquire and to grow. In this light, they function as methods of approaching life and learning from it. At the same time, for Dewey, the qualities are moral in that they literally form human character in a particular direction. They help characterize what he calls "the moral self." On the one hand, they function as attitudes that predispose the person to inquire and to learn in the first place. On the other hand, they fuel democratic sociability—the willingness to interact meaningfully with others who may differ in outlook and belief. Dewey's concept of readiness to learn is constituted by the moral traits touched on here and remains central to his perspective on the meaning of education. It sheds light on why he concludes *Democracy and Education* by describing an interest in learning from all life's contacts as the essential moral interest.

Interest, Situations, and Selves

To Emerson's statement that "All I know is reception," Dewey would reply, "All I am and have is what I learn from the contacts of life." That process depends on what Dewey calls "interest," a concept he introduces formally in chapter 10. His analysis falls between chapters devoted, respectively, to aims in education and to the nature and relation between experience and thinking. Aims provide direction rather than leaving human activity up to chance or random forces. Experience and thinking are where aims come alive and begin to be realized in the world. In chapter 10, Dewey emphasizes the centrality of the person or self as a kinetic agent in the transforming process of thought, experience, and action guided by aims.

Interest is a name for what Dewey describes as a "double" attitude on the part of a person engaged in life. On the one side, there is "solicitude" or concern regarding future consequences of particular acts and events. On the other side, there is intent and energy "to assure better, and avert worse, consequences" (p. 131). Thus, the double attitude of an interested person differs from the empty or null attitude of the mere spectator, for whom outcomes are indifferent and of no concern. Dewey acknowledges that people often equate interest and concern with personal preference. The concept preference reflects an economic picture of the world, with producers and consumers on one side and a world of consumable products on the other. Dewey parts company with that reductionist view of the relation between selves and world. In broad terms, he rejects the dualistic picture that self and mind have a separate existence from the world of events. Concepts like interest and concern, he argues, "suggest that a person is bound up with the possibilities inhering in objects. . . . [Interest and concern] are always attitudes toward *objects*— toward what is foreseen. We may call the phase of objective foresight intellectual, and the phase of personal concern emotional and volitional, but there is no separation *in* [my emphasis] the facts of the situation" (p. 131). Dewey's verbs "bound up" and "inhere" evoke the organic bonds between self and world. Quite literally, for Dewey, the self is bound to the world and has no existence apart from it.

More concretely, the self *emerges* or *finds expression* through interacting with "objects," by which Dewey denotes everything from a car racing toward us at a crossroads, to a book we take in hand to read, to a friend we call to set a time for a rendezvous, to an image of a garden we'd like to plant, and more. World and objects, which include the self, are coterminous. Dewey avers that we can employ language for heuristic purposes to distinguish "phases" of our experience, from the reflective to the emotional and volitional. For purposes of inquiry and understanding, this heuristic move can yield important dividends. However, *in* the actual experience of life's situations, the phases form part of a continuous whole. They are not separated.

"Such a separation," Dewey goes on to say in a key passage,

> could exist only if the personal attitudes [of interest and concern] ran their course in a world by themselves. But they are always responses to what is going on in the situation of which they are a part, and their successful or unsuccessful expression depends upon their interaction with other changes. Life activities flourish and fail only in connection with changes of the environment. They are literally bound up with these changes; our desires, emotions, and affections are but various ways in which our doings are tied up with the doings of things and persons about us. Instead of marking a purely personal or subjective realm, separated from the objective and impersonal, they indicate the non-existence of such a separate world. They afford convincing evidence that changes in things are not alien to the activities of a self, and that the career and welfare of the self are bound up with the movement of persons and things. Interest, concern, mean that self and world are engaged with each other in a developing situation. (p. 132)

Dewey repeats his verb "bound up" and weds to it the verb "tied up," thereby underscoring the organic connection between person and world. He also repeats the term "situation," a concept whose meaning comes to light if we contrast it with two others in Dewey's ecological lexicon. According to Dewey, my "surroundings" include everything and anything that may affect my existence as a living creature. My "environment," however, consists of only those things that factor into a course of sustained action within my surroundings. For example, if I am a teacher, my environment includes the students and subject matter I teach, the school in which I work, the colleagues with whom I interact, and so forth. This environment differs from my surroundings. The public transportation I take in the morning and afternoon, what I eat for dinner, the brand of light bulbs I use in the bathroom, and a countless array of other objects, are not part of my environment as a teacher even though they do constitute my surroundings as a living being. The distinction is not hard and fast. In principle, any element of my surroundings could become a part of my environment. For example, I may take pains to prepare a particularly healthy dinner one evening because I'm worried about getting under the weather and don't want to miss a day in school. Through reflection and foresight, the dinner has metamorphosed into an element in my environment as teacher.

"Situations" figure prominently in Dewey's discussion of self and interest because they constitute the fabric of lived experience in environments. They are the medium in which, and through which, people engage objects. Dewey has in view an image of a human life as a more or less continuous process of entering, transforming, and leaving scenes of activity. For example, a student in my second period history class asks me a question about the document we're studying, and I move to respond. We have simultaneously created and entered a situation. The "we," however, includes more than the student and myself. It includes every other student who has overheard the question, it includes the question, it includes the document, it includes whatever transpired right before the posing of the question that in one way or another created the very possibility of the action, it includes the environmental circumstances that have licensed the student to speak and me to listen, and much, much more. It includes the student's prior learning as a student of history, as a student in my classroom, as a student in this school, and, once more, the list goes on. Dewey would contend that the student and I have no selfhood whatsoever outside of these situations. Literally, we do not *live* in the past or future; we live only in the present moment. In that moment, we can project a future—for example, an upcoming essay assignment and how the study of the document figures into it. In that same moment, we can draw on the past—our memories of a previous discussion of a similar kind of text. Nonetheless, all projecting and all remembrance take form in the present moment.

Moreover, the quality of the situations humans create, enter, transform, and leave, will influence formatively their very constitution as persons. A wide variety and richness of objects and environmental conditions will make possible situations that fund the self in substantial ways, fueling its growth so that in all subsequent situations it has greater resources and energies to bring to bear, thereby generating an ascending spiral of experience and quality of life. In other words, the more the self can infuse into a situation, the richer the situation, and the richer the possible incremental transformation of the self. This outcome will be that much more assured if situations increasingly feature greater infusions from the world by way of objects, including other selves enjoying a comparable experience.

On the other side, where the grass is not greener but dried out, an impoverished environment marked by limited objects will have a correspondingly diminishing effect on what Dewey calls "the career and welfare" of the self. Dewey's intense awareness of this important and fateful fact (or so it is to him) constitutes a driving energy behind *Democracy and Education*. Dewey is outraged by his societal surroundings, which thwart or cripple the life chances of many persons. He is inspired by a vision of how to reconstruct environments as a mode, on the one hand, of slowly transforming surroundings, and, on the other hand, of generating conditions for fruitful situations.

According to Dewey, the self dwells in situations, and it is through them that it substantiates, literally, its very identity as a self, as a person. At the same time, it is through the medium of interest that the self engages in situations or meets and transforms the world (however modestly), and thereby grows as a self. Through the self's agency, the world becomes a scene of facts and objects. Prior to human conduct, the world is, so to speak, a pure expression of chemical, biological, geological, atmospheric, and other forces. But that world becomes transformed when the self interacts with it in ways that convert raw surroundings into environments and situations. The latter are distinctively human contributions to the known universe (even while physical forces continue to operate within them, variously constraining and liberating the scope of human affairs). "The developing course of action," Dewey writes at the end of chapter 10, "whose end and conditions are perceived, is the unity which holds together what are often divided into an independent mind on one side and an independent world of objects and facts on the other" (p. 145). Self and world reside together in situations, in developing courses of action. For Dewey, the social and moral implications of this outlook give rise to the idea of the associative mode of life, that is, to democracy.

After emphasizing the crucial place of situations in human life, Dewey turns again to everyday notions of interest. Persons take "an interest" in politics, in sports, in history, in the weather, in the stock market, and so forth. They engage in legal or business proceedings by showing that "their interests" are involved. And people demonstrate, through a posture of involvement and engrossment, that they are "interested in" whatever it is they are doing. Drawing on his previous analysis, Dewey ascends from these understandings to another formulation of his view of self and interest: "To be interested is to be absorbed in, wrapped up in, carried away by, some object. To take an interest is to be on the alert, to care about, to be attentive. We say of an interested person both that he has lost himself in some affair and that he has found himself in it. Both terms express the engrossment of the self *in* an object" (p. 133, my emphasis). Once more, we witness Dewey connecting self and world. Quite literally, he suggests, the self "loses" and "finds" itself in its involvement with objects, with the latter understood, it bears repeating, not as inert things—only a spectator of life sees the world as such—but as anything that draws out simultaneously both focus and solicitude. On the one hand, with every new encounter the self loses an aspect of its prior identity because it is now infused with, and has infused, the new object. But that fact means the self has found a new aspect through its interaction with that very same object.

For example, the stamp collector examining the one-thousandth addition to her collection has lost and found her self. Regardless of—or, better, because of all the previous stamps she has organized and studied—the new stamp alters her perception, understanding, knowledge, and sensibility, however minutely in scale compared to the totality of her life as a collector. The bus driver turning the corner at a busy boulevard for the tenth time that day (and perhaps the one-thousandth time in his career) undergoes a transformation in the self—he loses and finds his self, however minimally—via his interaction with the vehicles, the pedestrians, the passengers, the weather, his mood, and more, that were not the same on the previous trips. The effects of these typically microscopic self-transformations may not make themselves known or visible for some time. What seems to happen is that the effects cumulate until one surprising day, in those moments of sudden illumination that help people mark the contours of their lives, the stamp collector realizes that she has enjoyed collecting the little pieces of gummed paper because of their beauty and insight into human history, while the bus driver realizes he has enjoyed guiding the huge metal conveyer down city streets because of the endless variety of people, weather, and events that come his way.

The examples presume that the stamp collector and the bus driver are not simply going through the motions. They are not plodding through one repetitive act after another, nor are they merely accumulating impressions or information like a sensory machine. For Dewey, learning always implies a transformation in the self, however subtle. That fact accounts for why learning differs from merely gathering and memorizing information. On the one hand, a person can be a veritable encyclopedia but remain profoundly unlearned, unable to meet life situations that call for responsiveness, responsibility, and imagination. On the other hand, unlike the human encyclopedia who can go on adding material ad nauseam, a person who has learned has always lost as well as found something. When I study a new document in history, my overall assumptions and view of history alter, however microscopically—in a literal sense, I lose my previous conception, and I find a fresh one. As I prepare dinner using a new recipe, my very understanding of cooking evolves, however hard to discern (at the moment) the change may be—once more, I have lost and found an outlook. As I get to know another person, my insight and affections shift, and I lose my initial impressions and find others. I can remember, perhaps for a long time, my prior conceptions of history, cooking, and the other person. However, my relation with these objects (in Dewey's sense of the term) and my lived engagement with them are dynamic, not static, a distinction that provides another way to describe the ongoing process of losing and finding.

Dewey underscores this perspective by turning next to problematic ways in which the idea of interest is construed in school practices. He laments how routinely interest is equated solely with the one-way "effects" of various things on students' personal advantage or disadvantage, success or failure, pleasure or pain (p. 133). That presumption mirrors the dualistic view that self and mind exist in complete separation from the world. Operating in this mind-set (or set mind), people find it hard to conceive, literally, that the universe of objects called the curriculum could in fact constitute the vehicle for the very formation of students' selves through their engagement with it. Instead, because people too often regard the curriculum as things to cover rather than as objects formative of life, they focus willy-nilly, and often despite their best intentions, on inducements, baits, appeals, excitation, "fun," and more, in an effort to get students to attend to subject matter. (See Zahorik, 1996, for a particularly demoralizing study of some educators' tendency to "flee" from the curriculum because they regard it as a body of things rather than potential objects in Dewey's sense.) The upshot, Dewey complains, is that much of schooling becomes simply a matter of getting through the time, for educators and students alike. It is merely something that has to be done, rather than an occasion of and for life.

Dewey's response to this state of affairs is not to recommend philosophy in-service courses for educators so that they can acquire the proper understanding of the idea of interest. Dewey urges instead greater study of what actually happens when teachers spark situations that call out learning and growth (cf. MW.3.249–272). One thing they do, he emphasizes, "is to discover objects and modes of action, which are connected with present powers [of students]." "The function of this material," he argues, "in engaging activity and carrying it on consistently and continuously *is* its interest. If the material operates in this way, there is no call either to hunt for devices which will make it interesting or to appeal to arbitrary, semi-coerced effort" (pp. 133–34). A root meaning of interest, Dewey points out, highlights that which is "between" a beginning and end point. At the beginning of a lesson are the students' present powers of understanding, expression, imagination, reflection, and more. The teacher aspires to draw out and to expand, broaden, and deepen these powers through activity as rich as possible in subject matter and meaning. The activity may comprise countless situations featuring lecture, discussion, small group work, individual work, and other modes of work perhaps not identifiable through any current educational lexicon. At the end of the lesson, ideally, are new understandings regarding the subject matter at hand. Those understandings imply more than solely a new increment of information, and, as such, they indicate a transformation in the selves of students, however modest in scope. In between the beginning and end of the lesson resides a temporal process, a movement of engagement and experiment, of reaction and response, of uncertainty and incipient understanding, on the part of teacher and students alike. "These intermediate conditions are of interest," Dewey writes, "precisely because the development of existing activities into the foreseen and desired end depends upon them. To be means for the achieving of present tendencies, to be 'between' the agent and his end, to be of interest, are different names for the same thing" (p. 134).

Dewey counsels teachers not to fixate on who students are apart from subject matter. There is no call to regard students as having predetermined, final selves with final interests to whom subject matter must be utterly alien and remote. There is no need to be intimidated by the tiresome refrain to "make it relevant," as if students come to class as consumers with their tastes and preferences neatly lined up, rather than as bundles of energy, confusion, insight, doubt, accomplishment, innocence, worldliness, and more. To presume that relevance trumps the development of readiness and receptivity makes no more sense than presuming that teachers' selves and interests are frozen and hardened. The key to perception is remembering that students, the subject matter, teachers themselves, the evolving environment, the flow of situations, are all potentially dynamic and capable of fueling conditions for growth. According to Dewey, the fusion of self and interest in learning emerges in and through activity, not through first lining up in one column students' "interests," and then lining up in another column elements of the subject matter and trying to figure out a match. Educational work is not fitting together the fixed pieces of a human jigsaw puzzle. It is an art of living. It is an associative mode of living.

Interest and Self Become the Moral Self

In the final chapter of the book, Dewey reminds readers that educational work can be understood as a process of moral education. Every society seeks to form its young in some particular direction, and all choices of direction presume that "this is better than that" or, more strongly, that "this is good to be and that is bad to be." In short, every educational scheme is value-laden and saturated with moral presuppositions regarding who and what persons should become. Consequently, the kind of moral education a society fashions will mirror the kind of society it aspires to remain or to become.

In chapter 7 of *Democracy and Education*, Dewey argues that a society that wishes to be democratic in substance rather than solely in name must invest itself in the form of education to which he has devoted his entire book. This education will pivot around concepts such as growth, the reconstruction of experience, and more, highlighted throughout his text. Dewey argues that if democracy constitutes "a mode of associated living, of conjoint communicated experience" (93), its educational practice must cultivate that very mode. The fusion of self and interest he has taken pains to elucidate will not be oriented toward just any set of objects and relations, whether preset or not. Rather, it should be directed toward "learning from all the contacts of life," precisely because that phrase constitutes another way to describe democracy. An interest in such learning becomes moral, for Dewey, because it is the *best* enactment of interest for individuals and society alike if they wish to grow rather than remain static. If persons are mutually engaged with one another's ideas, actions, and hopes, their selves widen and deepen in insight, knowledge, sensitivity, and capacity to grow in communicative and expressive ways. In so doing, persons constantly position themselves to expand their learning through each successive interaction, in a dynamic spiral of give-and-take. They lose and find their selves. They lose limited horizons and perceptions and find broader ones, however microscopically the change may be on each occasion. At the same time, society itself becomes transformed through such interactions. As it more and more features such contacts, its surroundings, environments, and situations take on a greater transactive character. They fuel mutual engagement. They lend it wider import and greater meaning.

Dewey does not suggest that educators and the public must deploy the particular vocabulary he develops, nor does he contend that they must always keep uppermost a democratic, moral consciousness. Elsewhere he argues that there is no sign of a better balanced nature than to know when it is important to raise moral considerations. Outside that Aristotelian mean, persons may either lack moral sensitivity or they may become so self-conscious and lacerated by uncertainty that they fall into what Dewey calls "a mania of doubt" (LW.7.170). Moreover, in the everyday work of the school and classroom it is out of the question to make moral matters supreme at every moment (MW.4.267–268). If teachers and students constantly stood upon a meta-platform from where they incessantly asked, What are the moral meanings and consequences of our thoughts and actions? nothing would get accomplished. There is a time for such questions, and determining that time constitutes part of the art of teaching and learning.

Rather than afflicting people with carrying a twenty-four-hour moral monitor, Dewey emphasizes (again drawing on Aristotle) the crucial role of habit in human thought and conduct. Habit can carry much of the burden of conduct so long as the practice of education fuses it with "an interest in learning from all the contacts of life." For Dewey, habit can constitute an empowering, kinetic constituent of personhood. It does not imply passively dwelling in a rut, a condition he would characterize as "routine" or as "habituation." According to Dewey, teaching and learning should be generating two sorts of habits, both of which help bring into being the associative mode of living. On the one hand, he highlights the development of socially responsive habits of thinking and communicating that constitute, he argues, "a character which not only does the particular deed socially necessary but one which is interested in that continuous readjustment which is essential to growth" (p. 370). On the other hand, Dewey underscores the development of habits of think-ing, inquiring, imagining, communicating, and more, which are distinc-tive to individuals and enable them to pursue activities and callings in ways that reach beyond or alter conventional practice and expectation.

For Dewey, the associative mode of life requires both kinds of habit and trajectory. Social habits of mind and outlook developed in isolation from the personal may breed conformity and, ironically, a reduction in the diversity of "contacts" people encounter and thus a decline in the quality of life for all. At their worst, such habits support a tyrannical form of popular opinion or groupthink. At the same time, personal habits of mind and outlook, coddled in isolation from the social, may breed idio-syncratic, capricious, and even explosive modes of conduct. Such an outlook, Dewey claims, "often makes an individual so insensitive in his relations to others as to develop an illusion of being really able to stand and act alone—an unnamed form of insanity which is responsible for a large part of the remediable suffering of the world" (p. 49). When Dewey describes this condition as one of insanity, he echoes once more his view that self and world are bound up together. To forget that and to presume one is an island unto oneself is literally, for Dewey, to lose one's mind.

Through an education in and for the associative mode of life, people develop the capacity "nobly to share" (p. 369) in a communicative, expressive give-and-take. Echoing his affinity with Emerson and roman-tic poets such as Wordsworth, Dewey's use of the term "nobility" lends grandeur to the often mundane, everyday process of living. The term rarely comes to mind in witnessing a typical elementary school classroom, adult evening class, or auto mechanics workshop. It does not spring to heart in watching customers in a restaurant, riders on a train, or people walking their dogs. However, for Dewey genuine human nobility, and dignity, dwell in any moment in which individuals are losing and finding themselves in shared, expanding activity. In such moments, and without knowing it, people often put forward their best efforts, best imagination, best aspirations, and best communications, however modest in scope and range. That condition can hold for the teacher assisting a child with an arithmetic problem, an action that can have subtle effects on others in the room, and it can hold for the person walking the dog, whose presence in the public park can add, however imperceptibly, to the meaning and enjoyment of others. At the same time, for Dewey, an education in and for the associative mode of life liberates individuality precisely by generating continuous situations for expressivity, for the enactment and evolution of personal style. Moreover, this dynamic process helps cultivate, if not in so many words, the disposition to regard individuality as "precious" (p. 315). Dewey employs that diamond-studded term to underscore his belief that a worthy society is composed of worthy, distinctive individuals, and vice versa (p. 128). The one is dependent on the other.

Dewey concludes his book with an image of the moral self because he believes it can carry the weight of *all* his preceding analysis. That image fuses self, interest, growth, and the democratic prospect. Dewey dramatizes this viewpoint in the final chapter, "Theories of Morals." He rehearses in a new key his sustained critique of the dualistic thinking that persistently, and confoundingly in his view, leads people to separate their selves and minds from the world. That thinking leads people to splinter life into separate, allegedly unrelated categories—mind and body, education and living, philosophy and action—and, for Dewey, the results are particularly problematic with regard to moral thought and practice. He criticizes familiar moral theories that presume, he contends, either (1) that morality has only to do only with the "inner," or with motives and intentions, or (2) that morality has only to do with the "outer," or with consequences and effects in the world, or (3) that morality has only to do with principles that should guide conduct, or (4) that morality has only to do with character and virtue. Dewey regards these elements—motives, actions, principles, and character—as aspects of a single course of human experience. To support his claim, he takes yet another pass at describing the relation between self and interest. However, where the initial analysis in chapter 10 had been descriptive and critical, seeking to debunk hard and fast divisions between the self and world, Dewey's penultimate treatment is reconstructive, fashioned through a moral prism.

For example, Dewey affirms why principled conduct is so widely admired. However, he rejects the assumption that it is so because it harbors no element of self-interest. Principled action is not selfless action. Nor does it express some hidden self-aggrandizing impulse. The confusion here, Dewey suggests, derives from "a false notion" of the relation between self and interest. The first wrong step is presuming that "the self is a fixed and hence isolated quantity." "As a consequence," Dewey writes, "there is a rigid dilemma between acting for an interest of the self and without interest. If the self is something fixed antecedent to action, then acting from interest means trying to get more in the way of possessions for the self—whether in the way of fame, approval of others, power over others, pecuniary profit, or pleasure. Then the reaction from this view as a cynical depreciation of human nature leads to the view that men who act nobly act with no interest at all" (p. 361). However, Dewey retorts, to anyone not caught up in this theoretical controversy it must be plain as day that a person would not carry on with an activity unless he or she were interested in it (or were coerced, a separate condition). Other things being equal, a doctor who remains at her post when an epidemic breaks out in the community must be interested in her vocation. But it would "distort" her acts, Dewey argues, to claim that they necessarily mask an ulterior end such as a will to power or desire for personal glory.

What we need, Dewey urges, is the right lens on the issue. "The moment we recognize that the self is not something ready-made, but something in continuous formation through choice of action, the whole situation clears up" (p. 361). The doctor's interest in keeping at her work means her self is found *in* the work—once more, the preposition to which Dewey turns is literal in meaning. If the doctor packed her bags at the first sign of an epidemic, she would be a different kind of self. The "mistake" in our thinking, Dewey suggests, resides in the false notion that the doctor's work is merely a means to an end, that she has a prior, "ready-made" self to which her actions in the world are purely mercenary.

However, without action, there is no self. Without interest, there is no self. Without the world, there is no self. There may be brute existence, but not human life. Dewey implies that the idea that the self exists prior to engagement with the world is a house of cards generated, in part, by linguistic practices that persistently place before us distinctions between subjects, verbs, and predicates. These distinctions are real and invaluable for any number of purposes, but they distort perspective when people reify them into separate worlds. When people do that, they generate conundrums such as "the problem" of the relation between interest and the self. For Dewey, however, self and interest "are two names for the same fact; the kind and amount of interest actively taken in a thing reveals and measures the quality of selfhood which exists. Bear in mind that interest means the active or moving *identity* of the self with a certain object, and the whole alleged dilemma falls to the ground" (p. 362).

People can and do act selfishly. In some cases, as Dewey has previously suggested, their action can literally be insane, or mindless (or selfless in the sense of not developing as a human being). However, persons also act from unselfish interest. According to Dewey, if we survey the range of interests typically evoked by the term unselfishness, we discern what he calls "two intimately associated features": "(i) The generous self consciously identifies itself with the *full* range of relationships implied in its activity, instead of drawing a sharp line between itself and considerations which are excluded as alien or indifferent; (ii) it readjusts and expands its *past* ideas of itself to take in new consequences as they become perceptible" (362). In the course of medical school and her subsequent career, the doctor may have had no inkling that she would one day end up in the midst of an epidemic. However, if she is the sort of doctor who works hard at her practice, who seeks to learn from it, and who cultivates both her knowledge and her prowess in working well with patients, then when the epidemic strikes she will move to do what she can—unselfishly, as popular parlance has it, but in fact as a continued and expanding expression of self and interest. "The wider or larger self which means inclusion instead of denial of relationships is identical with a self which enlarges in order to assume previously unforeseen ties" (p. 362). The self can grow, transform, and mature. It can be funded by experience. Memory and foresight can move richly and deeply in a self.

Such a self, penultimately, embodies an interest in learning from all the contacts of life. But that means both self and interest are becoming moral. Thus, Dewey transforms the unselfish self into "the generous self." The "un" in unselfish is too passive to do justice to the active, expanding nature of the self and its actions. The generous self gives to the world, as do all such selves whatever their callings or doings. Posed differently, that self generates life, in the literal sense of acting in ways that expand and widen the human domain. The doctor's work during the epidemic saves lives, and each such life may go on to affect countless others. The bus driver who acts patiently with passengers and traffic renders the journey more peaceful and graceful for all, with who knows what consequences for their subsequent conduct, however subtle in effect. The waiter who helps orchestrate the meal into a more enjoyable and satisfying experience for customers may influence their mood, leading them toward better acts in their own right, however modest in scope. The teacher who helps students learn and develop may be positioning them to have an educative influence on people they themselves meet down the road.

These generous selves are not saintly or otherworldly. There is nothing romantic or rose-colored about what they do. Dewey describes as straightforwardly as he can what it means to be a self coming into the world more fully and comprehensively, in whatever circumstances in which it finds itself—saving lives, driving buses, waiting tables, teaching children. All such persons, in their own distinctive ways, are cultivating and expressing what Dewey has called traits of method or moral traits. However subtly, they are growing in their open-mindedness, their wholeheartedness, their directness, and their responsibility. These and related traits motor the expanding fusion of self, interest, and world. The doctor, the driver, the waiter, and the teacher learn to deal with difficulty and challenge rather than to ignore or push them away, just as they learn to realize more deeply the rewards and satisfactions of living. They "take the lean with the fat," as Dewey puts it (p. 363). Their interest, their selves, expand through meeting life in its manifold forms, and through resolving difficulty and frustration.

With his talk of the generous self, Dewey sounds the closing notes of the chapter and book. He takes up explicitly the idea of moral education as the primary aim of the school. He attacks the alleged separation between the intellectual and the moral aspects of educating. In the previous chapter he had argued that knowledge is best understood not as a noun, in which it denotes a disembodied body of material, but rather as a verb, as that which renders action more assured and significant. Now, he makes a comparable move with the moral. Rather than marking out a fixed set of principles, motives, or virtues divorced from matters of knowledge, the moral points to their fusion in ideas, in thoughts, and in acts that support the growth of the associative mode of life. "A narrow and moralistic view of morals," he writes, "is responsible for the failure to recognize that all the aims and values which are desirable in education are themselves moral" (p. 369).

Dewey deploys the term "moral knowledge" to capture what students and teachers learn through activities that are saturated with interaction between themselves and the most challenging subject matter they are equipped to tackle. Dewey calls this learning moral knowledge because "it builds up a social interest and confers the intelligence needed to make that interest effective in practice" (p. 366). Dewey means that in such a process students acquire more than rote information alone, or that which "has only a technical worth," as he puts it. Rather, they learn that ideas, interpretations, explanations, and ways of knowing have consequences. These things are *alive*, they are part of *their* lives, and they expand the scene of life. Posed differently, if school subjects are "acquired under conditions where their social significance is realized"—by "realized" Dewey means literally brought to life—"they feed moral interest and develop moral insight" (p. 366). Education in this spirit funds the generous self, the moral self, with the habits, resources, skills, and perspective to realize the meaning of generosity as giving and as generative. At the same time, such an education widens the "receptive self," the capacity to take and accept as well as to give, in the dynamic relation to which Dewey constantly points and to which he owed a primordial debt to Emerson.

Conclusion: Dewey's Moral Image of the World

Democracy and Education is many books in one, and among these can be found his book of the moral self. That book often reads like a philosophical primer for the art of living, the mirror twin for Dewey of the art of democracy. As we have seen, he strives for a point of harmony or balance between the individual and society, even as both undergo constant transformation. The individual person is not reducible, and should never be reduced to, a mere social cipher or effect of nature and nurture. Society is not reducible, and should not be reduced to, a mere aggregate of individuals discharging their respective preferences. To maintain capacity for growth on the part of individuals and society, people need an education in artfulness, which is another name for the associative mode of living since the latter depends on communication and personal expressivity. In turn, artfulness and the associative mode of living are realizations of "an interest in learning from all the contacts of life." This high-flying vocabulary comes to earth in the life of the moral self.

Dewey's egalitarian impulses lead him to the view that the art of living, as a metaphor for a life that is purposeful and growing, is not the provenance of an economic or cultural elite. On the contrary, members of the elite may more commonly put on a pose and enact a simulacrum of the artful life rather than the genuine thing. They may be too removed from heart-felt and mind-felt generosity, generativity, and receptivity. For Dewey, all human lives can be artful, marked by communication and expressivity in distinctive, irreproducible ways. That very individuality is crucial for democracy, for a meaningful associative mode of life. Without it, democracy sinks into a numbing conformity. Without social interaction, however, the individual may sink into solipsism, isolated from the contacts that stimulate the self to grow and truly live. The work of education means, in part, triggering situations in and through which people, whether young or old, can cultivate social and personal habits that bring them into the world. Open-mindedness, wholeheartedness, directness, and responsibility, as traits of method, fuel artfulness in whatever work or duties a person performs. As moral traits, those same qualities propel persons to engage others in meaningful ways. Artful life and moral life, for Dewey, fuse when constituted by an interest in learning from all the contacts of life.

Dewey's democratic attitude toward people, however, constitutes an upward egalitarianism. He expects a great deal from every human being (himself first and foremost), not only to give and take to the best of their ability, but to be dedicated to growing in this capacity. The very concept, moral self, implies a profound valuation, a commanding ideal of an ascending mode of conduct in which some ways of thinking and doing, as we have seen, are better than others. There is nothing soft or forgiving about his egalitarian impulse. He might delight in the democratic formulation of "an aristocracy of everyone," but he would caution that it must be an aristocracy of both being *and* becoming, not of settled attainment. He explicitly rejected the idea that his educational outlook was "child-centered"; it is no more so than it is "adult-centered." If anything, it would be better described as "growth-centered," and that posture entails a critical attitude toward anything—ideas, ideals, practices, principles—that gets in the way of growth.

With these thoughts in mind, at the start of this chapter I described Dewey's concluding sentence in the text as bearing a double meaning. It closes the book, and it apparently sentences readers to accept Dewey's images of the associative mode of life and the moral self that animate his educational vision. The idea of being "sentenced" to a particular mode of education constitutes more than a poetic conceit. Education is inconceivable without a constraint or limit. Without something to push against, there is no way to gain traction for growth. The constraint typically takes the form of claims like "these are the most important things to study and learn" or "here is the most worthwhile curriculum, pedagogy, and assessment strategy." All such formulations say "no," in effect, to alternatives, thereby constraining practice. However, in a more primordial sense, the image of being sentenced to education points to an aspect of the human condition—namely, that people cannot purchase or borrow their personhood. A person becomes a self, a realized human being, through education. As the cliche has it, education is a process, not a product to be bought in a self-service (or self-serving) cafeteria. For Dewey, the education people embrace makes all the difference for the way of life they will end up leading.

Dewey's imposing final sentence challenges readers to contemplate the alternatives to an interest in learning from all the contacts of life. Certainly, such an interest does not mean endorsing, accepting, admiring, respecting, tolerating, or resonating with any and all contacts. Some of them may be reprehensible, ugly, nasty, terrifying, violent, corrupting, and outrageous. For Dewey, however, the right response—the moral response—to these facts of life is not blind aversion, dogmatic condemnation, or cowardly withdrawal. The moral response is to learn from them. Since learning involves communication, the moral response means somehow engaging the contacts, somehow interacting or communicating with them, or, at a minimum, seeking out others with whom to communicate about them and perhaps taking action of one sort or another. Such communication and action, moreover, must cohere with the democratic principle of promoting rather than reducing human association. Whatever action might be contemplated and undertaken in the face of a repugnant contact, it must proceed as if those who find the contact repugnant might themselves one day be perceived and treated as such. The response must be formative rather than merely destructive in method and aim.

All of this constitutes, to say the least, a very tall order. A voice sobered by the vagaries of human conduct on the planet can hardly help asking: Is this moral image of self and world attainable? Has Dewey crafted an uninhabitable end-in-view for human conduct? Is it really possible to become persons constituted by an interest in learning from *all* the contacts of life? Moreover, is it in fact reasonable, or even ethically and politically healthy, to expect such things of people? What are the dangers of ideals such as those that Dewey advances? Do they lead more often than not to disappointment, rather than to making a difference in the struggle for a more just and artful world? Should people strive to dwell without such ideals, and turn to *Democracy and Education* for poetic enjoyment but not for ideas to live by? Perhaps Dewey's work is best approached as a humanist Book of Hours, which, like its medieval counterpart, refreshes and restores the individual in moments of repose, yet is hardly a realistic guide for society. For me, Dewey's achievement, as indirect as it is straightforward, is to press these questions to their limit. His book of the moral self asks its readers to confront their own sense of limit and possibility. That urging embodies not just an ideal but a reminder, as needful today as ever, that the quality of human life is not preordained.

Note

1. Unless otherwise indicated, all page references are from MW.9.

References

Dewey, John. (1977). Emerson—the philosopher of democracy. In J. A. Boydston (Ed.), *John Dewey, the middle works 1899–1924: Vol. 3. Essays on the new empiricism 1903–1906* (pp. 184–192). Carbondale: Southern Illinois University Press.

Dewey, John. (1977). The relation of theory to practice in education. In J. A. Boydston (Ed.), *John Dewey, the middle works 1899–1924: Vol. 3. Essays on the new empiricism 1903–1906* (pp. 249–272). Carbondale: Southern Illinois University Press.

Dewey, John. (1977). Moral principles in education. In J. A. Boydston (Ed.), *John Dewey, the middle works 1899–1924: Vol. 4. Essays on pragmatism and truth 1907–1909* (pp. 265–291). Carbondale: Southern Illinois University Press.

Dewey, John. (1985). Democracy and education. In J. A. Boydston (Ed.), *John Dewey, the middle works 1899–1924: Vol. 9. Democracy and education 1916.* Carbondale: Southern Illinois University Press.

Dewey, John. (1989). Theory of the moral life. In J. A. Boydston (Ed.), *John Dewey, the later works 1925–1953: Vol. 7. Ethics* (pp. 159–310). Carbondale: Southern Illinois University Press.

Dewey, John. (1989). How we think. In J. A. Boydston (Ed.), *John Dewey, the later works 1925–1953: Vol. 8. Essays and How we think* (Rev. ed.) (pp. 105–352). Carbondale: Southern Illinois University Press.

Emerson, Ralph Waldo. (1983/1844). Experience. In *Ralph Waldo Emerson. Essays & lectures* (pp. 471–492) New York: The Library of America.

Kant, Immanuel. (1985/1785). *Foundations of the metaphysics of morals* (L. W. Beck, trans.). Englewood Cliffs: Prentice-Hall.

Nehamas, Alexander. (1998). *The art of living: Socratic reflections from Plato to Foucault.* Berkeley: University of California Press.

Zahorik, John. (1996). Elementary and secondary teachers' reports of how they make learning interesting. *Elementary School Journal,* 96 (5), 551–564.

List of Contributors

GERT BIESTA is Professor of Educational Theory at the University of Exeter, and Visiting Professor for Education and Democratic Citizenship at Orebro University, Sweden. His latest book is *Beyond Learning: Democratic Education for a Human Future* (2006).

SHARON FEIMAN-NEMSER is the Mandel Professor of Jewish Education at Brandeis University. A scholar of teacher education and learning to teach, she has designed and taught in progressive teacher education programs at the University of Chicago, Michigan State University, and Brandeis University.

GARY D FENSTERMACHER is Professor of Educational Foundations at the University of Michigan. His primary scholarly interests are in the philosophy of teaching and teaching policy. His more recent work includes the fourth edition of *Approaches to Teaching* (coauthored with Jonas Soltis).

DAVID T. HANSEN is Professor and Director of the Program in Philosophy and Education, Teachers College, Columbia University. His scholarly interests center around the philosophy and practice of teaching, the nature of inquiry, and the criticism of educational values. He has written widely on these topics, including *The Call to Teach* (1995) and *Exploring the Moral Heart of Teaching* (2001).

LARRY A. HICKMAN is director of the Center for Dewey Studies at Southern Illinois University, Carbondale. He is the author of *John Dewey's Pragmatic Technology* (1990) and *Philosophical Tools for Technological Culture* (2001). He is also the editor of *Technology as a Human Affair* (1990), *Reading Dewey* (1998), *The Essential Dewey* (with Thomas Alexander, 1998), and *The Correspondence of John Dewey, 1871–1952* (1999, 2001, 2005).

HERBERT M. KLIEBARD is a Professor of Curriculum and Instruction and Educational Policy Studies at the University of Wisconsin-Madison. He is the author of *Forging the American Curriculum* (1992), *The Struggle for the American Curriculum* (2004), *Schooled to Work* (1999), *Changing Course: American Curriculum Reform in the 20th Century* (2002), among many others.

ELIZABETH MINNICH, who was Core Professor at the Union Institute's Graduate College and has taught at East Carolina University (Whichard Visiting Distinguished Professor), and Scripps College (Hartley Burr Alexander Chair for Public Philosophy), is Senior Fellow, Association of American Colleges and Universities. Her books include *Transforming Knowledge* (1990) and *The Fox in the Henhouse: How Privatization Threatens Democracy* (2005, coauthored with Si Kahn).

REBA N. PAGE is a Professor of Education at the University of California, Riverside, where she studies and teaches about curriculum, interpretive research methodologies, and the sociocultural foundations of education.

NAOKO SAITO is Associate Professor at the Graduate School of Education, Kyoto University. She was a postdoctoral fellow of the National Academy of Education/Spenser Foundation (2002–2003). Her recent publications include *The Gleam of Light: Moral Perfectionism and Education in Dewey and Emerson* (2005) and a number of articles on American philosophy as it relates to education, as well as the first Japanese translation of Stanley Cavell's work, *The Senses of Walden* (*Sensu obu Waruden*, 2005).

Index